ANGLO-AMERICAN POLICY TOWARDS THE FREE FRENCH

Anglo-American Policy towards the Free French

G. E. Maguire
Lecturer in British and American Studies
University of Paris XII – Val de Marne

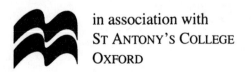

in association with
ST ANTONY'S COLLEGE
OXFORD

First published in Great Britain 1995 by
MACMILLAN PRESS LTD
Houndmills, Basingstoke, Hampshire RG21 6XS
and London
Companies and representatives
throughout the world

This book is published in the *St Antony's Series*
General editor: Alex Pravda

A catalogue record for this book is available from the British Library.

ISBN 0–333–63239–7

First published in the United States of America 1995 by
ST. MARTIN'S PRESS, INC.,
Scholarly and Reference Division,
175 Fifth Avenue,
New York, N.Y. 10010

ISBN 0–312–12710–3

Library of Congress Cataloging-in-Publication Data
Maguire G. E.
Anglo-American policy towards the free French / G. E. Maguire.
p.   cm. — (St. Antony's series)
"In association with St. Antony's College, Oxford."
Includes bibliographical references and index.
1.World War, 1939–1945—Diplomatic history.   2. France—Foreign
relations—Great Britain.   3. Great Britain—Foreign relations-
-France.   4. United States—Foreign relations—France.   5. France-
-Foreign relations—United States.   I. Title.   II. Series: St.
Antony's series (St. Martin's Press)
D752.M34   1995
940.53'2—dc20   95–11453
                                                                          CIP

10   9   8   7   6   5   4   3   2   1
04   03   02   01   00   99   98   97   96   95

Printed and bound in Great Britain by
Antony Rowe Ltd, Chippenham, Wiltshire

This book is lovingly dedicated to the memory of
my father

Thomas William Maguire, 1930–87

and of my niece

Sharon Maureen Ford, 1981–86

Contents

Acknowledgements

The list of persons and institutions who have assisted me in this research is quite long. To begin with, in Paris, I would like to thank the staff of the *Archives Nationales* – and particularly the *section contemporaine* – who gave me numberless special authorisations to consult officially closed papers and private archives. I must also thank the ever helpful staff of the American Library and the American University Library. I would also like to express gratitude to the staff at the Archives of the Ministry of Defence in Vincennes. Finally, I must give particularly heartfelt thanks to the staff of the archives and library of the Ministry of Foreign Affairs at the *Quai d'Orsay*. I must especially thank the staff of the library who gave me special authorisation to do research there. On the archives side, I am particularly grateful to Pierre Fournié who was ever ready to order documents for me at short notice; Catherine Oudin who allowed me to consult the oral archives and Anne-Marie Pannier who let me use her office to listen to cassettes. Finally, I must express my boundless gratitude to Marie-Andrée Guyot who secured my admittance to the library and helped me in many other ways.

In Britain I would like to thank the staffs of Churchill College Archives in Cambridge and the Middle East Centre of St Antony's College, Oxford, as well as that of the Bodleian Library. I must also express my gratitude to Colonel Aylmer who allowed me to consult the Spears Papers. No list would be complete without acknowledging the excellent service of the Public Record Office in Kew. I would also like to thank Dr Michael Hawcroft of Keble College Oxford who arranged for my accomodation there and Lynette Cawthra who was ever indulgent in allowing me to stay at her place in London when I needed to do research. Finally, I certainly cannot forget all the help given me by Fr Philip Whitmore and the priests, nuns and staff of Clergy House at Westminster Cathedral.

In the United States I must thank the staffs of the Roosevelt, Eisenhower and Truman Libraries who were very helpful. I must also recognise the assistance I received at the National Archives in Washington and especially that of Mr John Taylor in the Military Reference section. The archives of the Citadel in Charleston, South Carolina and the Historical Society of York County in York, Pennsylvania also kindly allowed me access to the Mark Clark and the Jacob Devers Papers respectively. Again, no list of acknowledgements would be complete without an expression of gratitude to one of the world's wonders, the Library of Congress, where

I consulted the Hull and Leahy Papers and innumerable books and where the newspaper and journals department were kind enough to do an exhaustive search of all Free French journals and newspapers in their possession. Finally I must thank my nephew Joseph Ford who served as a research assistant and greatly facilitated my work.

I cannot of course forget those who have assisted me in more personal capacities. I must particularly thank my mother, Gloria Smith, and my niece, Marie Ford, who made possible my research in Washington. I also owe special thanks to the Lopez family who were ever ready to be of assistance. Nor can I forget the help rendered by Roger and Line Zuber, my father and mother-in-law, who proofread and criticised the manuscript. I must also thank Professor Bernard Cottret of the University of Versailles-St Quentin who was ever ready with encouragement and who provided a forum for some of my ideas. Last but not least, I must thank my family. They put up with a great deal while this book was being researched and written, including long absences and endless hours locked in my office. Special thanks to Tommy and Kevin for being so understanding and to Henri for combining understanding and encouragement with proofreading and criticism. I could not have written this without them.

Paris   G. E. MAGUIRE

1 De Gaulle in London and the Formation of Free France, 1940–42

In beginning any history of Anglo-American relations with the Free French, the first things to be considered are exactly what was Free France and from which circumstances did it emerge. On 10 May 1940 – which co-incidentally was the day Churchill became Prime Minister – the Germans invaded Belgium, the Netherlands, Luxembourg and France. From the very start the war went badly for the Allies. Churchill, becoming alarmed at his own ignorance of events, decided to send Sir Edward Louis Spears MP, one of Churchill's closest friends and former chief British liaison officer from World War I, to Paris as his personal representative with the French premier, Paul Reynaud. What Spears discovered in June 1940 gave him a profound shock. His main job was to try to convince the French government to continue resistance, but this proved impossible. Virtually from the time of his arrival in Paris, Spears looked desperately for a second Joan of Arc; someone who could, as he put it, 'Awaken France out of her stupor, exorcise this awful spell, rekindle the sacred fire that once burnt so brightly in the hearts of all her sons'.[1] When Reynaud resigned on 16 June – allowing Marshal Philippe Pétain to come to power and ask for an armistice – Spears set out to find someone who was willing to come to London and organise resistance there. All the major figures of the government refused. Most of those who wanted to continue the war were not, in fact, convinced that all possibility of resistance was over as the later, ill-fated voyage of the *Massilia* shows.[2] Churchill and most English leaders also felt that France might still decide to continue the fight if the armistice terms were too harsh. Spears found only one man, the relatively unknown Under-Secretary of State for defence in the last Reynaud government and brevet general, who shared his vision and who was ready to assume the mantle of Joan of Arc – Charles de Gaulle. On 17 June 1940 Spears and de Gaulle left Bordeaux, the last refuge of the last government of the Third Republic, to rebegin French resistance in London. So it was that Charles de Gaulle entered the world stage in what may seem to us – who know his later career – a rather improbable role: that of a rebel fleeing France to throw himself into British arms.

Much has been made of de Gaulle's early career, of his rebellion against accepted military tactics and of his books stressing the importance of tank warfare. In fact, de Gaulle's claim to military foresight has generally been overstated, as many of his ideas had already been voiced by the British theorist Basil Liddell-Hart. A great deal has also been written about his relationship with Pétain. The Marshal had no children, but at a certain period of his life he seems to have been looking for a spiritual son. In 1913 he noticed the young second-lieutenant de Gaulle and made him his protégé. With Pétain's assistance de Gaulle rose rapidly in the army. Pétain had long been wanting to write a book on his military ideas but felt himself to be an ungifted writer. He noticed de Gaulle's talent and as an ultimate sign of favouritism asked the latter to write that book for him. Pétain seems to have envisaged the work being published under his name, which was not an idea that appealed to de Gaulle – not generally known for his self-effacement. The two men quarrelled, and the book was later published in a revised form only under de Gaulle's name. De Gaulle's career reached a standstill. It seems clear that de Gaulle knew Pétain well and knew that he would never leave metropolitan France. He also knew that Pétain's natural pessimism would make him effectively unable to resist German demands or allow others to do so. One can, perhaps, even see a Freudian element in de Gaulle, who had been considered by Pétain as his spiritual son, organising resistance to his rule.[3]

As a focal point for this resistance, de Gaulle founded Free France. In order to understand this movement, let us begin by considering three early texts by de Gaulle: his call for resistance on 18 June 1940, his justification on 8 July 1940 of the English attack on the French fleet at Oran, and finally, the Brazzaville Manifesto of 27 October 1940. The first of these has become one of the most famous speeches in modern French history, and yet it is only one page long. Essentially, it is an immediate response to Pétain's announcement that he would seek an armistice. De Gaulle begins by saying that the heads of the French army – those responsible for France's military defeat – have formed a government and have asked for an armistice. They are thus doubly guilty for, by ruining the army, they have brought about the physical defeat of France – and they are now ready to negotiate the moral fall of France. De Gaulle does not question the German army's victory but insists that it is only 'the tanks, the planes, and the tactics of the Germans, far more than the fact that we were outnumbered, that forced our armies to retreat'. The defeat, therefore, is not definitive because 'the same means that have defeated us can one day bring victory.' The reason for this is simple because, as he repeats three times for emphasis, 'France is not alone.' The war that was being fought was not, as Pétain and so many others believed, the end of a European war but rather the beginning of a world war: Britain would resist and one day the United States would fight and, with its greater number of tanks and planes and its superior tactics, would win. All the mistakes that had been made, all the suffering that they would cause, could not change the fact that in the universe there existed the means of destroying the enemy. In this fact, he insists, lies the destiny of the world, and for this reason he calls everyone who can provide a useful service to come to Britain and continue the fight. He concludes by saying that the flame of French resistance must not go out and will not go out. The surprise of the 'Appeal of June 18th' can be immense for those who are used to the portrayal of de Gaulle as a staunch nationalist with 'a certain idea of France'. In this appeal he rejects all the insular considerations of Pétain and his followers, and against the narrowness of what they consider best for France he places universal concerns. Insularity is rejected in favour of a world vision, and we see de Gaulle as internationalist.

On 8 July de Gaulle went farther still by making himself the champion of the Anglo-French alliance in spite of Britain's assault on the French fleet at Oran.[4] This too was a response to Pétain and his government who had savagely attacked the British action. He told the French that they must see things from the only point of view that counts – that 'of victory and deliverance'. Pétain's government had made a 'dishonourable pledge' which meant that, although French leaders said they would never surrender the fleet, once the armistice had been signed they were hardly in a position to resist German demands. One day the Germans would have used the French fleet either against Britain or against the French Empire. This being the case de Gaulle states quite categorically that in his opinion it was better for it to have been destroyed. England was fighting for its life, and it was only by England's victory that France could be reborn. The fate of the two countries is thus united, and de Gaulle addresses both peoples, with a mixture of disgust and hope, praising neither but insisting that they must remain together. The French must, therefore, continue to fight with the English, and here we see the explosion of all popular stereotypes concerning de Gaulle. If, in the 'Appeal of June 18th' we see de Gaulle as internationalist, in this speech we see him as someone who believes that France and Britain are linked together and must remain linked together. The alliance must not be broken.

The third key text that we will consider here is the Brazzaville Manifesto, and like the other two it is a reply to Vichy. On 24 October 1940, Pétain met with Hitler at Montoire and established the basis for Franco-German collaboration. Once again de Gaulle's response was immediate, and this time the moral issue is clearly stated. As in his 8 July speech, de

Gaulle insists that what is at stake is not only France's borders, empire or independence but her soul. France's leaders have betrayed the nation to a 'horrible servitude' that the people refuse to accept. The Vichy government, thus, has no popular base, and for this reason is not a legitimate government but only an instrument used by France's enemies to subjugate the French people. It is, therefore, unconstitutional and cannot be the real government of France. A new power is necessary in order to direct the French effort in the war, and events have forced on de Gaulle 'this sacred duty'. De Gaulle himself, therefore, is the real government and will exercise his powers in the name of France and promises to account for his actions to the representatives of the French people when they can finally be freely chosen. Finally, he calls the nation to war: to union with the allies and to battle against their enemies. Following this statement he announces the formation of the Defence Council of the Empire. This speech shocked both the English and especially the Americans by de Gaulle's proclamation of himself as the rightful government of France without, as they saw it, any constitutional legitimacy. In fact the early days of Free France show a preoccupation by all its members with establishing the legality of their movement. The Brazzaville Manifesto shows the influence of the jurist René Cassin, one of the first to rally to de Gaulle. When Cassin had asked de Gaulle on what basis he justified their movement, de Gaulle had answered simply: 'We are France.'[5] This answer, however, satisfied no one, and Cassin set out to prove the legality of the Free French movement. To do so, of course, meant that he had to first show the illegality of Vichy, which was not easy given the troubled history of France and the fact that Pétain had come to power through the normal democratic process of the Third Republic. Already in September 1940 Cassin had written:

> On the organic and constitutional plan the reconstitution of a central power must also be envisaged. In the present state of things, the unity of Free France asserts itself in the man who has always been head of the Free French movement . . . It is he who must in principle provisionally accumulate the powers of President of the Republic, of ministers and of Parliament.[6]

In a series of articles in *La France Libre* during December 1940, Cassin tried to defend the logic of this belief. He wanted to show that Vichy represented a break with French history, but his attempts are not terribly convincing, and his logic contorted at best. He insisted that Free France represented the popular will and therefore legitimacy resided in it. However in 1940 it was certainly not true that Free France enjoyed widespread popular support. What we must remember is that Cassin, de Gaulle and most other Free French leaders were deeply troubled by the movement's lack of political legitimacy. In the final analysis Free France could only be a legitimate movement because Vichy, from their point of view, was immoral.

It is not surprising therefore to note that de Gaulle frequently speaks of the war in religious terms. For him it is part of the eternal battle between good and evil, with the Anglo-American democracies representing good. France is one of the historic champions of liberty, and thus its soul is with the Allies. De Gaulle himself is the chosen servant of France, 'the Madonna in the frescos'.[7] But if the Allies are fighting for good, they are also a threat to France. The Vichy government had allied itself with the future losers of the war. If there were no alternative French government France would be among the losers, and the victors would be able to do with it as they wished. The Free French, rightly or wrongly, suspected both the Americans and the British of having designs on the French empire. Somehow or other an unbroken commitment by France to the Allied cause must be shown to have existed in order to protect French sovereignty both during the war and at the future peace conference and to guarantee that her own security requirements would be considered. In July 1940 de Gaulle stated that: 'For her honour, for her life, France must be present at the victory. In that way she will refind her liberty and her grandeur.'[8] This explains the Free French oversensibility when questions of national sovereignty were involved. Their extreme weakness made them feel insecure and, while the Allies could protect them from the Germans, there was no one to protect them from the Allies – except, perhaps, the Anglo-American press. It was necessary therefore to be extremely vigilant, and, lacking other more persuasive powers, to react in a verbally violent fashion. In their view they were the trustees of the Republic and had to make sure that the Third Republic was passed on intact to the Fourth Republic. Their conduct however did lead to many misunderstandings with the Allies.

Furthermore, it was necessary for another reason. If de Gaulle could criticize Vichy as being only a puppet government for Berlin, it was obvious that Vichy could and would answer that Free France was controlled by the British – by the hated British that had attacked their fleet at Oran. De Gaulle, thus, had to be very vocal about asserting French sovereignty in order to show that Vichy was wrong, that he was not a British tool. Furthermore, it did serve one other useful purpose. Every kick that de Gaulle administered to the Anglo-Americans served also to illustrate the hollowness of the Pétainist belief that France would receive a greater role in a Europe dominated by Nazi Germany than in one dominated by the English-speaking democracies. No member of any of Pétain's governments would have dared to treat the Germans the way de Gaulle treated the Anglo-Americans. The very fact that they tolerated him showed that France's interests lay in an Allied victory. France had throughout her history been a deeply divided nation – both socially and economically – as the strength of both the fascist and the communist movements shows. The Republic had never been fully accepted by a large number of its citizens and many right-wing ideologues had insisted that democracy was a British idea alien to France. The Republicans replied that liberty was indeed a French conception while the communists considered the whole debate irrelevant for the end result was always the same – exploitation of the workers. De Gaulle feared that if the Anglo-Americans marched victorious into such a deeply divided France, civil war would be the result. The only thing to do then was to create French unity behind the Allies. The right-wing had to be discredited and the left-wing neutralised. The French must be shown to have been throughout the war wholeheartedly on the side of the Allies. And thus, from the realms of the mystical we descend to the more prosaic land of the practical. If the foundation of Free France was a moral judgment, it was also based upon the practical need to protect French interests, and for this also an alternative government was necessary. Thus from every point of view most Frenchmen who believed in an Allied victory saw the need for the creation of a 'free' France or rather its recreation.

The first step was to recreate the French Army that had been shattered by the German blitzkrieg. There must be concrete proof that France was still fighting at the side of the Allies. When de Gaulle arrived in London he had very little money and only one follower, his aide-de-camp Geoffroy de Courcel. His only immediate assets were that he was known to the British government, having been sent by Reynaud on a mission to London a few days before the latter resigned, and in General Spears he had a devoted ally who was one of Churchill's closest friends. His first offices in fact were lent to him by Spears. René Cassin described his arrival there on 26 June in his diary:

> [De Gaulle] was until then alone with three or four officers in three rooms . . . But he was happy at my coming: 'You've arrived at just the right moment,' he said, 'to help me' . . . He put me in charge of preparing the draft of an agreement with Churchill; he had been recognized by him as head of the Free French. An army has to be created.[9]

The task that de Gaulle had set himself must have seemed like an impossible one. Throughout the summer of 1940 men and weapons trickled in but a lot more left. Some preferred to join the British Army – which could only infuriate someone as obsessed with protecting French sovereignty as de Gaulle was – while some simply returned to France. Others, like Alexis Léger, the former permanent secretary of the Ministry of Foreign Affairs, and Jean Monnet, the future father of the European Community, could see no particular interest in supporting de Gaulle, whom they both mistrusted as an unworthy custodian of Republican ideals. Still others, like General Emile Béthouart, one of de Gaulle's personal friends, returned to France in order to reorganize the army there, so that it would be ready to fight beside the Allies when the latter arrived.

The men who did rally to de Gaulle were an oddly assorted group. To begin with, there were very few important civilian figures, other than Cassin, Gaston Palewski, Paul Reynaud's former chief of staff at the ministry of finance, René Pleven, a businessman who had been part of the Anglo-French Air Mission in Washington, and Maurice Dejean, a diplomat who took over the direction of foreign affairs until de Gaulle fired him in 1942 for being too tender with the British. Among the military the selection was no greater: Colonel Philippe de Hautecloque (alias Leclerc), Colonel Pierre Koenig, a foreign-legion officer who had risen from the ranks and Captain André Dewavrin (alias Passy), who organized the Free French intelligence services.[10] By far the most important person, either military or civil, to rally to de Gaulle in those early months was undoubtedly General Georges Catroux, the Governor General for Indochina. Catroux himself arrived in London under something of a cloud since he had failed to rally Indochina and had indeed been forced to give in to certain Japanese demands. Although he made a very strong case in favour of his action and although he was much superior to de Gaulle in both military rank and political experience, this fact effectively prevented him from being a threat to de Gaulle's leadership of the movement.[11] Catroux would serve de Gaulle both faithfully and well, first in Syria, then as one of the architects of French unity in North Africa, and finally as ambassador to the Soviet Union. Two naval officers round out the list: Captain Georges Thierry d'Argenlieu, a Carmelite monk who had returned to the navy at the beginning of the war and Vice-Admiral Emile Muselier, who, like Catroux, was senior to de Gaulle and who would, through his constant intriguing, play a role in the early history of Free France that would be almost as negative as Catroux's was positive. The numbers of enlisted men were also small; most chose to be repatriated to France. Furthermore, the attack on Oran and the disastrous Anglo-Free French assault on Dakar in September 1940 also had a negative effect on recruitment. The British Government estimated that in the summer of 1940 the Free French Army numbered at most around 4000 men of whom a large number were in hospital or convalescing. The navy had about 1000 men, while the air force had only about 150 men.[12] Naval and military schools were founded to train additional officers, but for a long time air force training had to be done as part of the regular RAF programme.

The only immediate way of increasing the size of this tiny army was to acquire French territory and thus whatever segment of the French army that was present in it. De Gaulle also felt the need to give his movement a base on French soil. From the time of the armistice certain French possessions had signalled a desire to continue the fight. The first to do so was the New Hebrides (22 July) which was part of an Anglo-French condominium. It was, however, far too remote to be of much use for de Gaulle's purposes. The next colony to rally was Chad (26 August), whose black governor, Félix Eboué, was known for his high intelligence and his devotion to democratic ideals. On the following day Leclerc and Col. Boislambert rallied the French mandated Cameroon – which was obviously closely linked economically to British Cameroon – and Leclerc became its governor. The 28th of August saw the rallying of the Congo and the 29th that of Oubangui-Chari. After these came Tahiti (2 September), the five French ports in India (9 September) and, on 24 September, New Caledonia. No other colonies would rally without a battle until 1943. The final early colony to rally to de Gaulle was Gabon (12 November) after several weeks of combat.

An analysis of these colonies suggests that the primary motivation for adhering to Free France was an economic one. The New Hebrides, the Cameroon and the five French ports in India were obviously too closely linked to the British to cut the connection without grave economic consequences. Furthermore, New Caledonia was almost as closely tied to Australia and New Zealand. The other colonies to rally were also in the midst of grave economic crises and were offered substantial aid by the British. This lesson, however, was not immediately understood for it was not applied to the attempt to capture Dakar.[13] Given its strategic importance on the Atlantic, Dakar was a prize of some importance and had earlier shown some signs of being inclined towards continuing the fight. It was originally supposed to be primarily a Free French operation, but, given the strength of Dakar's defences, it was felt that British assistance was necessary. This assistance, however, was insufficient to meet the unexpected arrival of Vichy warships and the hostility of the defenders. The attackers were forced to retreat, and the whole episode served to undermine any confidence that the British military had in the Free French. Both de Gaulle and the British Government were severely criticized in the press, particularly in the United States. Dakar certainly contributed to the

Americans' negative view of de Gaulle and to their determination to keep the Free French away from any of their later plans for invading French territory.

Free France had certainly gained a great deal through the establishment of its small empire. To begin with, it now had a home on French territory – even though, for practical purposes, its offices remained centralized in London – and a place to train its army. More importantly, French Equatorial Africa was of major strategic importance. It was just south of Libya where Britain's most important battles were to be fought over the next two years. Furthermore, with the Mediterranean cut off by Axis forces, it guaranteed the British an alternative supply route to Egypt and the Sudan by air, and it prevented the Belgian Congo from being isolated. It also allowed a French army to re-enter the war fighting from French territory, for de Gaulle quickly ordered Leclerc to invade Libya. Finally, because of its proximity to South America, the possibilities of Pointe Noire in the Congo as an army base could not fail to interest the Americans. De Gaulle had thus acquired an area of vital importance to both the British and the Americans, and a place from which to relaunch French participation in the war. The problem was that all this area needed to be administered. And so, willingly or not, de Gaulle and Free France were drawn into the business of government.

When de Gaulle arrived in London in June 1940, he seems to have only perceived himself as a military leader. He, as well as the British, certainly expected more important political leaders to follow him, and his first concerns were military – to show the world that some part at least of the French Army was still fighting with the Allies. By the end of the summer, however, it was clear that no major politicans were going to come and that the Free French were beginning to face important problems relating to the issue of sovereignty. One such case was the not surprising refusal of Vichy to issue passports or visas to adherents of Free France. Some kind of authority had to be constituted to do this. A second and more difficult problem was that of Frenchmen enlisting in the British Army. De Gaulle was not fundamentally opposed to their doing so, provided that they first requested his authorisation.[14] A third case was Egypt, where the French had important financial interests, particularly in the Suez Canal. Egypt of course, although nominally independent, was effectively dominated by Britain – a situation which the king and many other Egyptians resented. The rupture of the Anglo-French alliance not surprisingly threw much of Egypt into a fever of Francophilia – for Pétain's government – which meant that there was no question of Free France being recognized. Furthermore, much of the staff of the Suez Canal, who after all tended to have important economic interests and an imperialistic outlook, inclined towards Pétain as well. The danger therefore was great that if Britain felt particularly threatened – which with the war moving into Africa would certainly happen – she could simply take over full control of the Canal, which from the Free French point of view would have been a tragedy. This was avoided primarily thanks to one man, Baron Louis de Benoist, the chief administrator of the Suez Canal Company. He immediately perceived the delicate situation of French interests in the Canal, and in June 1940 became one of the first to rally to de Gaulle. He convinced the British of his loyalty to their cause and kept under control any Pétainist leanings of his staff. It was something of a *tour de force* that, in spite of Rommel's later push into Egypt, the French role in the Suez Canal Company – they were responsible for its security – was never questioned by the British.[15]

But, of course, the most serious problem was that of administering the empire. As we have seen, the main reason why most colonies rallied to de Gaulle in 1940 was to secure economic benefits from the British government, and they were almost immediately admitted to the sterling zone. They quickly became dependent on Great Britain for trade, and there was even some question of replacing the franc with the pound. Agreement, however, was reached to maintain the franc at a fixed and rather advantageous rate of exchange with the pound, although the situation did greatly worry de Gaulle and other Free French leaders. Cassin saw in this a fundamental problem for the future, for, as he put it: 'No marriage is possible unless there are two partners'. The French were so weak that Cassin feared that, without a central authority, individual colonies would be absorbed by the British. His goal was to reconstitute the French Empire.[16] De Gaulle shared his vision and that is why he objected violently to the British and later the Americans dealing directly with people on the spot rather than the more time consuming process of going through the Gaullist headquarters at Carlton Gardens in London. This also explains early attempts to interest the Americans in the Free French colonies: they were looking for another trading partner who could dilute British dominance.

If the Free French had their reasons for constituting a central authority, the British had theirs for recognizing it. The first reason, of course, was the need for military assistance, since for a short time at least there was a definite hope that de Gaulle could rally important forces. When de Gaulle arrived in London on 17 June, Spears took him to 10 Downing Street where Churchill authorized him to broadcast the next day. The War Cabinet, however, immediately annulled this decision, on the grounds that de Gaulle was 'persona non grata to the present French Government'.[17] Spears had to go and see all the members of the War Cabinet and convince them to allow the broadcast. He secured this by telling them about the large number of planes that the French air force had in Bordeaux. He dangled before them the prospect of a significant increase in air power at a time when the Battle of Britain was expected to begin at any moment.[18] The problem for de Gaulle, however, was that Pétain obviously had so much more to offer than did Free France. The British were thus continually tempted by the possibility that Vichy, or later General Weygand in North Africa, might re-enter the war as British allies. Not infrequently Pétain actually played on this hope and sent various messages that hinted at a new Anglo-French entente. This had the obvious effect of dampening English enthusiasm for de Gaulle, although, with the passage of time, the British lost all confidence in Pétain. Weygand was another matter. He had been sent by Pétain on 7 September 1940 as Delegate General of the French Government to North Africa; he was to be a kind of supreme authority there. In this position he began to make overtures towards both the British and the Americans. We shall see in the next chapter that the Americans also were greatly interested in Weygand. In January 1941 Weygand actually went so far as to say that he wanted to re-enter the war but he lacked material. No less a cynic than Alexander Cadogan, the permanent under-secretary of the Foreign Office, felt that the British should avoid getting involved in the Balkans and instead should 'clean up Africa and get the victorious "Army of the Nile" alongside Weygand in Tunisia'.[19] Hopes in Weygand, however, proved to be as illusory as those in Pétain. But there remained the possibility that, by negotiating with Vichy representatives in French colonies (most notably in Syria, Djibouti and Madagascar), the British could end fighting early and achieve their objectives of insuring that the Axis could not operate from that particular colony. Once again, these hopes were disappointed.

The second reason the British aided de Gaulle during this period was that they perceived that he was having a psychological effect in France. Not surprisingly General Spears was the first on the British side at least to understand this. Spears worked tirelessly to convince Churchill and the government to break completely with Vichy. Spears became virtually obsessed with enhancing de Gaulle's image – to the point of persuading the war cabinet to continue with the ill-fated expedition to Dakar, in spite of the opposition of British military leaders, simply because de Gaulle wanted it. He firmly believed that de Gaulle should be made the focal point of French resistance. Spears argued that the French would always suspect any English propaganda and, therefore, the way to make the French re-enter the war was not to tell them that Britain would liberate France or, even worse, seek an understanding with Vichy. The only way was to have an independent Frenchman like de Gaulle who could show them himself that this is where their interests lay. In other words, the British could not effectively respond to Vichy's attacks, only de Gaulle could do so for them – but only if he demonstrated that he was truly independent.

Very few persons listened to Spears at first and, as we shall soon see, even he became disillusioned and turned against de Gaulle. However the British, whose intelligence services had excellent contacts in France, could not escape the fact that during the period in question, 1940–1942, support for de Gaulle in France was definitely growing. Soon, the Foreign Office became the faithful champions of de Gaulle. Robert Parr for example, the consul in Brazzaville, wrote in the summer of 1941 that for the future stability of France it was necessary that some Frenchmen must return as victors. He felt 'that General de Gaulle's troops should form the spearhead of the action which sweeps France clear of the enemy [and] is essential to his country's moral redemption.'[20] Eden considered this analysis to be so important that he printed it and passed it to members of the cabinet. The British were beginning to understand what Cassin and de Gaulle had feared from the beginning: that civil war was a possibility in a deeply divided France.

The third major reason why the British supported de Gaulle was the very practical one that they needed someone to administer the French territories that had rallied, and to organize those French forces that had joined them. Contrary to Free French suspicions, the British had no designs on the French empire. In fact, they were generally too busy trying to keep their own empire, which was threatened not only by the Germans and the Japanese but also by the Americans who were, for example, loud in their support of Indian nationalism. Arab nationalism was another factor that worried them and, as we shall see, nearly pushed them to a confrontation with the French in Syria and Lebanon. The British thus were playing a holding game. Furthermore, all their propaganda – and especially the Atlantic Charter – insisted this was a war of liberty against tyranny. They could hardly continue to argue this if they were taking over French territory. Finally, from the very beginning it was clear that the decisive battle in Europe would take place in France, and it was therefore important to try to ensure that the French population would be friendly.

The British thus never seriously thought of abandoning Free France, although they were periodically tempted to find a replacement for de Gaulle. Their first official support for the movement came on 28 June 1940, five days after Laval entered Pétain's government, when de Gaulle was officially recognized as 'the Leader of all free Frenchmen, wherever they may be, who rally to him in support of the Allied cause'.[21] After a series of conversations between William Strang of the Foreign Office and René Cassin, an agreement was reached between the two sides on 7 August 1940 to supply Free France's military needs. The British also announced that they would recognize a 'Council of Defence', consisting of anti-Vichy elements in the Free French colonies and promised to restore France's 'former greatness' and independence. This did not go as far as de Gaulle wanted, who thought that the British should guarantee 'the territorial integrity of France and the French Empire'. Their refusal to do so only added to Free France's suspicion that the English were seriously considering extending their empire at the expense of the French. In fact, the British seem to have refused this guarantee because they were not sure that they would be strong enough to restore all the French empire and did not want to get themselves into impossible commitments over colonies like Indochina which was falling more and more under Japanese influence.[22] By autumn the British were paying Free French soldiers, providing supplies, equipment, accommodation and training facilities, as well as being the ultimate defenders of Free French colonies. Even de Gaulle's headquarters at Carlton Gardens was provided by the British Government.

The next step in Anglo-Free French relations came in October 1940 when, as we have seen, de Gaulle issued the Brazzaville Manifesto and set up the Defence Council of the Empire. The assertion that this council was in some way the legal heir of the Third Republic was greeted with misgiving by the British government who refused to recognise it as having any constitutional or judicial role. On 24 December 1940, they recognised it but only in the earlier, mainly military terms.[23] Soon after this, however, Anglo-Free French relations exploded in one of their most spectacular episodes. On 1 January 1941, MI5 arrested Admiral Muselier, accusing him of having betrayed the Dakar expedition to Vichy. According to Alexander Cadogan, de Gaulle worked himself into a passion over Muselier, insisting that he was innocent. Cadogan found himself in secret sympathy with de Gaulle because, as he confided in his diary, there really was no case against him, and he felt that 'it was that baby Dictator Winston who ordered immediate (and premature) action.'[24] On 9 January it was discovered that the evidence against Muselier was a forgery, and the prime minister was forced to release Muselier and to apologise to de Gaulle (he refused to apologise to Muselier, leaving that for the Foreign Office). De Gaulle himself surprised Churchill by accepting the apology very graciously, saying that 'he had no desire to press the matter' and that 'as for Admiral Muselier . . . he personally did not count and that what mattered alone was that the war should go on.'[25] In fact, de Gaulle did not like Muselier, whose promiscuity, drug-taking and constant intriguing for power antagonized the leader of Free France. He defended Muselier only because an issue of sovereignty was involved. De Gaulle believed that he should have been allowed to investigate the charges against Muselier and, had they been shown to be correct, decide on a punishment. He was offended by the fact that the British government had thrown in prison one of his own subordinates without consulting him first.

After this, Anglo-Free French relations calmed down for a while, and a relatively fruitful collaboration resulted. In early December the British had begun a counter-offensive against the Italians in Libya, and de Gaulle had sent a battalion of Free French to participate in this campaign. Two days later (11 December) the British with Free French assistance were victorious at Sidi Barani in Egypt. Throughout early 1941 the Italians were pushed further and further into Libya, while the Free French began to see action in the Ethiopian campaign as well. The arrival of German reinforcements under Rommel in Libya meant, however, that the African campaign began to go much less well for the British and their Free French allies. From April 1941 they found themselves being gradually pushed back towards Egypt. Meanwhile, a nationalist revolt against the British started in Iraq, on which the Axis tried to capitalize. Admiral François Darlan, now Vice-President of the National Council, Minister of Foreign Affairs and effectively head of Pétain's government, allowed the Luftwaffe to use Syria as a base from which to bomb the British in Iraq, and this in turn led to a decision to attack Syria with Free French assistance. This episode will be considered in more detail in Chapter 3, but we must say here that the armistice ending the Syrian campaign was felt by the Free French to have been a betrayal of their cause by the British. Once again they felt that they had been sold out in order to obtain illusory benefits from Vichy, and this provoked one of the greatest crises in Anglo-Free French relations during the war.

Autumn 1941 saw another major development in the Free French movement with the formation of the French National Committee on 24 September. This took place against a background of more intrigue involving Muselier, although this time the British were his champions. The problem was that Muselier did not want to join the Committee which he considered to be too much under de Gaulle's thumb and, to make his point, went around to various British officials, including the Admiralty and Lord Bessborough who headed the French Welfare Office, complaining about de Gaulle's dictatorial tendencies. De Gaulle in turn claimed that Muselier had committed an act of 'military rebellion' by threatening to give the Free French Navy to the British. The Admiralty pressured Muselier to agree finally to join the Committee, but he did so only with reluctance and complained about it to Lord Bessborough. The latter in turn wrote a letter to Churchill, saying that 'a Committee of Yes-men' had been created that would only confirm 'de Gaulle in his dictatorship'. This, of course, infuriated Churchill who immediately wrote to Anthony Eden, the Foreign Secretary, that:

> This is very unpleasant. Our intention was to compel de Gaulle to accept a suitable Council. All we have done is to compel Muselier & Co to submit themselves to de Gaulle. I understood you were going to make sure that the resulting Government represented what we want. It is evident that this business will require the closest watching, and that our weight in the immediate future must be thrown more heavily against de Gaulle than I hoped would be necessary.[26]

De Gaulle, however, had already found allies at the Foreign Office, most especially Sir Alexander Cadogan. Cadogan was infuriated and complained in his diary: 'What the Hell has it [the Council] got to do with [Bessborough]? whose only business . . . is to arrange Punch and Judy shows for Free French children!'[27] Eden agreed with him and wrote back to Churchill that:

> There are too many cooks stirring this broth. I still think that, having decided that de Gaulle should set up a Council, we could not out of the materials available in this country have materially improved the Council, even if we had chosen every member ourselves. Lord Bessborough, like other critics speaks of 'yes-men', but does not tell us where the 'no-men' are to be found. The decision to try to bring Muselier and de Gaulle together was made by the Cabinet.[28]

For the moment, Muselier's intrigues were stopped, but not for long. In March 1942, de Gaulle finally got rid of Muselier, in spite of British objections. The Cabinet had come to the conclusion that there were, indeed, 'too many cooks stirring this broth'. Because of the uniqueness of the Free French position, no normal liaison organisation was established. There were a multiplicity of groups that dealt with the Free French. The most important was the Spears Mission – named after its founder, General Spears. The mission had been conceived of as essentially military in nature – not surprisingly since de Gaulle's movement had been originally seen as a military one – and reported to the Minister of Defence (Churchill) through Desmond Morton, chairman of the Committee on (Allied) Resistance, and Morton reported directly to the Prime Minister. As we have seen Lord Bessborough also dealt with the Free French as did the Vansittart Committee. The most important thing to note here is that, although they had representatives on the Morton and Vansittart Committees, all of these groups were outside the control of the Foreign Office. As the Free French movement grew in importance, it was natural that the Foreign Office would try to assert its own qualifications for liaison work and would, indeed, try to suppress its rivals. This is exactly what happened, and Eden and the Foreign Office gradually assumed control of all liaison with the Free French. This appealed to de Gaulle for two reasons. The first was, of course, that proper diplomatic representation appealed to his strong sense of French sovereignty. The second was that he was finding Spears's excessive love for France to be very dangerous for the development of the Free French movement. By the summer of 1941, Spears had been sent to Syria, and the Foreign Office had asserted their supremacy over dealings with the Free French.

In spite of this, Anglo-French friction continued. Although people like Spears could serve as particular irritants, the fact remained that British policy did not have the same aims as Free French policy, for the British were essentially interested in winning the war, while the Free French directed their energies towards the re-establishment of France as a great power. From June 1940 onwards, conflict was bound to occur and to continue. Although certain personalities might increase the friction between the two sides, they were not fundamentally responsible for that friction. For one thing, as we have seen, very often during this early period British policy towards de Gaulle was determined by British policy towards Vichy. In many cases French soldiers were repatriated before de Gaulle or one of his representatives had a chance to speak to them about the Free French movement. Early on, in the rush of preparing for the Battle of Britain, the British actually more or less forgot about many of de Gaulle's recruits who were placed in unsanitary conditions in various camps. Desmond Morton, one of Churchill's assistants, wrote to the prime minister about one such camp:

> ... it has been arranged that the 1400 Frenchmen now at Olympia will all be given facilities for a shower-bath this evening ... All the men will be provided with the necessary soap, towels, etc, which they have lacked hitherto, and clean underclothes ... As regards the rumour that the soldiers were verminous, I am assured that this is a premature statement but not by a very great margin.[29]

One can imagine how these soldiers felt, many of whom had left their families in France, often at great risk, to throw in their lot with an ally who had bombed their fleet and detained them in appalling conditions. Furthermore, in this early period, military considerations were often thought more important than political ones, and here again the French and British were certain to conflict. The British military often actively discouraged recruitment for the Free French on the grounds that it might make Pétain and Weygand more anti-British. Finally, there was Britain's all important relationship with the United States, and the latter was less than excited by the Free French. Here again was room for conflict.

The basic problem was that during this early period, the Free French were almost completely dependent on the British. This dependence had a two-fold effect. It made the French feel resentful and jealous. Paradoxically, the very fact that Britain continued to resist the Germans, although deeply wished for by all Free Frenchmen, increased their resentment and jealousy. The Free French were humiliated by the fact that their country had been the only one to sign an armistice with the enemy, and Britain's resistance made them feel even more ashamed. In other words, the French had an inferiority complex – a fact which the most observant British commentators could not fail to realise – and for this reason they overreacted when questions of sovereignty or culture were involved. On the other hand, the British felt that the Free French owed them something, even if it were only proper behaviour and a sense of gratitude. They developed a corresponding sense of superiority. As time passed, however, the British became more and more convinced that they too needed the Free French. De Gaulle, in spite of his occasionally bizarre behaviour and always suspicious attitude, was fundamentally a dependable ally. Once territory was under the control of Free France there was no risk of any intriguing with the Axis, and to the British this was all important. The history of Anglo-Free French relations from 1940 to 1942 is one of differing goals, incomprehension, but also of mutual need and admiration. Throughout this period, however, their relationship became more and more complicated by the United States's growing involvement in the war. By 1942 British policy towards the Free French no longer really existed: it had become Anglo-American policy. Washington now had a strong voice in the question.

2 Free France and the United States, 1940–42

Even more than Britain's, America's policy towards the Free French during this early period was shaped by relations with Vichy. In late 1940 Admiral William Leahy, personal friend of Roosevelt and major military figure, was appointed ambassador to Vichy. He stayed until Laval's return to power in April 1942, but even after this an American representative remained until Vichy finally broke diplomatic relations after the Allied invasion of North Africa in November 1942. The maintenance of relations with Vichy inevitably entailed a certain neglect of Free France, and this in turn led to a great deal of bitterness among the latter. An examination of the French literature on the subject shows how much this was felt by the French. In fact there is much that can be said on both sides because, although there was a great deal wrong with the Free French organization, particularly in the United States, there is no doubt that the Americans – and especially Roosevelt – frequently behaved in a very petty way. Both sides suspected each other of the worst motives: the Free French often accused the Americans of wishing to perpetuate Vichy, and the Americans suspected de Gaulle of wanting to establish a dictatorship in France. While neither side was right, there was some evidence to support both interpretations. One thing is certain: American policy towards both Vichy and Free France was much more nuanced and complicated than it has been traditionally viewed. It certainly merits a detailed examination based on recently released documents.

To begin with, if the Americans were not fond of de Gaulle, they just as certainly did not like Vichy. One of the most criticized architects of American policy was Admiral Leahy who, while undoubtedly hostile to de Gaulle, was far from being pro-Vichy. In fact he held no illusions about the Pétain government, writing that:

> It is discouraging, from the point of view of those of us who are confirmed believers in representative government, to see France completely in the hands of a dictator, a benevolent dictator for so long a time as the Marshal survives; but so much of a 'Bill of Rights' as did previously exist in France has been abrogated and what are, in effect, *lettres de cachet* are now employed to get rid of opposition.[1]

Towards the end of his period in Vichy, he came to the conclusion that he had achieved nothing and that there was nothing he could do as ambassador that would, as he put it, 'give some semblance of backbone to a jellyfish'. His assessment was that most people at Vichy would only respond to 'positive action', a term that is not defined but probably meant physical force.[2] Leahy's antipathy towards de Gaulle, thus, did not stem from a corresponding fondness for Vichy. An examination of archival sources shows that the same thing is true for other major Americans dealing with France. Cordell Hull, the American Secretary of State, certainly did not like Vichy either – a point which is illustrated by his ultra sensitivity to any criticism of the United States's Vichy policy. Even Roosevelt held few illusions about Vichy.

In fact, American policy towards Vichy was based on very pragmatic considerations. To begin with, they felt that in the summer of 1940 Marshal Pétain had given the French what they wanted – peace. There is no doubt that, reeling under the shock of the German blitzkrieg, almost everyone in France supported the Armistice and felt grateful to Pétain and his followers for remaining in the country to share their hardship. As we have seen, de Gaulle and his movement attracted few supporters during this period. The Americans, unlike the British, did not feel the same sense of moral indignation about the Armistice. The Americans had not been fighting in 1940, and they did not feel betrayed by it as the British had. Furthermore, the British had survived the blitz and, thus, felt morally superior to the French. To the British, France had indeed 'fallen' – except for General de Gaulle – while to the Americans the situation was more complex. For a certain period of time, Pétain could be viewed as trying to 'shield' France from the worst consequences of their military defeat.[3]

American policy towards Vichy was therefore partly shaped by the fact that America was not, from June 1940 to December 1941, a belligerent. They could hardly wholeheartedly condemn Vichy for not fighting. Furthermore, although confined to a non-belligerent position, Roosevelt wished to do as much as possible to assist Britain. The President himself explained American policy to Vichy in the following terms:

> In spite of the severity of this blow [the defeat of France], there remained intact important French assets which might still be salvaged from the wreck. It was to this end, and in pursuance of our avowed policy of rendering all possible assistance to the hard-pressed peoples of the British Commonwealth and Empire, that this Government decided to maintain official – I stress the word official – relations with Marshal

Pétain's regime which Hitler permitted to function in a limited way at Vichy.[4]

As we have seen, the French fleet and the French Empire – particularly North Africa which bordered the Libyan field of battle – were considered by the British to be serious threats if they fell into German hands. It is, therefore, not surprising that Roosevelt would try to aid the British by asserting diplomatic influence on the French about these questions. The policy was thus – at the beginning – a logical one. It must also be said that no one near Roosevelt seemed to have doubted that the United States would one day enter the war and reconquer Europe. Therefore, the policy made sense from a second point of view: it maintained a visible, generally positive American presence in France and North Africa at a period when the French felt isolated, and in this way the Americans hoped to prepare their own future invasion of France. Much has been made of American use of Vichy as its 'eyes' in conquered Europe and North Africa, but many in the administration felt that it was even more important simply to maintain a pro-American opinion in the hopes that American troops would one day be welcome.[5] The only trouble was that, at least in terms of the Vichy government, the policy achieved nothing. Neither Pétain nor Darlan cared very much about what the Americans felt. As we saw in the previous chapter, de Gaulle was alone among French leaders in placing a high value on American power. The only major result of the Vichy policy was that it irritated America's natural ally.

Actually, it is a mistake to think that the Gaullists were fundamentally hostile to America's Vichy connection. They could perceive the logic of it and, more importantly, they were convinced that Vichy would only disappoint any hopes placed in it, and that in the end the Americans would be forced to deal with the Free French. After Pearl Harbor the Americans, both by words and actions, began to make it clear to Free France that they understood this. H. Freeman 'Doc' Matthews of the State Department, who had been in Vichy with Leahy and who could hardly be termed pro-de Gaulle, told the Free French that there was no misunderstanding in Washington about Vichy. He insisted that if the Allies were able to guarantee that the Germans could not touch the remains of French military strength, relations between Washington and Vichy would end instantly.[6] The opening of American military bases in Free French territory in 1942 showed the United States's desire and need to work with the Gaullists. It is safe to say that most members of Free France did not become seriously alarmed by the Vichy connection until after the 'Darlan Deal' in November 1942. What hurt the Free French was the American refusal – at least during this early period – to recognize them, not as a government but simply as Allies. One of their major aims was, as we have seen, to keep France in the war fighting at the side of the Allies, so that she could be present at the peace conference and share in the victory. If the most important of these Allies refused to acknowledge Free France's contribution, then those aims were in danger. The Free French were far more hurt by being kept from joining the United Nations pact against the Axis than by America's relations with Vichy. One State Department report noted that the Free French had been 'hurt' to see all flags but their own flying at meetings. They wanted to know what they were considered to be: 'Nothing more than canon meat?'[7] Adrien Tixier, the Free French representative in Washington, admitted to having been much more concerned by this refusal than by American relations with Vichy.[8] It seemed to them to be – and in fact was – a deliberately petty act. The story of how American-Free French relations descended to such a level is a sad one that reflects little credit on either side. It must not be forgotten, though, that this relationship had a constructive side to it that increased in importance as the war went on, and eventually dominated the question.

The problem probably began with the Free French organization in the United States. In those tragic days of June 1940, as we have seen, General de Gaulle had few recruits and, for this reason, he did not choose his representatives in America – they chose him. These early representatives were thus self-appointed and often barely known to de Gaulle. An organisation was also founded, 'France Forever', which was based in New York and had more of a cultural and fund-raising aspect. Unfortunately, none of the major French personalities in the United States – Alexis Léger, Jean Monnet, Eve Curie and Jacques Maritain among others – would rally to de Gaulle. There were other reasons why the Free French were not very popular in America. It soon became clear that there were serious problems with the Free French movement in the United States. To begin with, 'France Forever' not only did not raise any money to contribute to the Free French budget, it actually had to be financed by London. Given the material wealth of the United States, this seemed incredible to many people. They were of course hampered by the Neutrality Act, which at that time made it illegal to raise money for a belligerent government. The British, however, refused to accept this argument, insisting that since de Gaulle was neither a government nor the agent of a government, the Neutrality law could not apply to his movement. Both the British Consulate-General in New York and the Embassy in Washington agreed that the real problem was with 'France Forever', which was a remarkably ineffective organisation given to infighting and society parties.[9] The head of 'France Forever'

was Eugène Houdry who was generally considered to be honest but totally
out of his depth. The vice-president was close friends with Vichy sympathizers and had several times 'forgotten' to pass on information destined
for the British consul or Siéyès. Another former member of the Committee
had been guilty of passing bad cheques, while yet another member was
strongly suspected of Vichy sympathies. All in all the organisation gave
a bad impression.[10]

There were other, even more serious problems with the Gaullist organization in the United States. For one thing, there was an almost complete
failure to keep accounts or to forward them to London. There were also
frequent requests to the British consulate for financial advances, and this
practice de Gaulle disapproved of completely.[11] In one case a sum of $15 000
was advanced by the War Office without de Gaulle having been informed
of it by his subordinates in the United States. When the British government told him of this transaction, he had no idea why the money had been
requested. After this episode, de Gaulle was forced to instruct British con-
sulates to refuse to give advances unless they had been previously approved
by Carlton Gardens – excepting, of course, advances needed to transport
volunteers. De Gaulle also ordered someone to be appointed who would be
responsible for the accounts and who would deal with the financial department at Carlton Gardens.[12] There were also numerous stories of volunteers
for the Free French Army being effectively turned away by the American
branch of the organisation.[13] Furthermore, the Free French representatives
in the United States were sending no reports back to London – in spite of
the fact that some, at least, of them had relatively high salaries.[14]

Furthermore, there was a sharp personal antagonism between Free
France's two main representatives, Jacques de Siéyès and Marie-Adrien
(Maurice) Garreau-Dombasle. Siéyès, who was a close personal friend of
de Gaulle and completely devoted to him, had the title of de Gaulle's
personal representative and was in charge of recruiting, while Garreau-
Dombasle, a diplomat, took care of political and economic questions. The
problem was that both men insisted that the other was his subordinate.
Their infighting became quite heated and instead of sending reports on the
Free French movement in the United States, they sent letters to de Gaulle
insulting each other. It was generally agreed that Siéyès, at least, was honest
although incompetent. There was considerably more doubt about Garreau.
The latter finally offered his resignation in early June 1941, although he
remained with 'France Forever'. De Gaulle accepted his resignation on the
condition that he would publicly insist that no personal disagreements
were involved and that he was simply too busy to do the job. Unfortunately,
Garreau considered this to be useless because everybody knew the truth.[15]

Needless to say, it was generally considered that the situation in the United States needed to be investigated and put in order. In May 1941, officials at the Foreign Office began to discuss the possibility of sending René Pleven to Washington. They were frankly worried by the American attitude to Free France. As one official noted:

> Vichy have now done more than ever we could do to disillusion American official and unofficial opinion about themselves . . . But the fact remains that Gen de Gaulle is badly represented in the USA, and the lack of sympathy for the movement is certainly accounted for to a considerable extent by the poor figure cut by its sponsors.[16]

On 18 May, Anthony Eden approved such a visit . By the end of May, de Gaulle had come to the same conclusion, and on 2 June he wrote to Siéyès announcing the imminent arrival of Pleven and insisting that the latter was empowered to act in de Gaulle's name during his mission. Pleven's orders, de Gaulle wrote, would be de Gaulle's orders.[17] Pleven left for Washington later that month. De Gaulle had secured British agreement to assist Pleven in every way possible and in return he told Pleven to keep Lord Halifax, the British Ambassador in Washington, informed of his activities.[18] It is nothing short of remarkable that in the midst of one of the most serious Anglo-Free French crises of the war – that over Syria in the summer of 1941 – we see at the same time one of the best examples of Anglo-Free French cooperation during Pleven's visit to the United States. There is no doubt that the British Embassy did everything it could to further the Free French cause with the Americans, and that in return Pleven honoured de Gaulle's undertaking to keep the Foreign Office informed of everything.

Pleven was the logical choice for this mission because he had been part of the Anglo-French Air Mission in Washington in 1939–40 and counted among his friends the American Under-Secretary for War, John McCloy. He also possessed unquestionable integrity and important administrative skills. Upon arrival, though, Pleven discovered that the situation was worse than anyone in London had realized. In January 1941 de Gaulle had sent one of his followers, Gérard de Saint-André, on a special mission to New York in order to investigate problems in the Free French organisation there. When Pleven arrived, he discovered that Saint-André had made an agreement with a New Yorker that allowed the latter to act as an intermediary between Free France and the Treasury Department on the question of unfreezing French assets in the United States. Part of the agreement was that if these assets were unfrozen, a rather large commission would be paid to the New Yorker. Worse still, Saint-André had received the accord of Siéyès and neither one had informed Carlton Gardens. Pleven immediately went to the Treasury Department and revealed what had happened. Fortunately, according to American law, the whole transaction had absolutely no legal value.[19]

It was, of course, clear that new men had to be found to represent Free France in America. Pleven was probably the best choice to do this, but he wished to return to Carlton Gardens and continue his work there. He tried to interest Alexis Léger in the job, but the latter preferred to remain aloof from the movement. Realizing that there was no single person who had the force and reputation for such a position, Pleven decided to form a delegation. He wrote to de Gaulle that he had found two men who were capable of leading the delegation: Etienne Boegner, an industrialist whose father was head of the French federation of Protestant Churches, and Adrien Tixier, director of the International Labour Office in Washington. Pleven himself seems to have preferred Boegner for the job, and there is no doubt that he was better viewed by the State Department. De Gaulle however chose Tixier, who was friends with both René Cassin and John Winant, the American ambassador to Great Britain. De Gaulle seems to have felt that his movement had been too often portrayed in the United States as being extremely right-wing and that a known leftist and labour leader would stand in well with the administration that had developed the New Deal. Boegner was placed in charge of economic questions while Raoul Roussy de Sales, a prominent and gravely ill French thinker, was responsible for press and public relations. Siéyès remained in charge of recruitment, while a young diplomat named Raoul Aglion took over the movement in New York. 'France Forever' was also reformed and suspected Vichy sympathizers and other undesirables were forced out.

Pleven also spent a great deal of time meeting with representatives of the American government. Not surprisingly, he was warmly received at the War Department, which quickly decided to send a fact-finding mission to Free French Africa. He also met with the Vice-President, Henry Wallace, and with many officials at the Treasury Department and with the United States Trade Commissioner. He primarily tried to interest the Americans in buying products from Free French colonies, such as lead, nickel, zinc and vanilla. In general, he was well received in the United States – almost everywhere, in fact, except at the State Department. In spite of Halifax's best efforts, no senior official there would meet with Pleven at first. However, as the summer progressed, Vichy's stock declined considerably and Free France's correspondingly rose. To begin with, an anti-British coup had taken place in Iraq in early April 1941, and Vichy had, on 11 May, decided to allow German planes to fly from Syrian bases to support the rebels. This had greatly shocked American opinion, but what was even more upsetting was that when, in June, the British and Free French had invaded Syria, the Vichy French had resisted bitterly. Furthermore, in July, Vichy allowed Japanese forces to occupy Indochina. The State Department reacted strongly, and the Under-Secretary of State, Sumner Welles, issued a statement saying that:

> Under these circumstances, this Government is impelled to question whether the French Government at Vichy in fact proposes to maintain its declared policy to preserve for the French people the territories both at home and abroad which have long been under French sovereignty . . . The United States will be governed by the manifest effectiveness with which those authorities endeavour to protect these territories from domination and control by those powers which are seeking to extend their rule by force and conquest or by the threat thereof.[20]

The implication of this statement was quite clear, and Pleven felt that it signified 'a major turning point' in United States policy. No one could doubt the willingness of Free France to defend its colonies against the Axis.

In reality, Free France had never been entirely without friends in the State Department. Perhaps their most important ally was Anthony Biddle, the American Ambassador to the exiled governments in London. In June 1940, when the French government fled Paris for Bordeaux, the American Ambassador to France, William Bullitt, had stayed behind in Paris to give whatever protection he could to the city. Biddle had, in his place, represented American interests in Bordeaux and had been disgusted by what he had found there. He was convinced that the American policy towards Vichy – and particularly Weygand – was wrong and disagreed with Robert Murphy's requests for assistance to North Africa. In May 1941, he explained to Harold Mack of the Foreign Office that:

> You and I were south of the Loire last June; Bob Murphy was north of the Loire. We were standing by the wringer and saw the dirty water coming. Bob Murphy went to Vichy afterwards and only saw the water which was comparatively clean after several rinsings. He consequently has no idea of the depth of defeat and degradation to which the men of Bordeaux and the men of Vichy have sunk. I would take Weygand over to America and blanket him. People like him are best liquidated and we should try and find some energetic officer to put in his place.

Given his title it was natural that, until an official representative to de Gaulle could be appointed, he acted as unofficial liaison with the Free French. He sent highly positive reports back to Washington and did his best to interest the State Department in Free France. In April 1941 he asked Ben Burman, who was going to Free French Africa on behalf of the United Press and *Readers Digest*, to investigate the situation there, and Burman did indeed send a glowing report. Here we see for the first time what will become commonplace in American relations with the Free French: the people on the spot, either in Free French colonies or near their head-quarters in London, will have a much higher opinion of the Gaullists than will those in Washington. This, of course, is at least partly linked to the low level of Free French representation in the United States, which in spite of Pleven's reorganization remained troubled throughout the war. One thing is certain: the meagre results of their Vichy policy, the strategical importance of Free French Africa, the Biddle reports and the Pleven visit were all conspiring to force the United States Government towards de Gaulle and Free France.[21]

The problem was that, like in Britain, many different groups and individuals were responsible for policy towards the Free French. As we have seen, the Treasury and the War Department were both generally well-disposed towards the Gaullists. The State Department was evolving in its views, but there remained the ultimate authority, President Franklin Roosevelt. It is important to remember that no major redirection of American policy could be achieved without the President's consent. However, Pleven did get some important results. He got the State Department to recognize a Free French delegation which, although not given full diplomatic status, would be the channel for official dealings between the two. He made notable progress towards one of his most important goals: getting the French admitted to Lend–Lease in their own right. This programme was devised by Roosevelt to assist the British war effort; its goal was to provide military equipment without accumulating the massive debts that had destabilised the world's economy after World War I. Material would be lent or leased to those countries whose defence was considered vital to that of the United States, and payment could be made in kind (Reciprocal Aid) or settled after the war. At the time of Pleven's visit the Free French were allowed to order supplies under Lend–Lease but as part of the British programme. On 11 November 1941 Roosevelt signed a statement admitting the Free French officially to Lend–Lease. Furthermore, the State Department decided to add one of their representatives to the military mission to Free French Africa. This, however, quickly gave rise to another crisis in American–Free French relations. The State Department had requested that this visit should remain a secret, at least until the mission arrived in Africa. In an article that contained an interview with de Gaulle, George Weller of the *Chicago Daily News* announced this mission and, what is more, revealed that de Gaulle had offered the United States naval bases at Douala, Pointe Noire and Port Gentil. He went on to state that de Gaulle wanted an immediate break between the United States and Vichy. Pleven was petrified when he saw the interview, and de Gaulle immediately denied most of it. All of this could only infuriate Vichy, and it is perhaps symptomatic of the deterioration in American relations with that government that the State Department did not seem very upset about the incident. It did, however, only add to their belief that the Free French were unreliable.

The military mission to Free French Africa was the next episode in the saga of America and de Gaulle. Its leader was Colonel Cunningham from the War Department. Cunningham had been chosen because he spoke fluent French and had a French wife. It was not unwise to think that he would be sympathetic to the Free French, and the first impression he gave was quite a good one. The American Consul at Leopoldville wrote to Hull that Cunningham was the best possible choice for such an appointment and that the French had been greatly impressed by him.[22] Unfortunately this good impression did not last long. He irritated both the War and State Departments by giving an interview to the *New York Times* which exaggerated the importance of the mission and his role within it. What is worse, he quickly became involved in Free French politics, offering advice on all subjects to them, and when questioned about this wrote rather aggressive replies to Washington. He was also extremely liberal in his promises of aid – promises which often had not been approved in Washington. He told de Gaulle, for example, that Roosevelt had promised to provide everything necessary for a Free French victory.[23] On 20 December, Hull ordered Cunningham to return to the United States, which he did in January. He had certainly violated Free French sovereignty by injecting himself into their local affairs.[24] He managed to irritate both de Gaulle and the State Department by his attitude. On the other hand, he had clearly done a great deal of work and gathered a lot of information. As a result of his trip, the War Department became more and more interested in establishing a base at Pointe Noire, and this was finally done the following year.

The Cunningham Mission, however, was eclipsed by the Free French invasion of Saint-Pierre and Miquelon. De Gaulle had announced his intention to rally these two tiny islands off the coast of Canada in September 1940 but had been prevented from doing so by the Canadian government.[25] Late in 1941 de Gaulle decided that it was time to try again and sent Muselier to North America. In fact, both Canada and the United States had become increasingly alarmed by the powerful shortwave radio station on St Pierre. It was known that Vichy was transmitting meteorological reports from there to the Axis, and it seemed likely that they could be sending other, even more damaging information. By late 1941 Canada, the United States and Great Britain all felt that something had to be done about the situation, but the problem was that no one could agree on what to do. The British wanted the Free French to take over the islands, while the Americans preferred a Canadian expedition to neutralize the radio station. De Gaulle, who was as usual worried about French sovereignty being violated, felt that the Free French had to rally the islands. On 15 December 1941, the American Minister in Canada telephoned Washington to say that Muselier had arrived there and was authorized by de Gaulle to take over the islands. The following day, Ray Atherton of the European Division of the State Department told the American Minister that the President had announced his opposition to any attempt by the Free French to rally the islands. On the 17th, Muselier accepted this and agreed to take no action. The following day, however, he received an order from de Gaulle to seize the islands. Muselier obeyed and on the 24th invaded. A plebiscite taken immediately afterwards showed overwhelming support for Free France. The American Government, however, was furious – particularly Cordell Hull. The Secretary of State was certainly in an overwrought condition already from his negotiations with the Japanese that had ended a few weeks earlier with the attack on Pearl Harbor and the destruction of much of the Pacific fleet. Psychologically, it was not the best moment to do something that risked upsetting Hull. The Secretary of State's reaction was immediate. He issued an ill-advised statement, saying that 'three so-called Free French ships' had taken over the islands and during the next few weeks worked hard to remove the Free French in order to placate Vichy. The press had, however, almost unanimously welcomed the invasion, and Hull's statement was greeted with derision – some papers describing Hull as the 'so-called Secretary of State'. Hull only made matters worse by trying to explain that 'so-called' had referred to the ships not to the Free French, which led some papers to suggest that Hull might have thought the invasion had been conducted on surfboards or pink elephants. The whole episode was convincing proof of the unpopularity of the American Government's Vichy policy in the nation. From this point of view, de Gaulle certainly gained his point, but he did so at the cost of totally alienating most of the Department of State for a long period of time. Furthermore Muselier, who as we have already seen was deeply hostile to de Gaulle, did his best to convince the State Department of his sincerity and of de Gaulle's dictatorial ambitions. He was sowing on fertile ground. However, strangely enough, what seemed to irritate Hull even more than the actual invasion was Churchill's speech in defence of de Gaulle in Ottawa a few days after the invasion. In a conversation with the British minister in Washington, Sir Ronald Campbell, Hull showed that his anger was greater against the British than against the French, and he criticised the British Government for 'fomenting against the United States for British benefit the bitter agitation against this country over the islands'. In an amazing contortion of logical reasoning, Hull accused Churchill of giving 'trouble-making people a pretext to make it appear that the British were the only friends the Free French had, and, inferentially, that the United States was not their friend'. The man who had talked of the 'so-called Free French' now was worried that, because of the British, they might not think he was their friend! He went on to say that Churchill was trying to show that the British were anti-Vichy, while the United States supported that Government![26] Clearly Hull, at least, was uncomfortable with America's French policy and equally clearly he was highly suspicious of the British. Furthermore, a memorandum by Hopkins shows that Hull had wanted to handle the whole question through normal diplomatic channels and had resented Roosevelt's decision to take it up directly with Churchill.[27] The United States finally accepted the Free French action, recognizing that only a change of regime was involved and not a change of sovereignty. However, the Americans did revenge themselves on de Gaulle. Roosevelt had originally agreed to phrase the Declaration of the United Nations of allies against the Axis in a way that would allow the Free French to participate. When the pact was signed on New Year's Day, 1942, the Free French were not present.

Strangely enough, on 15 January 1942, in the midst of all the uproar over St Pierre and Miquelon, the Americans signed an agreement with the Free French which allowed the United States to establish military bases in Free French possessions in the Pacific. In March the Americans landed over 40 000 troops under Major-General Alexander Patch in New Caledonia. In a stroke the Americans entered into a colonial situation of overwhelming complexity.[28] For one thing, New Caledonia contained many different ethnic groups: there were the original inhabitants, the Kanaks; a large number of imported Asian workers; a few Japanese, and of course the French settlers who dominated the island. The situation was further complicated by a personality conflict between the governor, Henri Sautot, who was generally loved by the settlers, and the High Commissioner for the Pacific, Admiral Georges Thierry d'Argenlieu, who was intensely disliked by the New Caledonians for his rather high-handed methods but was one of de Gaulle's favourites. Patch, of course, knew absolutely nothing about the internal situation in New Caledonia. Furthermore, Patch's army had been put together quickly and was neither well-trained nor well-equipped. To add to Patch's problems, New Caledonia was very clearly threatened. The Pacific War had started very badly for the Allies; Pearl Harbor had been quickly followed by the fall of Singapore and the occupation of Sumatra and Java. By May both Australia and New Caledonia were directly threatened. On 4 May the Battle of the Coral Sea began which would decide the limits of Japanese expansion. It is against this dire military menace that the events in New Caledonia must be judged.

D'Argenlieu had originally expected to be in command of any American Force in New Caledonia but had been informed by the Combined Chiefs of Staff that this would be impossible. They emphasized, however, that his position would be no different from British governors in areas were there were leased bases.[29] D'Argenlieu appears to have been quite disappointed by not receiving command of the expedition, and he reacted in a way that could only appeal to de Gaulle – he became obsessed with protecting French sovereignty. This argument also worked to his advantage because Sautot was much more friendly to the Americans and ready to accommodate them. Furthermore, Sautot showed a tendency to reach agreements with the Americans without consulting d'Argenlieu, which, of course, only served to increase the latter's irritation. Patch, meanwhile, took a dislike to d'Argenlieu and wrote to General George Marshall, Chief of Staff of the United States Army, suggesting that, since the New Caledonians disliked d'Argenlieu so much, it would be a good thing if he could be transferred.[30] It is unclear whether the Americans presented this suggestion to de Gaulle or not.

De Gaulle, of course, firmly supported d'Argenlieu and his method of governing the island and of treating the Americans. In a letter of 8 April, de Gaulle stated that he would prefer it if Sautot and d'Argenlieu could work together, but if this was impossible he would recall Sautot to London. In his letter he included a message of recall and left it to d'Argenlieu's discretion as to if and when it would be used.[31] D'Argenlieu presented this message to Sautot on 30 April, and Sautot, although obviously upset, at first agreed to leave. The problem was that Sautot was so popular and d'Argenlieu so disliked in New Caledonia that the population was soon demanding, not only that Sautot should remain, but that d'Argenlieu should be recalled instead. At this point, on 5 May, d'Argenlieu panicked and abducted Sautot and four of his leading supporters – all important citizens of New Caledonia – and sent them sailing towards New Zealand. The situation then rapidly spun out of control in New Caledonia, as a general strike was called and numerous demonstrations took place. D'Argenlieu was forced to ask the Americans to restore order, but Patch refused, insisting that he must remain neutral. Patch reported to Marshall that he was most concerned by the fact that d'Argenlieu could not have undertaken such an action unless American troops had been present to maintain order. The very act implied American support, and this in turn, Patch felt, might discredit the Americans to the New Caledonians. The next day Patch wrote once again insisting that: 'The source of trouble is d'Argenlieu and his mission.'[32]

By 9 May the situation was escalating out of control: demonstrations were becoming violent; business had been practically halted; d'Argenlieu was himself a prisoner of his opponents, and a Japanese aircraft carrier was within range of New Caledonia. Patch decided that he had to intervene and requested permission to declare martial law. The American Admiral Stark in London, who was responsible for relations there with the Free French, went to see de Gaulle. The latter, after voicing numerous complaints which he had received from d'Argenlieu about the Americans, reluctantly agreed to Patch's request. In view of the danger facing New Caledonia he really had no other choice. It was agreed that Patch would specify that a state of siege had been declared only because of the military situation and with the accord of de Gaulle. Patch would also assume responsibility for the security of d'Argenlieu who would be free to send coded telegrams to de Gaulle. Furthermore, it was agreed that Patch would neither become nor name the new governor. Instead, de Gaulle promptly named a new governor who was in Africa. Until his arrival, Patch would be in charge and issue orders. Finally, strict censorship was imposed, and de Gaulle was not forced to give any kind of guarantee about d'Argenlieu's future status.[33] In his reports d'Argenlieu had been giving a rather slanted version of events, insisting that the trouble was caused by Vichy sympathizers working in unison with the Americans. It was the sad result of America's Vichy policy and of de Gaulle's suspicious nature that the latter never doubted such an explanation. He even went so far as to tell d'Argenlieu to beware of any message supposedly from de Gaulle that the Americans might give him and to insist that he should only rely on coded telegrams directly from Carlton Gardens.[34] It was a particularly sad episode that only served to confirm both sides – incorrectly – in the bad opinion they had of each other.

Furthermore, Pleven's attempt to clean up the Free French organization in the United States had not worked. 'France Forever' continued its infighting and backbiting. Even the delegation in Washington continued to have problems. To begin with, Raoul Roussy de Sales, who was much the most prominent and respected member of the delegation, died soon after his appointment. This was an immense loss to the Free French movement. Furthermore, Adrien Tixier, the head of the delegation, was also jealous of Etienne Boegner who was well-considered by the State Department, and he managed to turn de Gaulle against Boegner on the grounds that the latter was too pro-American. Boegner was soon forced out of the movement, leading Adolph Berle, the main State Department official responsible for the Free French, to tell Tixier:

> I observed that it was difficult for us here to appraise the De Gaulle movement when our principal news was of would-be de Gaulle supporters who were being constantly eliminated from the movement. Political movements usually aimed to gain adherents, not to exclude people.[35]

Tixier himself was not a trained diplomat, and his bluntness and rudeness quickly offended State Department sensibilities. His left wing associations quickly attracted the wrath of J. Edgar Hoover, who did his best to find incriminating evidence against him but without any real success.[36] Worse still, Tixier was lying to de Gaulle about his meetings with State Department officials, insisting that he had taken a much firmer stand than had been the case. This the Americans quickly discovered through their own sources in Free French headquarters, and it only served to further irritate the State Department.[37] Needless to say, Tixier was hated by the State Department.[38] However, this did not mean that the State Department – and particularly Berle – had given up on the Gaullist movement. On the same day as his unfortunate interview with Tixier cited above, Berle wrote to his superior saying that:

> The Free French situation presents a dilemma. On the one hand, we may be faced with a complete break with Vichy at any time. On the other hand, there is the de Gaulle movement which consists of a substantial military force under de Gaulle's military command; the de Gaulle name as a symbol, and an almost complete lack of political *savoir faire* . . .

Berle did feel that the Free French movement was important, and that the United States should work to construct a sound relationship with it, but he felt that this would have to be done in London, where a high quality American representative could talk directly with de Gaulle.[39]

In early September, just before the invasion of North Africa, the State and War Departments conducted a study of whether or not the Free French should be recognized by the United States. All major officials dealing with the French were asked to give their opinion, and the general consensus was against recognition for very pragmatic reasons. First, it was felt that recognition would give no military benefit to the United States because the Free French in most places were only too willing to be of military assistance. Second, many people believed that with the invasion of North Africa imminent and the situation still tense in Syria and Lebanon, it might actually have negative consequences to recognise the Free French.[40] Most officials realised that de Gaulle was sincerely committed to the Allied cause, that he was an important symbol in France, and that the Free French were popular and Vichy unpopular among the American public. Many of them also admitted that his following in France was likely to increase and that it might be damaging for the United States in the future to have delayed recognition of de Gaulle.

The Americans did not like Vichy, but they were certainly very unsure about de Gaulle and the Free French movement. Like the British, they had been shocked by his claim in the Brazzaville Manifesto that he represented the legal government of France, but, unlike the British, they did not know him well. They only noticed that in his early speeches he spoke in a rather hazy fashion of 'liberty' but never talked of restoring the Republic. They were suspicious that he was not really a democrat and might try to institute a dictatorship in France. In fact, de Gaulle had a solid reason in those early years for not talking of the Republic, for the German blitzkrieg of 1940 had discredited the Third Republic in France, and de Gaulle recognized this. In July 1941 de Gaulle wrote to Cassin that:

> We must continue to be prudent in the expression of our political position, in spite of the difficulties this semi-obscurity might create for us in the United States. If we simply proclaim that we are fighting for democracy we might get some fleeting praise from the Americans but we would lose a great deal on the French side, which is the most important. The mass of French people for the moment confuse the word democracy with the parliamentary regime that existed before the war. Our own supporters, whatever their political point of view, and especially our soldiers, are, by a great majority, convinced of this. That regime is condemned by the facts and by public opinion.[41]

However, as the war progressed, and Vichy became more and more discredited, the Republic gained in popularity. Correspondingly, the Free French developed their notions of the illegality of Vichy. Earlier they had stated that French governmental authority had been invested in de Gaulle and then in the French National Committee. In June 1942, they went further and openly formulated the idea of republican continuity. They stated in a memorandum which they sent to the American government that the French had freely entered the war and that their duly elected government had formally agreed not to conclude a separate peace from the British. The Government and the French national will had committed the nation to fight the Axis until the final victory. Adolph Berle immediately understood what the Gaullists were claiming. He wrote that the document:

> Had asserted a sort of principle of legitimacy by insisting that France was still at war with Germany, owing to the action of the Third French Republic. In a sense, it suggested that the Third French Republic was still alive. Monsieur Tixier said that it did do just that.[42]

The Free French had taken on the mantle of the Republic.

The Americans, however, were not convinced by de Gaulle's embrace of republicanism. In October 1942 de Gaulle wrote a letter to Roosevelt to try and explain why Free France was necessary. He stated that:

> If France, liberated by the victory of the democracies, felt herself to be a conquered nation, it is feared that her bitterness, her humiliation and her divided loyalties, far from turning her towards the democracies, might lay her open to other influences. You know what these are. This is not an imaginary danger, for the social structure of the country is going to find itself more or less shattered by privations and spoliation.

He insisted that Free France considered itself only a provisional authority that would last only until a rightful government could be elected. In explaining his own actions, he said:

> A member of the last regular Government of the III Republic, I openly declared in favour of France remaining in the war. The Government which, in its despair and panic had seized power, ordered the cease fire . . . However you look at it, I was alone. Should I have remained silent?[43]

It is sad to say that American–Free French relations had degenerated to such a point that this letter was greeted with derision at the State Department. Ray Atherton wrote to Sumner Welles that: 'It is two years too late and takes some ten pages of introduction to get down into the very little meat there is in it.'[44] It was not a good portent for the future that, on the eve of the invasion of North Africa, the Americans and the Free French viewed each other with suspicion. However, each side clearly understood that they needed each other.

3 Lebanon and Syria

The events in Syria and Lebanon during World War II form one of the strangest stories of that war. Crises occurred repeatedly in that region and were fuelled by personality conflicts between General Sir Edward Spears – who, as we will remember, had brought de Gaulle to London – and almost every French official in the area. However, there was much more to the problem than a simple question of individuals. To begin with, there was the strategic significance of the Levant which was of immense importance to the British who otherwise had few interests there. The British and Free French had moved into this area initially because the Germans were using it as a base to attack the British. As long as the Suez Canal remained threatened the British would consider these territories to be extremely important, and even afterwards they would remain vital because many Allied supplies for the Pacific War passed through the Suez Canal. These regions also bordered the powder-keg of Palestine, which was under British mandate and was threatening to explode into violence between Jew, Arab and British occupier. Any events in Lebanon and Syria would automatically have significant repercussions in Palestine, and, needless to say, the British wanted to avoid this at all costs. The Middle East was also vital as a whole because of the importance of its oil supplies to the war effort. The British therefore could not risk irritating Arab opinion for it might have severe consequences on their war effort. The French on the other hand – true to their policy of retaining the empire – did not wish to grant full independence until after the war. Most French were not fundamentally opposed to independence, but rather did not want to do so from a position of weakness. They were thus determined to hold on to Syria and Lebanon at least until the end of the war, while the British were equally determined to force them to give a real measure of independence to these nations – although they wished the French to maintain a privileged position in the Levant similar to the British position in Iraq or Egypt.

Syria, which included a partially autonomous Lebanon, had been taken from the Ottoman Empire and placed under French mandate after World War I. The express aim of this mandate had been for the French to prepare Syria for independence as quickly as possible. A nationalist revolt had broken out there in 1925 and dragged on until 1936, when independence was promised by the government but voted down in the Chamber of Deputies. The Syrians were therefore an extremely dissatisfied people. Churchill had been seriously considering moving into Syria since the summer of 1940 and, during de Gaulle's absence from England for the Dakar expedition, had sent General Catroux there immediately after his arrival in Britain in September 1940.[1] From Cairo, Catroux studied the situation in the Levant closely. His observations led him to make several important conclusions. First, he realized that the French Army in the Levant was overwhelmingly hostile to Free France, and in March 1941 he warned that the army would resist any attempt to rally Syria and Lebanon.[2] Second, it was clear that nationalist troubles were breaking out in the area. These troubles were based primarily, according to Catroux, on the native population's dissatisfaction with the scarcity and expense of most basic food items and their anger over high taxation and repressive measures imposed by General Dentz, the Vichy High Commissioner. According to Catroux, the nationalists were taking advantage of this situation in order to exploit this dissatisfaction for their own purposes. They succeeded in their aim for the protests quickly became political and hostile to the maintenance of the Mandate. Panicked by the reaction, Dentz had changed direction and made certain concessions to the Syrians and Lebanese, but this, in turn, had irritated the local French. Catroux's recommendation was that the British should ease their blockade and try to strengthen Dentz's hand, because otherwise the troubles in the Levant might spill over into Palestine and Transjordan and seriously hurt the war effort.[3]

The situation, however, changed dramatically in April when a nationalist revolt against the British started in Iraq. Darlan, then in charge of the Vichy government, agreed in May of that year to let the Germans use Syrian airfields in order to support the Iraqi rebels. In response to this, the British and Free French decided to seize Syria, hoping to exploit the deep discontent among all groups and rally the territories without serious fighting. However in June 1941, when the Free French entered Syria, bitter, fratricidal fighting broke out with the Vichy troops, and British reinforcements were called in. The Syrian venture marks the last time that Free French troops were used by the Allies in attempts to rally the French Empire. In combination with the fiasco of Dakar, the Syrian battle convinced the Allies that the Free French would provoke a far stronger resistance by Vichy troops than would the British or Americans. In Madagascar and North Africa the Free French would be kept completely out of the picture – at least until military operations had clearly ended.

In an effort to gain Syrian support and with a view both to Arab and American opinion, the British insisted that the long deferred independence had to be proclaimed, and Catroux and de Gaulle, with some reluctance, agreed. On the day that Free French and British troops entered Syria, 8 June, General Catroux from Cairo proclaimed the Syrians and Lebanese 'free and independent'. He announced that they could now form them-selves into one or more states as they wished.[4] Sir Miles Lampson, then British Minister in Cairo, also made a declaration guaranteeing that the British Government would support Syrian and Lebanese independence. Mindful of the economic problems that had so antagonized the population, he also said that if the Levant would join the Allies, the United Kingdom would lift the blockade and associate them with the Sterling bloc. This declaration thus morally committed the British to the independence of the Levant. To a certain extent this statement worked, for the Syrians, at least at first, welcomed the British as liberators. It was clear from the very beginning, however, that the French had reservations about this declaration. Catroux himself wrote to Eden in late May that he had prepared the document in the 'spirit of alliance', and in his opinion such a proclamation was far from 'indispensable to French interests'. It had been done primarily, he maintained, in order to help the British in their policy towards the Arabs. He went on to complain that, although he had agreed to this only to please the British and although Churchill himself had sent him to Cairo to deal with the Syrian question, he was completely excluded from all military preparations for the attack due to a War Office order.[5] There is no doubt then that even before Syria was attacked, a certain half-heartedness was displayed on both sides. The Free French were not terribly enthused by this proclamation of independence while the British military did not consider the Free French to be equal partners.

The situation only worsened when it became clear that Vichy was determined to resist and that their hostility was primarily directed against the Free French. The British commander-in-chief in the Middle East, General Wilson, said of Vichy officers: 'Their attitude appears to be that this is [their] first opportunity since defeat by Germany of vindicating [the] honour [of the] French Army and that Free French as traitors to France constitute suitable corpus vile.'[6] The British military quickly be-came alarmed by this fact. When the Vichy commander, General Dentz, asked for an armistice, the British authorities immediately agreed. This was signed at Saint-Jean-d'Acre on 14 July, with the approval of General Catroux. This agreement was immediately denounced by General de Gaulle, who felt injured by the attitude taken by the British military. He was particularly irritated because General Wilson, the British commander, had in an address on the radio spoken as if his troops had been fighting against the French. De Gaulle felt that Wilson should have realised that, on the contrary, the real France was fighting with his troops.[7] De Gaulle literally flew into a rage in the office of Oliver Lyttelton, the newly arrived British Minister in Cairo, over the terms of the armistice and even went so far as to hand an ultimatum to the British, informing them that on 24 July at 12 noon the Free French troops in Syria would no longer be under British command.[8] De Gaulle objected in particular to two things in the armistice: first, the Free French were not allowed to try to recruit volunteers from the Vichy forces and, second, there was no reference to the legal situation of Syria. De Gaulle insisted that France must retain a privileged position in Syria. In a letter to René Cassin, he stated quite clearly that he wanted to establish the Free French solidly in the Levant, both politically and militarily and that the British were trying to prevent him from doing so.[9] The problem for the British was to find a way of placating de Gaulle without antagonizing the Syrians so that peace might be maintained in the area. Spears said of the situation:

> The problem is to prevent the country going up in smoke, to help make out of Syria a solid bloc which will provide a safe basis for our armed forces to operate from whatever the circumstances may be.
>
> This object is to be achieved in a country where (a) native interests often are in conflict with each other. (b) Population is now to a great extent armed. (c) French of all categories intensely disliked. (d) Free French very jealous of the British. (e) Free French authorities are often in conflict with each other. (f) Complete dearth of administrative officials. (g) A great many British unconnected elements intensely distrusted by the French upon whom the natives will endeavour to play.[10]

Essentially, they had to find a way to keep Syria as French as possible while protecting British interests in the Arab world. The potential for conflict was obvious.

On 23 July, Oliver Lyttelton and de Gaulle reached agreement on an interpretation of the armistice that would be considerably more favourable to the Free French. The Lyttelton–de Gaulle accords stated clearly that the Free French had the right to present their point of view to Vichy personnel; that all war material was Free French property; and that the French had 'special obligations' in the Levant States.[11] De Gaulle pronounced himself to be satisfied with the agreement. The effect on the local population, however, was considerably less good. They were, in general, extremely disappointed that there was no visible sign of the independence they had been promised, and feared that they had simply traded one set of French for another.[12] Even in other matters, Franco-British relations continued to be troubled. De Gaulle clearly suspected the British of wanting to replace them in the Levant.[13] This led to frequent disputes with the military authorities whom de Gaulle constantly accused of ignoring the Lyttelton–de Gaulle accords.[14] The British military, on the other hand, felt they needed special powers in order to secure the military situation, and these powers necessarily overlapped into the political and economic domain. They desperately sought to maintain order and to do this they had to ensure adequate food supplies – which only the British could do since they controlled most of the shipping – and to establish some kind of a working arrangement between the French and the local governments.

In effect, the British were demanding that an informal Franco-British condominium had to be established in the Levant during the war because of its strategic importance. This involvement in Syrian and Lebanese affairs, while perfectly justifiable according to the British point of view, seemed to the French an unwarranted invasion into relations between France and the nations under its mandate. Given the long history of colonial rivalry between the two nations, many French people feared that this informal condominium would last beyond the war and that the British wished to take over completely in the Levant. The problem was complicated by the extremely weak condition of the Free French who were totally dependent on the British for everything. Catroux, for example, found it humiliating to have to ask for advances from Spears, a man he detested. In one case, he wrote to Carlton Gardens asking them to send whatever money they possibly could without requesting an advance from the British.[15] To aggravate matters further, both sides generally overreacted to the other's proposals. In early August, for example, the Free French tried to refuse any special rights to the British military which led General Wilson to threaten to impose martial law.[16] At the same time, the French refused a British request to have General Spears present at the negotiations to establish treaties with the Syrians and Lebanese. Catroux explained that this was a matter that only concerned France and the nations under her mandate: to allow a British representative to be present, he insisted, would injure the authority of the French negotiators.[17]

By now the situation had become further complicated by the personality of General Spears. Spears had done a great deal for the movement in its early days, but it was clear that he wanted to control it himself. Spears was certainly very jealous of his role in Free France. Early on he wrote to Churchill: 'The French situation is not a hopeful one nor is it likely to bring much credit to anyone in charge of it and that is why I venture to suggest that you put me in charge of the whole French question and let me be responsible to you.'[18] However much Churchill liked to inject himself and his friends in foreign affairs, he was not crazy enough to go that far. Spears continued to complain about French questions being discussed in his absence. In fact, from the very beginning, de Gaulle seems to have tried to develop his own links with British ministries and to circumvent

Spears. This led to numerous protests by Spears and members of his staff, who found that they frequently did not know about major questions involving the Free French.

Basically Spears felt more at home in France than in England, to a large extent because of his childhood. France was the country in which he had been born and raised while England was the country for which his parents had abandoned him. Because they had not registered his birth with French authorities, Spears was denied French citizenship and forced to be British. He reconciled his British nationality with his mystic love of France in a strange way: he could be French while remaining British through the military alliance of the two countries. When France fell, only de Gaulle gave him the possibility of maintaining that alliance, and he threw himself into the organization of Free France. The problem was that he wanted to direct the movement himself, and the only way he could do this, given his role, was to assert British control. He explained once that:

> The French must really have the courage to stand by and defend the position which every thinking man knows to be inevitable, namely that the F[ree] F[rench] Movement, although completely free and independent is but a very junior partner of the British Empire and everybody knows it, and that if we are to help them we must do it in our own way.[19]

This explains the strange transformation, which so puzzled his contemporaries, of a devoted Francophile into a champion of British imperialism. It also explains why de Gaulle, in particular, felt he had to go.

Spears had been sent to Syria and Lebanon in July 1941 as head of the British Mission to these countries. He was also in charge of relations with the Free French in this area since his relations with de Gaulle were still relatively amicable. De Gaulle's behaviour over the Franco-British armistice of that month alienated the two men completely. Spears's function changed when on 27 September Catroux declared Syria to be independent and on 26 November when he made the same announcement for the Lebanon. It was one thing to declare another country independent, it was another to actually give them the powers that would allow them to be so in reality. This the British insisted had to be done, while the Free French dragged their feet. Spears enthusiastically took up the nationalist cause and became one of the greatest champions of Syrian and Lebanese rights. In February 1942, in a gesture of recognition of Syrian and Lebanese independence, the British appointed Spears to be their first Minister in the Levant. He continued to cause trouble there and made an enemy of the normally diplomatic Catroux.[20] This upset the Foreign Office, who had found Catroux to be comprehending and accommodating towards British views. That

Spears had made an enemy of such a man could only reflect badly on him, and the Foreign Office as well as the Free French began to press for Spears's removal from the position. In this, however, they were blocked by the obstinacy of Churchill, who insisted that, although General Spears had many enemies, he had one friend – the prime minister.[21]

The retention of Spears in the Levant inevitably enflamed the situation and convinced many Frenchmen that the British really did want to assume control in those territories. De Gaulle, for one, felt that, 'if Spears' personality has undoubtedly added to the inconvenience of the situation, it cannot, nevertheless, be attributed solely to the ill-chosen actions of the British representative in Beirut, but is the result of the policy of the British Government itself.'[22] It confirmed all of de Gaulle's worst fears about the British and convinced him that the only policy he could adopt was one of unbending firmness towards the Allies. Paradoxically, it had another, perhaps even more damaging side effect: it persuaded those members of the Free French who did not believe that the British coveted the Levant, that the only real obstacle to Anglo-French entente in that region was Spears and Churchill. Many believed that once Spears was removed, the French would be allowed to pursue within certain limits their own policy in peace. On the British side, too, there was a similar effect. The controversy in the Levant turned Churchill bitterly against the Free French. At the same time, it convinced the Foreign Office that, if only Spears could be got rid of, the French and British could amicably work out solutions to all their differences.

In reality, the controversy over Spears simply disguised the fact that British and French policy in the Levant were basically different and, unfortunately, likely to come into conflict. It is important to remember that Spears was not so much pursuing a personal policy as exaggerating real aspects of British policy in the Levant in order to irritate the French. It also disguised another, highly significant fact: that both the British and French leadership were incurably Eurocentric: they wished to preserve their nations' power in a changing world. Whether they suspected each other or wished to work together, their essential premise was one of European dominance. They did not consider the Syrians and the Lebanese and their viewpoints more than was obviously necessary for the maintenance of their own power. Oliver Harvey of the Foreign Office shows this quite clearly in his diary:

Syria is incapable of governing herself and we have made it almost impossible for the French to do so. Who is to do so then if it is not us? Yet if we oust the French in this way, as they always said we were aiming to do, we raise the most appalling issue which will lie across our relations for a generation. And all this is muddled thinking. The P.M., H[is] M[ajesty's] Government] and the British people have no wish to take over Syria. Local pro-Arab officials in subordinate positions are of course working for it. Spears certainly did so in spite of F[oreign] O[ffice] instructions . . . Yet this policy is suicidal to British local interests which are identical with those of the French. We are both occupying Arab territory and the Arabs hate us both as Christians and Europeans. We should have emphasised French responsibility for the Levant by taking all our troops out.[23]

There can be no clearer statement that one of the main reasons for the British desire to re-establish the French empire was to protect their own empire. The world was in full transformation, and the trend of the future, as Roosevelt clearly understood, was independence.[24] Many among both the British and French felt that the two imperial powers had to work together to preserve their position in the world.

On the French side, Catroux was a very clear exponent of this idea. He actively sought to associate the British with French actions there. Catroux believed that, given the weakness of Free French forces in the Levant, he would have to call on the British if any serious trouble started there. From this he drew the conclusion that he should work with British authorities, except Spears of course, to decide questions affecting the Levant.[25] Since the only way to maintain the French presence in the Levant was through British power, the French had to work with the British and it should be shown to the native peoples that the two were united. In particular, he insisted that the British should be associated with any repression so as to lower their credit with the Syrians. Catroux felt that the British and French should decide things together and then impose their will on the Syrians. He described his methods in a letter on an accord over the wheat monopoly. The agreement was reached in two steps:

> First, I sought a compromise with the British in order to isolate the Syrians. This result was obtained in Cairo.
> Second, the decision that Casey [who had replaced Lyttelton as British Minister in Cairo] and I reached in common, was imposed, equally in common, by us on the Syrians.[26]

The Americans termed such methods as 'high-handed', but the Foreign Office generally accepted them.[27] Spears, however, refused to work in this manner and instead constantly intrigued with the Syrians and Lebanese. Upon his appointment as Minister, he had angered Catroux by calling on the Syrian and Lebanese presidents in order to present his credentials but not on the Frenchman. Catroux felt that, as the representative of the Mandatory power, he should have received at least a courtesy visit from Spears. He was also incensed by Spears's attempts to advise the Syrians and Lebanese. Catroux learned, for example, that Spears had invited Alfred Naccache, the Syrian president, to call an election, implying that he spoke for the British government. Spears had also suggested that, in the name of independence, the Syrian government should reduce the number of French advisers.[28] Spears was almost alone among the Europeans in that he tried to work with the Syrians and Lebanese and to understand and express their point of view – although even he was obsessed with the demon of British prestige.

Not surprisingly, throughout 1942, the situation worsened in the Levant. Given the personal hatreds that dominated the atmosphere, the smallest incidents took on a grotesque importance and threatened to spiral out of control. The British continued to press for elections, while the French continued to postpone them. The main development in 1942, however, was the growing involvement of yet another power in the controversy – the United States. It may seem surprising, but the Free French had actively sought to enlist American sympathies for their point of view in the Levant. They had been tempted to do this by the attitude of the American Consul in the area, Stephen Gwynn, who had expressed sympathy for the French point of view.[29] De Gaulle had been very favourably impressed by Gwynn at a meeting with him and had felt that: 'The United States Consul General takes the same view as we do.' Gwynn, however, appears to have far exceeded his instructions from the State Department during this conversation. De Gaulle's account of it reads:

> On taking leave, the American Consul General declared that his Government was going to intervene to bring the British back within the bounds of their rights and their agreements. It would be a good thing if M. Dejean had an interview with Stark and another with Bogomolov about this, and impressed on them, as I impressed on Gwynn, that we consider the matter has gone far enough and we intend to have the situation straightened out without delay.[30]

Earlier, in May, Catroux had visited Gwynn's superior the Consul-General in Kabul and presented to him the French point of view. Catroux stated that it was Spears's activities that had given rise to the belief that 'two rival authorities' were in confrontation in the Levant and that 'one was determined to replace the other'. He insisted that the British Legation was the source of problems in the Levant. Furthermore, Catroux restated all the arguments in support of the French presence in the Levant and emphasised that they would not be dislodged.[31]

Needless to say, de Gaulle's action in going to the Americans, as well as to the Russians, infuriated the British. It did not necessarily aid the French either, for, as we have seen, American governmental opinion – especially in the White House and the State Department – was far from enthusiastic about the Free French. In fact, American policy on the Levant was extremely nuanced, and they harboured suspicions towards both the British and the French. To a certain extent, American sympathies were with the British who were after all fighting a major battle in Egypt throughout 1942. The Division of European Affairs at the State Department, for example, felt that it was inexcusable that, with Egypt in danger, de Gaulle should try to force an issue in the Levant which might lead to conflict between the British and French there. Fear that recognition of the French National Committee would strengthen de Gaulle's position in Syria was one of the most frequently cited reasons against recognition.[32] The Office of Strategic Services (OSS), the American intelligence organisation at the time, was even more severe in its assessment:

> The recognition of de Gaulle would further intensify the already strained situation in Syria and Lebanon. The entire population of Syria and two-thirds of the population of Lebanon have been reported as hostile to French rule and consider the de Gaullists, who are opposed to the British plan for a general election, as the perpetuation of a vicious regime. If the recognition of de Gaulle would mean the surrender of the natives to the old French imperialism, the prestige of the United Nations among the peoples of the Near East would suffer another blow.[33]

The Americans did not want to be seen as supporters of French imperialism.

This did not mean, however, that they were not suspicious of the British. Many did believe that the British were trying to edge the French out of the Levant. Furthermore, it was difficult for any American to understand why the British were insisting on elections and self-government in the Levant while placing Gandhi and Nehru in prison in India. This de Gaulle clearly understood. He wrote to Pleven and Dejean that: 'As long as the Germans are advancing in the Caucasus and are almost up to the Nile Delta, and as long as Gandhi and Nehru are under arrest, we shall not hold elections.'[34] The British were also well aware that any demand for United States assistance in the Lebanon, particularly during the crises of 1943 and 1945, might have led to demands in other quarters for American intervention in India. This the British obviously did not want, so they did not press the Americans to show support for the British point of view in the Levant.[35]

As we shall see, Roosevelt did not even respond to Churchill's telegram attacking de Gaulle during the crisis of November 1943. It was not that his hostility to de Gaulle had disappeared but simply that he did not want to take sides in a dispute between imperialist powers over colonial territory. He knew that the American press would unfailingly draw the parallel of India and perhaps he himself was suspicious of British motives. American policy was also complicated by the existence of a large Lebanese community in the United States. The State Department's policy, therefore, was one of 'progressive implementation' of Syrian and Lebanese independence.[36] They felt it should be done step-by-step in relation to the military situation, but progress should clearly be evident. Roosevelt believed very strongly that the French should be obliged to honour their promise of independence.[37] In support of American policy, a certain Wadsworth was appointed American Consul-General to the two republics. In October 1943, the Department of State informed the British Embassy that:

> The United States Government . . . is not prepared to admit that France should enjoy a 'preeminent and privileged position' in Syria and the Lebanon. However, this Government is in substantial agreement with the views of the British Government as regards the possible conclusion of agreements defining the relationship of the French authorities to the new States.[38]

The Free French were unlikely to gain much by bringing the Americans into the dispute.

In the summer of 1942 de Gaulle paid a visit to the Levant, and as a result the situation there nearly reached a crisis point. Upon arrival in Beirut, de Gaulle sent a telegram to Churchill protesting that the British were constantly violating the de Gaulle–Lyttelton agreements. Churchill denied de Gaulle's charges and replied that: 'We are pursuing no political aims of our own in the Levant and we have not sought to undermine the French position there'. He insisted that: 'Our principal concern in the political sphere is to ensure that no policy is adopted which may jeopardize our military security or interfere with our prosecution of the war. It is for this reason that we expect to be fully consulted beforehand on major political developments.'[39] De Gaulle, however, refused to accept Churchill's guarantees and even went so far as to imply that British troops in the Levant should be placed under French command. By now, de Gaulle had succeeded in alerting Cordell Hull to the problem of Spears, and Hull, vigilant as always where the British were concerned, had asked the American ambassador in London to discuss the problem with Eden. Needless to say, the British were doubly infuriated, both by de Gaulle's letters to

Churchill and by the Frenchman's success in involving the Americans in the question. Wendell Wilkie, who had been the Republican candidate against Roosevelt in previous elections, had been sent on a special mission by the American Government in order to show that all parties were united in the war effort. De Gaulle succeeded in arranging for him to visit Beirut and had a long interview with him on 10 September. De Gaulle insisted on British misbehaviour in Syria and Lebanon and stated quite categorically that 'he had not taken the responsibility of shedding French blood in order to, afterwards, abandon, to a greater or lesser degree, the Levant States under French Mandate to British control.'[40] The British, of course, were particularly irritated because they were still fighting in Madagascar and were actively trying to negotiate a formula that would allow the Free French to take over administration of that island. They were also upset because of the looming invasion of North Africa, for which the final preparations were now being made. The eve of such a major operation hardly seemed to be the ideal time for de Gaulle to be stirring up trouble in French possessions. They thus tried to convince de Gaulle to return to Britain and, by dangling the bait of Madagascar, finally succeeded in late September. De Gaulle, however, arrrived in a nasty mood and showed this by firing the Commissioner for Foreign Affairs, Maurice Dejean, a few weeks after his return, on the grounds that Dejean was too pro-British. Fortunately, the events in North Africa soon drove the Syrian controversy out of everyone's head. Late 1942 and most of 1943 was taken up by the landings there and the eventual forging of a union between all the different French groups. The improving military situation, particularly after the German defeat in Tunisia in May 1943, meant that strategically the Levant was much less important and, therefore, much less controversial. Elections were held in Syria and Lebanon and new governments installed there. Although disagreements remained, things did seem to be relatively calm there.

It was obvious, however, that the situation had not improved between local French and British officials. They had even deteriorated to some extent because in March 1943 Catroux left the Levant in order to negotiate the union of the Free French with the North African French under Henri Giraud. His replacement as Delegate-General, Jean Helleu, did not have the same diplomatic ability as Catroux and, furthermore, appears to have suffered from a drinking problem. By July, Catroux was criticizing Helleu, and particularly his favouritism of the Christians, to no less a person than Spears![41] His performance certainly did not please the Committee, for a few months later, René Massigli, now Commissioner for Foreign Affairs, was intimating to Macmillan that Helleu would be soon replaced. The

Syrian elections took place in two stages during July 1943 in a relatively calm atmosphere and even Spears admitted that they had been held in a remarkably impartial manner.[42] The nationalists won an overwhelming victory, securing around 80 per cent of the seats in the Chamber. The Lebanese elections, however, were another matter. The elections took place against a background of charge and counter-charge, with both the French and British accusing the other of interference. Furthermore, the election results were a bad surprise for the French. They had expected a nationalist victory in Syria and so were hardly astonished when this occurred. However, in Lebanon they had expected a pro-French majority, and when the nationalists won there as well, it was something of a shock. The French had long hoped to make predominantly Christian Lebanon into a bastion of French influence in the Middle East and were obviously upset by the results. A government consisting of both Christians and Muslims was formed.

A deadlock quickly developed in relations between the two States and the French. Syria and Lebanon wanted to secure as much independence as they possibly could and were willing to take unilateral action, while the French wished to preserve as much as possible of their privileged position – and refused to grant further independence until it was secured by treaties. The Lebanese and Syrians did not want to consider treaties until they were sovereign states. Furthermore, as they watched the progression of the French drama, they came to the conclusion that it was best to obtain as much as they could as quickly as possible so as to take advantage of France's relative weakness. After the war France would be in a much stronger position and, therefore, would be able to refuse more easily. In early October, the Lebanese prime minister declared that only Lebanese officials could take part in the administration. He also proposed other changes to increase Lebanese sovereignty, including the designation of Arabic as the official language. The rights and privileges of France in its hoped for bastion of influence in the Middle East had been directly attacked. The British were unhappy with this announcement because they did, after all, hope to maintain the French position in the Levant, but they sympathized with the Lebanese wish to gain their promised independence.[43] The French insisted that the Mandate was still legally in existence and that they would, therefore, not recognise any constitutional change made without their consent. The Lebanese, however, were delighted and in late 1943 a strong wave of nationalist sentiment swept the nation – including both the Christians and the Muslims.[44] Helleu went off to consult Algiers and asked the Lebanese to take no action until his return as he would be able to offer some concessions. The Lebanese, however, went ahead and on 9 November voted the constitutional changes. Helleu responded on 11 November by dissolving the Chamber and arresting most of the government. He named Emile Eddé, known for his pro-French views, as the new president of Lebanon.

The Foreign Office was shocked by the event but tried to maintain a balanced view. They wrote the following analysis of the situation to Macmillan's office in Algiers:

> In the first instance the Lebanese Government having secured, largely if not entirely through support of HMG, the holding of elections resulting in formation of a representative administration, have attempted to take the bit in their teeth. Fortified by the belief ... that HMG would not allow the French Committee to impose a treaty on them before the end of the war, they have proceeded to lay before the newly elected Chamber proposals for modifications of the constitution to which the French, even if they were informed in advance, had certainly not agreed. So far as is known in London neither HMG nor their representatives have been offered an opportunity of expressing an opinion on this procedure, an opportunity to which they might well consider themselves entitled.

In other words, the British were irritated at the Lebanese because they had acted without asking British advice, and yet were confident that the British would have to support them. The French, however, the Foreign Office felt, were even worse:

> The French on their side have behaved even more foolishly. HMG have repeatedly informed the French Committee that they consider them bound to proceed, even in wartime and pending the conclusion of a treaty between France and the Levant States, to gradually fulfil independence granted to these States ... In the light of this situation there appears absolutely no reason why the French should not proceed to further concessions ... [45]

The first reaction of the British to the Lebanese crisis was one of irritation at both the Lebanese and the French. They were more upset at the French action, considering them to have behaved worse, but there is a notable lack of indignation in the early communications by the Foreign Office on the subject. The British limited themselves to two demands: the removal of Helleu and the release of the ministers. Eden, however, made it clear that they were ready to move in and use British forces to maintain order if the situation seemed to be getting out of control. [46]

In Lebanon, the immediate effect of this action was to unite the Christian and Muslim communities behind the imprisoned government. Demonstrations were taking place, and several of these turned violent. The *coup d' état*, which was effectively what had happened, shocked opinion in the Arab world. There were demonstrations not only throughout Lebanon but in Egypt as well. This naturally alarmed the British who feared that Helleu's action would have repercussions on their own position in Egypt. Palestine was also showing signs of reacting to the trouble. Things worsened considerably on 13 November when a peaceful delegation of around 50 Lebanese students mainly from the American University approached the British Legation in Beirut in order to speak with Spears, who was out. They were attacked by French marines and ten students were injured, one seriously. The British were incensed by this action, and Eden sent orders to Macmillan to make a sharp protest to the Committee, calling the episode 'intolerable'. His conclusion was that: 'The incident shows that the French cannot even control their own forces.'[47] On the same day, the British presented the French with another memorandum, threatening directly to use their troops to maintain order if the situation continued to deteriorate. They also offered to call a conference where French, British, American, Lebanese and Syrian representatives would come in order to agree to a provisional arrangement between France and the Levant States after the war.[48] Churchill also wrote to Roosevelt trying to anger the other, but the American president did not take the bait.[49]

In Algiers, meanwhile, Helleu's action had been as great a shock as it had been in London. Catroux told Macmillan that Helleu had not even asked the Committee for instructions; the whole thing had been done entirely on his own personal initiative. The Committee immediately decided to send Catroux to Beirut in order to investigate and deal with the problem. De Gaulle, however, refused to disavow the action. He insisted that Catroux should not blame Helleu publicly, for he felt that even though Helleu had been 'a little too forceful, France is solidly behind him in what he has done'.[50] He also wrote to Helleu to tell him that he would not disavow him. On the British reaction, he informed Helleu: 'I am convinced that London is bluffing, for the English have every reason to hope that disorders will not occur in the Lebanon or Syria.'[51] To the British, however, he was a bit more dramatic:

> De Gaulle said, first, that he knew the French position was weak and that they could not move a ship or a man unless the Allied Command agreed. If we forced the issue he would give orders to withdraw all the French officials and troops from the Levant and wait upon events, publishing the French case to the world.[52]

De Gaulle was calling what he saw as a bluff with a bluff of his own. Fortunately, Massigli and Catroux were determined to be more conciliatory.

The problem was that the British were becoming progressively more firm in their attitude. They were certainly being pushed in that direction by Richard Casey, the Minister of State in Cairo. On 14 November he wrote to the Foreign Office strongly suggesting that the situation was dangerous in the Lebanon and stated that the main reason that things had remained relatively calm until now was that the population was hoping for a British intervention. He felt that if the British waited too long to act, the Druze, in particular, might get out of hand. Furthermore, in a few days Beirut would face a dire shortage of food, and it would become a great temptation for many to plunder. He recommended that the British should give the French an ultimatum: that the British would occupy the country if, by 17 November, the Lebanese government had not been released.[53] Although Eden did not follow Casey's advice, it was certainly an idea that was appealing more and more to London. The Foreign Office was further upset by signs that the French were trying to gain time. For example, when Catroux arrived in Cairo on the fourteenth, he told Casey that he was too tired to meet with him before the following day. When Catroux did meet with him, he informed Casey that what should be a Franco-Lebanese conflict was seen throughout the world as a Franco-British conflict and insisted that the French could not lose face to the point of recalling Helleu and restoring the Lebanese government.[54]

On the seventeenth de Gaulle gave a speech in which he appeared to reject any compromise with the Lebanese. As a response to this, the British Government finally lost patience over the situation in Lebanon. Eden wrote to Casey that, if by the eighteenth there were no signs of the French agreeing to British demands, then Casey should fly to Beirut on the fol-lowing day and tell Catroux that the British would declare martial law on 21 November at 10 a.m. if the French had not complied. Meanwhile, in Algiers, Macmillan was issuing his own threats to Gaston Palewski, de Gaulle's political adviser:

> Finally I said that I thought Winston, Stalin and Roosevelt would soon be meeting and would have before them a long agenda. They would make short shrift of the Lebanese crisis. It would be easy to decide to place the Levant under joint Anglo-American military control. It would be decided without perhaps any discussion.[55]

This, of course, was hardly likely, since the Americans did not really want to get involved in any significant way, and the Russians issued no state-ment whatsoever during the whole crisis. Palewski, however, could not be sure. Casey, meanwhile, informed the Foreign Office and Macmillan that he had, from the very beginning, been insisting to Catroux that the ministers should be reinstated. This had not been one of Great Britain's original demands, but Eden was forced to support Casey and to add the reinstatement of the ministers to the two earlier demands.[56]

On the eighteenth, Casey received the order to go to Beirut and present an ultimatum to Catroux the next day, if the French showed no signs of agreeing to British demands. On 19 November Casey informed Catroux that unless the French had complied by 10 a.m. on 22 November the British would declare martial law. For Catroux, this was one of the most humiliating moments in his life. He had felt gravely embarrassed by Helleu's behaviour and had sincerely hoped to remedy the situation in the Levant, but he had been hampered by the extremely firm attitude of de Gaulle. The receipt of the ultimatum was to him a second Fashoda – much worse than the first, because this time Britain was France's ally and friend.[57] The situation could have turned nasty but for the newer members of the Committee, who had mainly come from the ranks of the resistance. They refused to break with the British. Already on the twentieth they agreed to recall Helleu and on the following day voted to release the ministers and reinstate the president. The fate of the ministers was left deliberately ambiguous. Only three members of the Committe voted against the proposal: de Gaulle, Pleven and Diethelm. Catroux on his own initiative decided to restore the ministers.

The Anglo-Americans were delighted by this result – not only because it fulfilled British demands. They were particularly thrilled because de Gaulle had been defeated by what was in effect his own government. The replacement of many members of the Committee by representatives of the resistance movement which had occurred recently had obviously decreased the power of de Gaulle. Macmillan said of the situation:

> The most interesting immediate feature in the picture is a further defeat of de Gaulle. Massigli says that he feels the difference between his almost dictatorial authority a few months ago and the present situation. The new members of the Cabinet are much more independent minded than the old and the new Assembly is confronting de Gaulle, who has no parliamentary experience, with a new problem.[58]

In other words, the Committee, with the addition of the Consultative Assembly which had been founded to provide a more democratic forum, were becoming representative enough to give de Gaulle a dose of what real political life was about. To both the Americans and the British this was a positive development. In particular it reassured the State Department who began to put aside its fears that de Gaulle would establish a dictatorship upon his arrival in France. By early 1944 there was little difference between State Department and Foreign Office policy towards the French.

The period after the Lebanese constitutional crisis shows a growing involvement of the United States and the Soviet Union in the Levant. The French still fought to maintain as much influence as possible which both the Syrians and Lebanese resisted. British policy did not change, and, until December 1944, Spears continued to cause trouble. One consequence of this battle for influence was that in late 1943 the Orthodox community began to seek the support of the Russians, which they had previously enjoyed before 1914. Stalin had no hesitations about playing this game, and the Russians became more and more involved.[59] In the spring of that year Tass opened an agency in Beirut and began to make contact with representatives of the local press. A Soviet chargé d'affaires was soon named.[60] A peculiar situation developed in which the French and British were fighting what was in effect a post-imperial struggle, while the Soviets and Americans were beginning a kind of pre-Cold War rivalry. All of this was immensely complicated by the tensions between and within the Christian and Muslim communities and the rising temperature next door in Palestine. To make matters worse, General Beynet, who had replaced Helleu, fed de Gaulle and the Minister for Foreign Affairs a series of reports that were designed to confirm all of de Gaulle's worst suspicions. In one despatch he went so far as to talk about: 'the regime of protectorate established by British political officials in Lebanon is being little by little transformed into direct control.'[61] Spears continued to be the villain of the piece in French eyes, at least until he was finally forced to leave.

Trouble began to come to a head over the problem of rearming the Syrian *gendarmerie*. The Syrian government had become alarmed by the fact that the *gendarmerie* had failed to contain some disturbances after the elections. They, therefore, asked the French urgently for one thousand rifles. The French replied with an offer of many fewer rifles which were, furthermore, antiquated, so the Syrians went to the British. The British military authorities, supported by Spears, offered a considerably greater number of rifles to both the Syrians and the Lebanese and these rifles were more modern than those possessed by the French. Needless to say, the French were up in arms over such a decision – especially since it was made without consulting them – for it would make maintaining any kind of French position in the Levant impossible. The Foreign Office severely criticized Spears's behaviour in this episode:

Thus at every stage Sir E. Spears has refused to carry out his instruc-tions and has plainly encouraged the C. in C. M[iddle] E[ast] and GOC

IXth Army to disregard the views of the F.O. Had this not been done, there is prima facie absolutely no reason why any difficulty should ever have occurred such that, at any rate, it could not have been arranged between London and Algiers.[62]

Spears also caused problems during the negotiations over the question of transferring the *'Troupes Spéciales'* to the Syrians and Lebanese. The 20 000 strong *'Troupes Spéciales'* were financed by Great Britain and consisted of Syrians and Lebanese. They could serve only in the Levant, and in theory they belonged to the Syrian and Lebanese states, but the French were given command of them for the duration of the war.[63] In the summer of 1944 negotiations were being conducted to transfer their control to the local governments. Spears caused trouble once again by suggesting that the French should not be able to increase the number of troops they had in the Levant. Of course, outside the *'Troupes Spéciales'*, this number was fairly small, and the French were outraged at this proposed clause to the agreement. As a result of this, the Foreign Office finally succeeded in recalling Spears. He returned to the Levant for a few months in autumn but was forced to resign in December.

This did not, however, mean the end of Franco-British tension in the Levant. The Syrians and Lebanese continued to complain that the French transfer of powers was going too slowly. The British were also increasingly preoccupied by the situation in Palestine where it seemed more and more likely that the Arabs would be obliged to accept a Jewish state. Churchill told Oliver Harvey that 'he didn't want to upset them [the Arabs] in Syria because of the pill – Zionism – which he knew they would have to swallow in Palestine.'[64] The British found themselves walking a delicate balancing act between the French and the Arabs. The French were trying to force the Syrians and Lebanese to sign treaties that would guarantee them a special position in the Levant. The local governments continued to resist French pressure. Furthermore, the United States and Russia became more and more involved in the dispute – both of them supporting the local States against the French. Wadsworth reported to Hull on a meeting with the Syrian foreign minister in which the latter had said he was willing to negotiate a treaty with the French only if he first negotiated one with the United States. When Wadsworth suggested instead that he propose a treaty simultaneously to all four powers, the Syrian foreign minister answered: 'All right. I will propose a treaty to you, to the British and to the Russians; but we can propose no treaty to the French until, first, they turn over the Army to us and, second, they have a recognized constituted government with which we can deal.'[65] If the French were sticking to legal niceties by insisting that the Mandate was still in force, the Syrians and Lebanese were equally legalistic in their continual statements that they could not negotiate with the French since they did not have a recognized government. Both sides used legalistic arguments in support of their own positions.

In spite of Spears's disappearance, tension continued and reached a crisis point in the spring of 1945. The British agreed to a suggestion by de Gaulle that they should both start withdrawing troops. In May, however, the French landed a small number of replacement troops in Syria and timed their arrival with the presentation of a new demand to the Syrian government to recognise France's special position. These two events caused an explosion in Syria and provoked strife between the French and the local people. On 29 May heavy fighting started in Damascus, and the French started shelling the city. The following day the Syrian president asked the Americans to intervene in the crisis, pointing out that the French were using Lend–Lease equipment against the Syrians.[66] The British, however were already seriously considering intervening, but they did not wish to fire upon an ally. The decision, therefore, was made to ask the French to remain in their barracks. On 31 May, Churchill felt obliged to send the following message to de Gaulle:

> In view of the grave situation which has arisen between your troops and the Levant States and severe fighting which has broken out, we have with profound regret ordered the Commander-in-Chief Middle East to intervene to prevent the further effusion of blood in the interests of security of the whole Middle East, which involves communications for war against Japan. In order to avoid collision between British and French troops we request you immediately to order French troops to cease fire and to withdraw to their barracks. Once firing has ceased and order has been restored we shall be prepared to begin tripartite discussions in London.[67]

De Gaulle agreed to allow the French troops to cease firing but insisted that they should retain their present positions. In spite of this, on 3 June the French withdrew from Damascus, and the British entered the city. Order was quickly restored throughout Syria, and in July an agreement was finally reached to transfer the *'Troupes Spéciales'*. The whole episode, however, had once again shown the world how weak the French really were.

While the story of events in Syria is only a sidelight in the history of Anglo-American relations with the Free French, it is nevertheless extremely important. To begin with it shows us to what an extent colonial rivalries still remained between the British and the French. The French, being in the weaker position, were the more suspicious and, given Spears's attitude, these suspicions were not entirely unjustified. This episode also shows that the British and French still possessed an imperialistic outlook for they only considered nationalist demands when they felt that doing so was the only way to preserve their own position. Lebanon and Syria also point towards the general direction of the future with Britain and France being replaced as dominant powers in the region by the United States and the Soviet Union. Although the Levant may have been only a distraction from the main centres of activity of World War II, it was also a prelude to what would come.

4 North Africa, 1940–42

On 8 November 1942 Allied troops under General Dwight D. Eisenhower began Operation 'Torch', the invasion of French North Africa, and this event marked America's first major action in the war. Although its primary objectives were attained, this operation can hardly be termed an unqualified success, and yet the Americans had been preparing it for a very long time. After the fall of France, Roosevelt, that arch but inconsistent anti-imperialist, developed an interest in that region. With the arrival of General Maxime Weygand, who preached a kind of semi-sedition, as Delegate General for North Africa – a post created for him – Roosevelt decided it was time to act. As we have seen, the president hoped that France and the French Empire would play an important role in his attempts to assist the British during the period from June 1940 to December 1941, when the United States was not yet at war. North Africa had major strategic interest because it lay next door to Britain's most important battlefields, those of Libya and Egypt. The French North African army was estimated to number around 120 000 and thus represented a substantial potential force. If Weygand could be convinced to re-enter the war, the Germans and the Italians would be surrounded. Furthermore, if particular attention were paid to important native figures like the Sultan of Morocco and the Bey of Tunis, it might also further Roosevelt's aim of decolonisation and result in economic advantages to the United States after the war. Therefore, from 1940 to 1942, America's French policy – to the detriment of de Gaulle – was concentrated on North Africa.

The man who played probably the largest role in the formulation of that policy was the diplomat Robert Murphy. Murphy had been at the American embassy in Paris and had remained there with Ambassador William Bullitt in June 1940. Together they later went to Bordeaux and then to Vichy. In the autumn of 1940 Murphy was asked to return to Washington where he was rushed to the White House for a conference with Roosevelt. The president had read Murphy's reports on North Africa and expressed a strong interest in any additional information that the diplomat could give. According to Murphy, Roosevelt was fascinated by the possibilities that the relative independence of North Africa offered. He asked Murphy to return to Vichy and try to get permission to make an inspection tour of North Africa. Murphy was to report on his findings directly to the president. For this reason, Murphy insists in his memoirs that:

The French African policy of the United States Government thus became the President's personal policy. He initiated it, he kept it going,
and he resisted pressures against it, until in the autumn of 1942 French
North Africa became the first major battleground where Americans fought
Germans.[1]

It was conducted in a way that was typical of Roosevelt because it went
outside the usual State Department channels. Roosevelt liked to make sure
that he alone held all the strings on foreign policy questions – at least
those that interested him.

Murphy did, indeed, succeed in making an inspection tour of North
Africa and even reached an agreement with Weygand – signed in February
1941 – that committed the Americans to providing certain supplies to
French North Africa, as long as these were not used by the Axis. In return
the Americans were allowed to appoint twelve vice-consuls to verify the
use made of these supplies. In reality, these vice-consuls were something
very like spies, who reported to Murphy on conditions in North Africa and
who made contact with various individuals and groups who wanted France
to re-enter the war on the side of the Allies. The twelve men had been
selected by the Army and Navy mainly because they spoke fluent French.
They were then turned over to the State Department. Neither the Army,
Navy or State Department gave them any training or any indication of
what they were to do. Virtually all of them had little knowledge of
conditions in North Africa, and some, in fact, had never even been there.[2]
It must be noted that almost no one in Washington knew much about
North Africa at that time and that no central intelligence gathering organization existed in the United States (and would not exist until the OSS
was founded after the American declaration of war). Each government
agency had its own organisation, and all of these separate groups were
often engaged in competing or contradictory operations. No one, of course,
wanted to help a rival, and thus it is not too surprising that these vice-
consuls received so little training.

Unfortunately, they were entering an exceedingly complex society. To
begin with, there were the Arabs. Most of these cared little about the
European War but, being discontented, were open to anti-French propaganda. The Americans did, however, quickly perceive that an Arab uprising
would be fatal to any Allied landing in North Africa and that, given their
own ignorance, they could not hope to govern them directly. Murphy, for
one, soon realized that the French would have to remain in power.[3] American military leaders obviously appreciated his arguments. The operation

was extremely risky, involving the transport of troops over thousands of miles and the uncertainty of French reactions. As Eisenhower explained in his memoirs: 'The Allied invasion of Africa was a most peculiar venture of armed forces into the field of international politics; we were invading a neutral country to create a friend.'[4] The military wanted to attack the Germans as quickly as possible from a secure position, and to do this they needed the cooperation of the French. They were not going to promote disorder by intriguing with the Arabs. The second major group in North Africa was the Jewish community, which under Vichy law was losing its relatively privileged position and becoming an ever more persecuted minority. Needless to say, the Jews generally looked with favour on the Republic, and many Gaullists came from their ranks. The problem was that Vichy's anti-Jewish policy was very popular among the Arabs who had long resented Jewish influence in North Africa. Later Allied insistence on the need to restore full rights to the Jews frequently met with resistance on the part of French authorities because they feared that it might provoke a hostile response from the Arabs – or at least said they did.

The final major group in North Africa was the French. However, the French of North Africa were intrinsically different from the French of mainland France because they were settlers or their descendents. They possessed a colonialist outlook that predisposed them to look with favour on socially conservative movements. Many Vichy policies were, thus, more popular in North Africa than in unoccupied France. Para-military organisations like the Service d'Ordre Légionnaire (SOL), which consisted of elite members of the Legion (Vichy veterans' organisation), who both strongly supported the National Revolution and sought to remove opponents of Vichy, had a large following. Furthermore there existed an important monarchist movement, and the Count of Paris, heir to the French throne, was near at hand. There was a small *Combat* resistance group under Professor René Capitant, but it had few members, and many of these tended to be on the left politically, which, given the political situation in North Africa, was hardly likely to ensure popularity. Free France's popularity further declined after the summer of 1941 when large elements of the Syrian army were sent to North Africa. These men had fought against the British and Free French and harboured grudges. They were not the only ones because many people remained bitter over the British attack at Oran and the Anglo-Gaullist attack on Dakar. A further complication was that old French demon of centralization. The entire North African economy was based on exports to France, and all economic activity was centred on Paris. The budget was decided there, and no central governmental structures existed in either North or West Africa. Weygand's title, in fact, had been mainly honorific. Furthermore, Algeria was officially part of France and as such had been administered by the Ministry of the Interior, while Tunisia and Morocco as protectorates were under the Foreign Ministry. It was thus unlikely – to say the least – that any French leader would voluntarily cut North Africa off from the mainland. It is perhaps just as well that the American spies were so ineffective because had they realized the complexity and explosiveness of North African society, they might never have counselled a landing there. Given all this, however, no one should be surprised that the Americans had so many difficulties there when they did arrive.

Murphy came to North Africa in late 1940 and found Weygand sympathetic but unwilling to break with the Marshal. The situation, however, changed dramatically in late 1941 when the British actually began to win important victories against the Italians in Libya. There was even some hope that the British might be able to go straight to Tunisia and link up with Weygand. This threat seriously alarmed both the Germans and Vichy: on 20 November Weygand was recalled to France. Rommel was sent to Libya and began to push the British back into Egypt. These events had two major consequences: although no real purge took place after Weygand's departure, military and political advancement in North Africa became more and more linked to an anti-Allied stance, while in Egypt the British felt one of their vital interests, the Suez Canal, to be more and more threatened. At one and the same time a greater impetus was given to a North African landing while the chances of a peaceful one became more remote. The British thus were unlikely to oppose the growing American involvement in North Africa. They were, however, in a difficult position, particularly in 1941. Given the British blockade, the Americans were forced to insure that the British approved of the Murphy–Weygand Accord and would allow American supply ships to pass. The British had some reservations about this deal because they felt that the Americans, and particularly Murphy, were too soft on Vichy. They also feared that North and West Africa might receive enough supplies to make their standard of living higher than that in Free French Africa, which would inevitably destabilize the latter. To avoid counter-revolution, the British were therefore forced to insure that French Equatorial Africa received at least as much from themselves at a time when Britain was struggling financially.[5] Furthermore, the British had been trying to get a similar agreement between themselves and Morocco. Given the Franco-British colonial rivalries in this area, it is not surprising that the French preferred American help and when they received it, forgot all about British offers. The British were quite willing to give place to the Americans in North Africa. A Foreign Office report on the United States and North Africa insisted that: 'It can only help the common cause that the United States Government should take a direct interest in the defence of North Africa.'[6] They thus gave their accord.

We must, therefore, not forget that the North African venture was the brainchild of Roosevelt and to a lesser extent of the State Department, all done with the support of the British. It certainly was not the pet project of the War Department. General Marshall, Chief of Staff of the United States Army, in particular was hostile towards the idea. He felt that action should be taken immediately in France in order to give maximum assistance to the hard-pressed Russians and to threaten Germany directly. The British wanted action to occur first in North Africa where it would assist their army in Egypt. It must be remembered that the battle of El Alamein, which halted Rommel's advance into Egypt, only occurred on 3 November 1942 – five days before the Allied landings in North Africa. Until that time the Suez Canal was threatened. The battle over Operation 'Torch' was thus not between the Americans and the British but between the British and the American War Department. Given Roosevelt's immense and long-term interest in North Africa, it was virtually certain that he would be unable to resist the idea of a landing there. Nor was it likely that the State Department would hesitate to support him because such an operation would validate their Vichy policy and calm Cordell Hull's conscience. When the decision had to be made, this is exactly what happened. Roosevelt, supported by the State Department, decided to send troops to North Africa. And Robert Murphy's work, which had at first been treated with indifference in many places in Washington, suddenly became vitally important.

In North Africa, Murphy found a number of people who were willing to work with him for an Allied landing. His main contacts were known as the Group of Five: Jacques Tarbé de Saint-Hardouin, a diplomat; Henri d'Astier de la Vigerie, a monarchist who had two brothers – one, François, was Charles de Gaulle's adjutant and the other, Emmanuel, was head of the left-wing resistance group '*Libération*'; Jacques Lemaigre-Dubreuil, a rich industrialist who had close connections to leading collaborationists and was widely rumoured to have been involved with the *Cagoule*, a violent right-wing group of the thirties; his even more dubious assistant, Jean Rigault; and Colonel Van Hecke, head of the North African *Chantiers de Jeunesse*, which was the Vichy form of national service for young men. Outside of this group there were two other important contacts: General Emile Béthouart, a personal friend of de Gaulle, who commanded the Casablanca division in Morocco; and General Charles Mast in Algiers, a monarchist closely associated with the Five. All of these men were willing to organize a rebellion in support of an American landing. There was, however, another man with whom Robert Murphy was in contact, Alain Darlan. He was the son of Admiral François Darlan, Commander in Chief of the French armed forces and Pétain's dauphin and as such heavily implicated in Franco-German collaboration. Darlan had been head of government at Vichy from February 1941 to April 1942. During his tenure he had met with Hitler, significantly strengthened anti-Jewish laws, increased attacks on the resistance, and instituted an oath of allegiance to the Marshal among top civil servants and military officers. Needless to say, Darlan was widely hated, and, although it seems clear that he had become progressively disillusioned by collaboration, his rather tentative overtures towards the Americans through his son met with little interest.[7]

The situation was further complicated in April 1942 when General Henri Honoré Giraud escaped from prison in Germany and went into hiding in unoccupied France. He had been stationed in North Africa during the 1930s and was believed to have a great deal of influence there. He had also come out strongly in favour of resisting the Germans – having written a widely publicised letter to his children from prison urging them to continue the fight – and was thus untainted by any important association with Vichy. This made him acceptable to both the Allies and Free France. De Gaulle, for example, had announced at a press conference that 'I personally, like all the French Army, have a great deal of consideration and admiration for General Giraud.'[8] He was also independent of all political movements, including Free France and, in fact, had very little interest in politics. Mast, for one, assured the Allies that Giraud was powerful enough to rally the North African army to the Allied cause. Given all this, it was irresistible for the Americans to get in contact with him and try to secure his assistance in the landings in North Africa. Furthermore, because of the harsh feelings in the Vichy French Army and Navy against the Gaullists, the decision was also made to exclude de Gaulle.

By the autumn of 1942 rumours were rife of an invasion of North Africa. De Gaulle, of course, thought that it would be an Allied invasion. Darlan, on the other hand, believed that the Germans would do so and once again approached Murphy. His emissary, Chrétien, surprised Murphy by asking only whether the Americans would be willing to supply North Africa's needs if Darlan sailed there with the French fleet in order to resist an eventual German aggression.[9] Darlan appears not to have considered the Americans capable of an invasion themselves and seems to have been totally surprised by their landings. In any case, Murphy quickly discovered that Mast and Giraud hated Darlan and would not work with him.[10] Although Churchill is supposed to have told the British Admiral Cunningham: 'Kiss Darlan's stern if you have to, but get the French Navy', it is clear that, for the moment at least, the Allies refused to work with Darlan.[11] Instead, they concentrated on Giraud.

It is clear that the War Department remained sceptical about Murphy's work in North Africa. They were unconvinced that they would receive French assistance in the landings and were planning to fight if necessary. Seeking to learn from the mistakes of Dakar, they prepared for a massive invasion, using 100 000 troops. However, most of these troops were inexperienced, and, given the difficulties of the operation, the War Department was forced to hope that the State Department was right. American soldiers were ordered not to fire until they were fired upon. Eisenhower, in his diary, expressed well the War Department's reservations on the campaign:

> However, study had conclusively shown that it was impossible to build up a force of sufficient strength to make tactical considerations the governing ones in undertaking this operation. The capacity of the ports and the relative slowness of the buildup made it clear that if the French forces in North Africa should oppose the landing as a unit and with their full strength, there would be little hope of carrying out the great purpose of sweeping to the eastward to gain control of the whole of North Africa. Consequently, the whole campaign had to be considered as depending entirely upon political factors – that is, upon the accuracy with which our political leaders could foresee the reactions of the French and Spanish armies in North Africa to this landing.

His conclusion was simple: 'Without going into the details of the various plans proposed, it is sufficient to say that, measured purely from a military standpoint, the risks of the projected operation were so great as to condemn it if military factors alone were considered.[12] Other worries weighed upon Eisenhower, such as how to preserve communications, if the French were hostile, between the three landing ports: Casablanca, Algiers and Oran. Then there was the further problem of reaching Tunisia as quickly as possible in order to fight the Axis. Eisenhower had had grave doubts for some time about the way the political part of the operation was organized. It is clear that he wanted to turn the French into allies and work with them. In August he told Bullitt that there was a need for very careful preparation in the area so that a civil administration, headed by a Frenchman, could be set up immediately after the Allies arrived. Eisenhower also expressed his distrust of Roosevelt's abilities in this area, saying that he was 'certain that the President could not possibly organize such an administration effectively because of his inclination to treat everyone outside the British Isles as natives.'[13] Everyone hoped that Murphy was right about French cooperation, but many people feared that he would be proved wrong. The military hoped for cooperation but prepared for conquest.[14] To make sure of the War Department's authority in this matter, Marshall asked Roosevelt to change Murphy's directive so that he was not attached to the State Department any longer but to Eisenhower's staff. The State Department thus was largely shut out of the North African adventure.[15] Given French grudges against the British and the Free French, Roosevelt insisted that 'Torch' should be an American controlled operation without Gaullist participation. He wrote to Churchill that: 'I consider it vital that sole responsibility be placed with Americans for relations with French military and civil authorities in Africa.'[16] Churchill agreed, stating that 'In the whole of Torch, military and political, I consider myself your Lieutenant.'[17]

As soon as the landings began there were three hitches that immediately occurred to the American plans. First, Giraud arrived in Gibraltar the day before the landings were due to take place and immediately disappointed the Americans. General Mark Clark, Eisenhower's deputy, was put in charge of negotiating with him. Clark was quite firm with Giraud and was overheard to tell him 'We would like the Honorable General to know that the time of his usefulness to the Americans for the restoration of the glory that once was France is *now*. We do not need you after tonight.'[18] Giraud insisted that, if the Allies wanted his help, he would have to be made supreme commander immediately. The Frenchman also wanted to transfer the operation from North Africa to southern France and carry out an invasion there. Eisenhower and Clark spent hours trying to explain to him that they had no authority to place themselves and their armies under another commander without the approval of the British and American governments, but Giraud refused to listen. The latter also refused to consider their arguments concerning the difficulties of changing an invasion from one of North Africa to one of France.[19] Needless to say, neither American was impressed with either the intelligence or the integrity of Giraud. Eisenhower wrote sarcastically to his Chief of Staff, General Bedell Smith:

So far as I'm concerned, my opinion of Giraud coincides with that of the PM. He wants to be a big shot, a bright and shining light, and the acclaimed saviour of France. But he will not (repeat and underline) take one single step or do any single thing that could possibly be interpreted as inimical to the interests of any Frenchman. Consequently, he did not want to get on the job at the beginning (when we needed him) and try to prevent fighting. To have done so might have identified him with a local civil war, so he has procrastinated, hoping that all would be over this morning and he could go as a knight in white armour and be the big hero to lead France to VICTORY.[20]

When Giraud finally did arrive in North Africa on 9 November – after the invasion had started – and called for an armistice, to his great shock he discovered that he had no effect whatsoever.

Meanwhile in North Africa the Allied conspirators began what was in effect a *coup d'état*. Béthouart in Morocco managed to sequester Noguès, the Resident General, in his residence, but the rebellion was quickly neutralized by Admiral Michelier, and Béthouart placed in prison. When General George Patton started his landings there a few hours later he met with fierce resistance. In Algiers, the Group of Five had also organized a rebellion in support of the Americans. It had all been prepared rather hastily and inadequately because they had only received four days' notice of the invasion. This was perhaps for the best because subsequent evidence has suggested that they were probably planning a monarchist coup and that had they been better organised they might have succeeded.[21] So here was the second complication to American plans: the rebellions were generally ineffective and did not stop French resistance. There was also a third hitch in their plans. On 5 November, Admiral Darlan left Vichy for Algiers in order to be with his son Alain who was near death from polio. This unexpected event would throw all plans into disorder. In the early hours of their rebellion, the Group of Five actually managed to hold Darlan in custody, but when the local authorities regained control of Algiers, they were forced to release him.

For Eisenhower the situation was dramatic. Everywhere there was resistance from the French and yet their groundplan called for turning the French into allies. Giraud and the local conspirators had completely failed to do this. The Americans were faced with two choices: they could negotiate with Darlan and see if he could end the fighting, or they could ignore him and begin a military conquest of North Africa. On the 9th Darlan approved an armistice for the Algiers area only, and Eisenhower sent Mark Clark to meet with him. Darlan, however, stipulated that he did not want to see Giraud. This, coupled with Giraud's earlier behaviour led Eisenhower to write: 'All of these frogs have a single thought – "ME"'. He went on to lament:

> It isn't this operation that's wearing me down – it's the petty intrigue and the necessity of dealing with little, selfish, conceited worms that call themselves men. Oh well – by the time this thing is over I'll probably be as crooked as any of them. Giraud, in his first conference with me, even made a point of his rank. Can you beat it? Yet he's supposed to be the high-minded man that is to rally all North Africa behind him and to save France.[22]

The negotiations took place over several days and revealed a clear difference between the Americans and the French in their attitude to Vichy. As
we have seen, although the Americans maintained relations with Vichy,
they had few illusions about that government. Darlan, on the other hand,
wanted his negotiations to have the approval of the Marshal. Clark was
surprised by the French commanders' insistence in obtaining Vichy's
authorisation and by the attitude of the North African leaders towards
Giraud and the other dissidents.[23] General Mendigal, the head of the air
force in North Africa exclaimed that: 'You had better put them in some
safe place. They are bitterly resented.' Clark was puzzled by such a reaction and could only reply: 'I don't understand. They helped us so much.'[24]
In response to this attitude Eisenhower wanted Giraud to work actively for
the Allies.[25] Unfortunately, when Giraud realized how little real influence
he had and how badly he was viewed by much of the army leadership he
simply wilted. All pretensions of grandeur faded away and within a few
days Eisenhower was writing to the Combined Chiefs of Staff that Giraud
was believed by French leaders to be guilty of some treachery in working
with the Americans and that, astonishingly enough, Giraud sympathized
with their attitude.[26] Faced with this, the Americans had no choice but to
continue their talks with Darlan.

Darlan, however, was determined to do nothing that would divide the
army – which on the whole was loyal to Pétain and detested dissidents,
as their reaction to Giraud shows – or give the Germans an excuse to
invade the unoccupied zone. On 11 November the Wehrmacht did exactly
that, and Darlan felt free to reach an agreement with the Americans. He
could now claim that Pétain was a prisoner and thus unable to voice his
support for Darlan's action.[27] He even felt strong enough to welcome Giraud
back into the fold although, of course, not de Gaulle. On 13 November,
Eisenhower and Cunningham arrived in Algiers and gave their agreement
to an accord with Darlan. On the same day Darlan gave orders for the
French to stop fighting the Americans and to start attacking the Axis in
Tunisia. Throughout North Africa, the French began actively to assist the
Americans. In spite of the failure of American preparations for the landing,
Eisenhower and Clark had achieved the desired result: the French were
back in the war, fighting with the Allies. The generals now could rush
troops as quickly as possible to Tunisia to attack the Germans. On 22
November the Clark–Darlan Accord was signed in Algiers which formal-
ized relations between the Allies and the North Africans, and although
Darlan failed to bring over the fleet, on 23 November French West Africa
rallied, giving the Americans control of Dakar. Eisenhower and Clark
might well feel that they had done their best.

If this is what they thought they were to be rudely awakened. Initial reaction to the 'Darlan Deal', as it was popularly called, ranged from viewing it as an unhappy temporary expedient to an outrage against all the ideals for which the Allies were fighting.[28] There was an enormous uproar among the British press and in Parliament. Aneurin Bevan, the Labour Party radical, gave an impassioned speech against the agreement, saying that:

> Darlan has so many crimes against him now that he can never expunge them. The man who stood on one side and connived at the slaughter of innocent French hostages, friends who gave their lives for us, is not a man with whom we dare cooperate.[29]

Churchill was forced to call a secret session of Parliament in order to justify the agreement. He gave one of his best speeches insisting that the agreement was necessary because: 'It makes a lot of difference to a soldier whether a man fires his gun at him or at his enemy; and even the soldier's wife or father might have a feeling about it too.'[30] The reaction was so hostile that Roosevelt was forced to call a press conference and state repeatedly that the agreement was only temporary.

Even in official circles the reaction was hardly enthusiastic. Cordell Hull had serious reservations about the agreement and asked Roosevelt whether it might not be possible to give Darlan a high-sounding title without any real power. He told the president that he 'thought it was unfortunate that this agreement had already been made' and felt that it would cause trouble.[31] The President's general attitude to the French question was summed up in the same conversation when he said that 'his first idea of a solution would be to place Admiral Darlan, General Giraud and a de Gaulle representative in one room alone and then give the government of the occupied territory to the man who came out.' Hull expressed his views quite clearly to Adrien Tixier and Admiral d'Argenlieu of the Free French:

> [He] added that if he were attacked by a thug on the street and someone came to his assistance he would welcome the assistance of his collaborator in destroying the would-be murderer but he would not cease to fight and ask his unexpected collaborator to tell him his name and antecedents . . . Mr. Hull pointed out that the British and American fleet were in control of the Mediterranean and this in itself controlled Darlan's approach to France.[32]

Hull was determined to reassert at least some State Department control over policy in North Africa. In late November he cabled Algiers about rumours that 'former notorious collaborationists' were arriving there and strongly suggested that they should be 'put over the border'. A few days later he told Marshall and Eisenhower that he wanted civil matters to be gradually turned over to the State Department.[33] Eisenhower readily agreed to this request.

On the British side, feelings were, if anything, more hostile. Churchill wrote to Roosevelt insisting that they could only have a very temporary agreement with Darlan because 'Darlan has an odious record.'[34] Eden was even more hostile. Alexander Cadogan felt that the agreement was 'dirty', but he did admit that it was probably a military necessity.[35] The British quickly regretted having given the Americans carte blanche in North Africa and were determined to send someone to North Africa who would have the rank of a cabinet minister and who would be forceful enough to assert British views in Algiers. For this job Churchill chose Harold Macmillan. Until this point Macmillan's political career had been unimpressive. He had remained outside the government during the 1930s because of his opposition to the policy of appeasement. Even when Churchill came to power he was only appointed junior minister at the Colonial Office. Now he was offered a political appointment that would change the whole direction of his career and make his reputation. His job was to 'report to the Prime Minister on the political situation and future plans for North Africa and to represent to the Commander in Chief the views of His Majesty's Government on political matters'.[36] He was expressly not attached to Eisenhower's headquarters. The British had decided to secure some independence for their own policy towards North Africa. However, for various reasons, Macmillan did not arrive in North Africa until after Darlan's death.

The man who undoubtedly benefitted the most by the Darlan flap was General Charles de Gaulle. At Roosevelt's insistence, de Gaulle had been told nothing beforehand about the landings. When he first heard of the landings in North Africa, de Gaulle was pleased and on the very day broadcast a speech calling on the French in North Africa to assist the Americans. Other leaders of Free France greeted the news even more enthusiastically. Giraud was universally well-considered for his opposition to the armistice, and it was felt that Free France would soon be in the picture working with him. De Gaulle certainly did not feel threatened by Giraud, writing to his subordinates that: 'if my estimation of his military qualities is correct, I consider him ill-equipped for the delicate task he presumes to take on'.[37]

Darlan, however, was another matter. Although de Gaulle privately admitted that the accord was probably necessary, Free France greeted it with immense hostility.[38] At the same time they were probably the major beneficiaries of it. Just after the landings, Cordell Hull had called a press conference and announced that the success of Operation 'Torch' was due to the Vichy policy for which the State Department had been so criticized. He was euphoric at his vindication. This euphoria did not last long, for the 'Darlan Deal' totally and completely, in one blow, discredited all of American policy towards the French and made suspect all of America's war aims. The press and public could not understand why a quisling like Darlan had been put in power by the United States government – which was supposed to be fighting a war in defence of democratic values – when a perfectly good democrat, Charles de Gaulle, who had always stood by the Allies, was treated with contempt. Aneurin Bevan voiced the opinion of many when he said: 'Do not try to put these traitorous quislings, these rats now leaving the sinking ship, in place of the men who stood staunchly by our side in our most difficult days.[39] Even Churchill was, in private, generous to de Gaulle:

[He] told the General that his position was magnificent. Darlan had no future. Giraud was finished politically. 'You stand for honesty,' he told the General. 'Yours is the true path, you alone will remain. Do not batter yourself against the Americans. It is useless and you will gain nothing. Have patience and they will come to you, for there is no alternative.[40]

At a cabinet meeting on 7 December, it was decided to accept the situation for the time being and to try to introduce more reputable French leaders into the North African government and let these people get rid of 'the unreliable elements'.[41] The Americans soon expressed their agreement with this policy.[42]

What is perhaps more important is that public opinion in France clearly turned towards de Gaulle at this period. The resistance, of course, was profoundly shocked by the 'Darlan Deal' and denounced it harshly in their newspapers. It certainly hastened the movement towards unification of the resistance and their recognition of de Gaulle's leadership. The nonresistance of Vichy to the German invasion of the unoccupied zone – only General de Lattre de Tassigny rebelled, and he was imprisoned by Vichy – completely destroyed whatever credit the Laval government had left in France. De Lattre later insisted that this was the turning point for France.[43] Furthermore, after the invasion of North Africa and the Soviet victory at Stalingrad a few months later, very few French people could really believe that the Germans would win the war. The only known and creditable leader working with the Allies who offered a real alternative to Vichy was de Gaulle. The 'Darlan Deal' and the invasion of unoccupied France showed this fact quite starkly. It is not surprising, therefore, that the French turned more and more towards him. It is for this reason that de Gaulle told Alexander Cadogan, after Darlan's assassination, that he regretted the Admiral's death, since the latter had been making 'numberless converts' for Free France.[44]

It was easier to say this afterwards than beforehand, for during his 40 days of rule in Algiers, Darlan seemed to be constantly strengthening his position. He had got the French to fight with the Allies and had rallied West Africa. He also managed, during his 40 days in power, the Herculean task of organizing governmental, administrative and economic structures for an area which, as we have seen, had previously been entirely dependent on France. Much to the embarrassment of the Allies, he took for himself the title of High Commissioner for North Africa and announced the formation of an 'Imperial Federation'. In constructing his government, Darlan was entirely without finances and had to borrow money from the Algiers branch of the Bank of France.[45] Once he had insured that his government had enough money to function at least until the end of the year, he proceeded to further concretise his goal of French unity in North Africa. He met with the Group of Five and offered them positions in his government, which most of them accepted. In this way, Henri d'Astier de la Vigerie became Secretary of the Interior and thus had under his, at least nominal, authority the forces of order in North Africa. In a series of *ordonnances* Darlan established the base of a government but also centred power in the High Commissioner, who would be assisted by an Imperial Council consisting of the governors and resident generals of North and West Africa, the Vice-Commissioner, General Bergeret, and the military and naval commanders-in-chief, Giraud and Michelier. The end result was that the Group of Five found their posts to be mainly honorific and that they themselves had little real power. During his remaining weeks, Darlan continued to increase the authority of himself and his friends – with one exception. Neither Darlan nor his friends, most of whom were army or navy officers, had any great expertise in economic matters. On 10 December Darlan named as his assistant in charge of economic questions, Alfred Pose, the director of the *Banque nationale du Commerce et de l'Industrie en Afrique*. His name had been suggested by one of the Five, Jacques Lemaigre-Dubreuil, and Darlan did not know him personally. He was chosen because of his expertise in financial matters, and he quickly proved his competence by preparing the budget for 1943 and floating a loan. Under pressure from the Americans, Darlan also began certain important steps towards liberalizing the regime, such as reinstating officers who had assisted the Allied landings.

Perhaps the most important achievement of the Darlan regime was the decision of the Americans – for which Giraud had done a great deal of work – to recreate the French Army. For the Americans, it was a way of giving France a part in the victory. However, they emphasised that: 'This army should not be the army of the North African civilian administration; it should be the army of the French people, and becomes the servant of the French authorities set up by the French people themselves once France has been freed.[46] Implicit in this statement is a condemnation of Darlan, for this army would not be that of Darlan's administration. This point is made quite clear. The same memorandum goes on to state that, 'any French organization outside of France [is] precluded from having a shadow of right to claim the leadership of the French people.' And in case anyone may not have completely understood, the author goes on to specify that the power of the North African authorities is confined to local affairs. This policy was the logical outcome of the decision to force France to re-enter the war on the side of the Allies. It would allow France a new and better role in World War II and would ultimately fulfil de Gaulle's ambition of having the French present at Germany's capitulation.

All of this feverish activity, however, did not change the fact that Darlan was, in many ways, a broken man. In spite of certain signs that Eisenhower and other Americans were warming towards him, it was clear that he was still considered to be a 'temporary expedient'. Already, on the day of the signing of the Clark–Darlan agreement, Darlan had written to Eisenhower that: 'Information coming from various parts tend to give credit to the opinion that "I am but a lemon which the Americans will drop after it is crushed".' He insisted in this letter that: 'I have acted neither through pride, nor ambition, nor intrigue, but because the place I held in my country made it my duty to act', and stated that when French sovereignty was firmly established he would return to civilian life.[47] It is significant that Roosevelt directed Eisenhower to reply by expressing his (Eisenhower's) appreciation of Darlan's assistance but to make sure that it was kept on the level of personal appreciation.[48] However friendly Eisenhower, Murphy, Clark and Cunningham might be with him, it was obvious that the Americans were not keen on his remaining in power. This was shown by the visit of General François d'Astier de la Vigerie, de Gaulle's adjutant and Henri d'Astier's brother. As early as 2 December, de Gaulle had requested Churchill to authorize this visit and had repeated his request to Admiral Harold Stark, the United States's representative who dealt with Free French matters in London. Eisenhower gave his accord on 13 December. Unfortunately, Eisenhower and Murphy proceeded to forget about this visit and, when d'Astier arrived on 20 December, no one was at the airport to meet him. Furthermore, they forgot to tell Darlan, who was furious when he discovered d'Astier's presence and wanted to arrest him.

It was a rather bad beginning for an attempt to construct French unity. Eisenhower gave in to Darlan on this question and made d'Astier leave the next day. However, d'Astier returned to London in a highly optimistic mood, for Darlan had apparently told him that he was seriously thinking of resigning.[49]

On the day before his assassination, Darlan remarked to Clark that 'I'd like to turn this thing over to General Giraud. He likes it here, and I don't.'[50] He made other similar statements to both Murphy and Clark. It is noteworthy, however, that he took very few personal precautions – although he was fully aware that there were a large number of plots against him. Murphy describes a rather strange conversation with Darlan the day before his death: 'You know,' he began, 'there are four plots in existence to assassinate me.' He went on in a detached manner, 'Suppose one of these plots is successful. What will you Americans do then?' He then pulled a document from his pocket and calmly discussed with Murphy who might succeed him. Murphy comments that: 'Darlan seemed sincerely disturbed over the prospect, but as though he were talking about the death of someone else, not himself.'[51]

The next day he was dead, having been shot by a young Gaullist named Fernand Bonnier de la Chapelle. Eisenhower was at that time absent from Algiers, but Clark immediately took charge and placed all Allied troops on alert. Guards were increased throughout the city. On meeting with French leaders, Clark was shocked to discover that some of them at least thought the Allies might be responsible for his death.[52] Under American pressure, Giraud was chosen to be Darlan's successor. Bonnier was court martialled and executed a few hours after the crime. This hasty application of justice raised all sorts of rumours, and the Darlan assassination remains to this day an even greater mystery than the more famous murder of John Kennedy. From the very beginning, no one believed that Bonnier de la Chapelle had acted independently. This was confirmed when, a few days after the assassination, a large number of arrests were made in Algiers. Virtually all of the Gaullist leaders in North Africa were either arrested or forced into hiding. It is probable that no one will ever know exactly who was responsible for Darlan's assassination. A few facts, however, are sure. One is that Henri d'Astier de la Vigerie and his assistant, the Abbé Cordier, were directly behind the assassination and convinced Bonnier that he was doing a noble act for which he would not be punished. To complicate things further, during his brief stay in Algiers, François d'Astier had given his brother a suitcase of money, and part of this money was given to Bonnier in payment for the assassination. Since François d'Astier was de Gaulle's adjutant, the Gaullists were indirectly implicated in the assassination.

Historians have raked what archives are available, searching for clues as to whether Darlan's assassination had been ordered by de Gaulle but have found no clear evidence. Recently opened documents shed only a little more light on the question. They do, however, establish a few important facts. First and foremost of these is the evidence of a secret report prepared by de Gaulle's intelligence agency, BCRA in June 1943. While it is clearly incorrect in parts, it makes some astounding assertions. For one thing, it claims that the royalists, such as Henri d'Astier, had planned on coordinating with the American landing on 8 November a coup in favour of the Count of Paris who was nearby. This failed because of Darlan's presence. According to this, and many other reports, Darlan's assassination was part of another coup attempt, which failed because neither the Americans nor the local police would play along. This document clearly suggests that Pose was involved in the planning of the assassination. However, it is wrong in other parts and, in its attacks on Giraud, is obviously motivated by politics. It also implies that Yves Châtel, the Governor General of Algeria, Jean Rigault of the Group of Five, and General Bergeret, the Assistant Commissioner were involved in the assassination. In the case of Bergeret, at least, this is clearly false. What is interesting is that both this document and other secret documents written just after the assassination and sent by Gaullists in North Africa to Carlton Gardens emphatically deny that the local Free French organization was involved in Darlan's assassination. Furthermore, the Gaullists were convinced that the arrests on the night of 29–30 December had been designed to frame them with Darlan's murder, discrediting the Free French movement and thus, as it were, killing two birds with one stone.[53]

Indeed, it appears that the real investigation into Darlan's death only began after the arrests. We may thus safely draw the conclusion that these arrests were made for other reasons. Furthermore, when General Bergeret – who was no friend of de Gaulle – did see the report of the investigation, he told the Americans that he believed de Gaulle had had no role in the assassination.[54] One immediate effect of the assassination was that it increased Allied pressure for a purge in the new Giraud administration. The first ones to go were Châtel and Rigault. The British and Americans then agreed to coordinate their policy. On 8 January, Hull and Marshall had written to Eisenhower:

Establishment in Algeria on soil of a department of France of single authority in place of both General Giraud's administration and French National Committee in London is envisaged. United States and British governments as well as other governments would recognize this authority as a De Facto administration provisionally exercising French Sovereignty over certain parts of France and over the whole French Empire (except Indo-China) pending establishment of government chosen as government or even as provisional government of France.[55]

Both the Americans and the British were thus committed to the pursuit of French unity. It was feared that because Henri d'Astier was the brother of François d'Astier, de Gaulle might react badly to his trial and that this might hamper unity. Furthermore, many Allied commentators feared that d'Astier's trial might become another Dreyfus case which would indirectly at least accuse the Gaullist movement. For the author of one British report, no moral issue was at stake:

It would appear that the plot to assassinate Admiral Darlan was a Monarchist–Fascist plot, the object of which was to create a situation of confusion from which certain personalities, particularly the Comte de Paris, might hope to profit. Thus the issue is not a political issue between supporters and opponents of the Vichy regime, or between patriots and traitors. It is simply a question of an attempted Monarchist–Fascist putsch which failed. When seen in its correct proportions there is no reason why this lamentable incident should be a disturbing factor in the process which the Allies earnestly desire of seeing all Frenchmen united in the common struggle against the enemy.[56]

It is perhaps more accurate to say that the Allied representatives in North Africa did not believe that the moral question was finding the assassin of Darlan (although later they would exclude Pose from his position in North Africa because of his implication in the murder), but rather to make sure that the Allies honoured their own beliefs.[57] The British Consulate General in Algiers said:

These arrests have caused extreme consternation and bewilderment amongst all non-Vichy minded Frenchmen in Algeria. The immediate effects of these arrests have been serious. The good faith of the Allies towards their Fifth column collaborators has been placed in jeopardy; all the work done by us to keep alive the spirit of resistance in France itself will have been wasted and any hope of organized assistance if, and when, the Allies invade France will be out of the question unless very early action is taken to obtain the fair trial and if found blameless, the release of all, and the re-employment of those among them who are officials.[58]

This report also expressed the conviction that the Gaullists were innocent and that the arrests were simply a 'red herring' to cover up a monarchist plot and to discredit republicanism. It was also feared that there might well be more assassinations and coup attempts if the situation were not stabilized immediately. Allied leaders in Algiers clearly felt that popular discontentment might become dangerous.[59] The need for union among the French was great. There was a further consideration for the Allies: Roosevelt and Churchill were due to meet soon at Casablanca. At a meeting between Smith, Cunningham, Murphy, Macmillan and Mack it was, therefore, decided to exert all their influence in obtaining the release of the men who had been arrested and to ensure that d'Astier's trial would, at least, be postponed until after the Casablanca Conference.[60] In other words, it was decided that in order to achieve French unity a cover-up was necessary. Giraud was prevailed upon to release the prisoners, to end investigations into Darlan's death, and to order the Count of Paris out of North Africa.[61]

Thus ended a particularly sad chapter in Anglo-American relations with the French. The Allies had invaded North Africa without any clear policy as to what they would do there. Much of this was because of Roosevelt's insistence that North Africa was an American operation, but the British cannot, by any means, escape blame for what happened. The Allies basically had three choices in North Africa. As the first they could have instituted a military government, but this was considered unfeasible by the War Department. Their second choice was to work only with the Gaullists and others who were friendly to the Allies, but they were relatively few in number and, furthermore, there was the risk that most of the French army would not rally and might indeed continue to fight. The third choice was to work with the existing authority, even though it was collaborationist. This is what was chosen, but, as we have seen, although it ended the fighting and prevented the army from splitting, it created an unstable atmosphere in North Africa and betrayed the very ideals for which the Anglo-Americans said they were fighting. It also had an extremely negative effect on resistance movements throughout Europe. Of course, much of this problem was not the fault of the Anglo-Americans but of the divisions among the French. Not illogically, the Allies reached the conclusion that the only way to prepare for the future invasion of France – and ensure that the events of North Africa did not repeat themselves – was to find a way to unify the French. Much of the success of any future military expeditions depended upon this.

5 Unity? 1943–44

In order to understand Anglo-American policy towards the union of French resistance movements, one must first consider the tensions that existed between the Americans and the British. British and American policy was bound to differ because the Americans were in a state of expansion on the international scene (like the Soviets), while the British were basically trying to preserve what they already had (like the French, although in a much less dramatic fashion).[1] Much has been written, for example about the British advocacy of a Mediterranean policy which, it was hoped, would protect the traditional British route of empire. It is also certain that the United States – and particularly Roosevelt – were quite insistent in their calls for the British to grant India independence, much to the irritation of the British.[2] It is safe to say that both the British and American governments suspected each other of wanting to profit at the expense of France's disaster. In the American case, their suspicion of British intentions is quite clear and had important repercussions in their relations with Charles de Gaulle. To begin with, he was virtually unknown to the Americans until he arrived in London. Murphy, who was attached to the American Embassy in Paris before the fall of France, wrote that the first time he had ever heard de Gaulle's name was during his broadcast on 18 June. No one at the American Embassy could understand why de Gaulle had suddenly become so important.[3] To many Americans he seemed to be a rabbit the British had pulled from their hats – a sudden, unexpected and fundamentally irrelevant British creation. His speech in defence of maintaining the Franco-British alliance after the British attack on Oran seemed only to confirm all these fears. It must be remembered that Bullitt and Murphy had stayed behind in Paris and that de Gaulle had only become a member of the French government on 6 June. They could not possibly have witnessed his attempts to rally Reynaud and other members of the government during those last days in Bordeaux. Only Biddle witnessed these scenes, and Biddle, as we have seen, was de Gaulle's main advocate with the State Department.

It must not be forgotten that Free France was, in its early days, entirely financed by the British government – a fact not lost on the Americans. Leahy, for example, termed de Gaulle the 'British-sponsored leader of the Free French'.[4] Throughout much of the war, and particularly during the first half of 1943, the Free French newspaper *La Marseillaise* was extremely harsh in its evaluation of American policy towards France and especially of Cordell Hull. Hull was very wounded by these comments, especially since he was not responsible for most of the decisions for which he was attacked. However, as during the Saint-Pierre and Miquelon affair, it is interesting to note that Hull, although angry with the Gaullists, reacted primarily against the British. The vice-president, Henry Wallace, describes Hull at a cabinet meeting as going into 'an indignant tirade against the British for the propaganda they had been putting out on behalf of de Gaulle and against the United States'. The president joined in, insisting that it was the 'old school tie crowd' that was responsible.[5] Commander Kittredge, who assisted Admiral Stark in his dealings with the French National Committee, said: 'Every criticism of the Administration's policy is attributed by Mr. Hull, first to Great Britain, and then to the use of British money employed by French agents.'[6] Leahy also clearly felt that this was the case, writing in his diary that: 'It is certain that Monsieur de Gaulle is interfering with our war effort, and that no action to stop his interference is taken by the British Government by which he is financed.'[7] 'Doc' Matthews, who had been with Leahy in Vichy and with Murphy in North Africa, was in London in early 1943. From there he fed Cordell Hull's anger and his distrust of the British:

> British prestige requires that General de Gaulle be given and maintained in a position of political primacy both during the war and in any early transitory period following the liberation of Continental France . . . If de Gaulle is a 'symbol' to the people of France, he is also a 'symbol' to the British Government, a symbol of justification for its whole French policy since June 1940. British prestige requires that 'the one French- man who stuck by us in the dark days of 1940' must be installed in France when the day of liberation comes.[8]

There is no doubt that there was a strong sense of rivalry between the State Department and the Foreign Office, and the State Department reacted almost instinctively with suspicion to anything strongly advocated by the Foreign Office. De Gaulle's strongest support in Britain, as we have seen, was in the Foreign Office. Matthews analysed the British position as follows:

> The Foreign Office, I am convinced, fears that American military lead- ership may now have long-term political consequences which are not to their liking. Quite understandably they regard the Mediterranean as a vital and legitimate British preserve, and they are not happy at seeing the United States playing the lead in that area or in their realisation of their less-favored position there with the French. In other words, they see Darlan as an American puppet . . . and in de Gaulle, for all his

difficulties of temperament, a leader who will support British long-term interests and who is subject to British influence. I think there is a certain suspicion by British 'imperialists', to use a much abused word, of American 'imperialist' intentions.[9]

Matthews was right that the British were as suspicious of the Americans as the Americans were of the British.

The basis of Hull and the State Department's antagonism towards Great Britain has been well-described in *The Juggler*.[10] Hull was a strong exponent of economic internationalism – he wanted equal access for all nations to world markets – and in his opinion the main obstacles to such a policy were the colonial empires, particularly that of Great Britain. The Secretary of State crusaded against the policy of imperial preference as one of the worst possible examples of economic nationalism. Hull was extremely suspicious of the British and feared that they might use their position during the war for imperial expansion. As we have seen, this was not true at all. Furthermore, the opening of imperial markets to outside competition would undeniably have benefitted the United States most of all. It is in this context that we must see Hull's – and much of the Roosevelt administration's (for Hull certainly was not alone in this belief) – opposition to de Gaulle. The Free French, it was feared, would be a willing tool of British expansionism.

Eden, in particular, received constant complaints from Hull about de Gaulle's statements. There was little, however, that he felt able to do. On one occasion, Eden went so far as to ask if the United States wanted him to stop funding de Gaulle, but Matthews immediately backed down.[11] Hull certainly was extremely sensitive to criticism. A British embassy report described Hull as 'most passionately concerned to justify his Department's policies at press conferences'.[12] There is also a great deal of evidence that some members, at least, of the State Department had been uncomfortable with the whole United States Vichy policy from the very beginning. Leahy in his memoirs spoke scornfully of the Department's position:

One of the first instructions I received from Roosevelt [on returning to Washington from Vichy] was to tell the State Department and the Board of Economic Warfare to resume the shipping of supplies to French West Africa and of infant relief to Occupied France. It being considered unsafe to give anybody any advance information on our military intentions to invade North Africa, some of these officials offered sharp objection. They clearly considered the President and me to be pro-Vichy. I considered them not sufficiently reliable to be trusted with vital military secrets.[13]

In fact, major foreign policy questions had been taken out of the State Department's hands at the beginning of World War II. This can be seen from the role assumed by Harry Hopkins after the war in Europe began. Hopkins had long been the president's favourite, although he rarely held any official position. During the 1930s he had mainly worked on domestic policy which, during the New Deal years, was the focal point of the administration.[14] However, even during this period, Roosevelt liked to keep ultimate control over foreign policy in his own hands. To this end he appointed as Under-Secretary of State Sumner Welles, who was, on many questions more knowledgeable than was Cordell Hull. Welles also was a close personal friend of Roosevelt, which was not the case of Hull. Furthermore, Welles took advantage of this fact to bypass Hull not infrequently and go directly to the President, while Roosevelt showed his preference by leaving Hull in Washington and taking Welles with him to his first summit meeting with Churchill. This inevitably fostered a great deal of jealousy between the two men. It reached such a point that they could not bear each other's company, and Hull would not invite Welles to official dinners he was giving. In such a circumstance, it was impossible for the two men to coordinate foreign policy together.

The situation became considerably worse when, in 1941, Sumner Welles committed an indiscretion that showed homosexual inclinations and word of it threatened to leak into the press. Hull immediately stated that Welles should resign because he could be blackmailed by an enemy agent and thus was a threat to the security of the nation. Of course, allegations of homosexuality were not something that a deeply religious southern gentleman was likely to be inclined to tolerate and, when coupled with the already poor relationship between the two men, the situation was certain to deteriorate. William Bullitt, the former ambassador to France and another close personal friend of Roosevelt, sided with Hull, probably because he hoped to get Welles's job. Roosevelt refused to abandon Welles, although the latter eventually did resign in 1943. The result of this episode was to distance Hull even further from the making of foreign policy and to exclude Bullitt from any kind of official position. The War Department and Harry Hopkins – a close personal friend of Roosevelt who also acted as a kind of unofficial liaison between the White House and the State Department – inevitably profited from this situation. It is significant that it was Harry Hopkins who was sent by Roosevelt to Britain in early 1941 in order to assess Britain's needs and that the result of this visit was the Lend–Lease bill. It is also significant that when Germany invaded the Soviet Union, Hopkins was also sent there. Hopkins attended most of the conferences with Roosevelt, while Hull was usually not even invited.

Churchill was often forced to leave Eden at home because Roosevelt did not want to be forced to invite Hull. In North Africa, Murphy, at least at first, reported primarily to Roosevelt and the whole arrangement with Darlan was mainly a War Department affair. During this period Hopkins, Marshall, Leahy and Eisenhower had a much greater role in the formulation of foreign policy than did Hull. This is proven by Hull's persistent requests to Leahy for information. In June 1943 Hull telephoned Leahy to request information on the political situation in North Africa. Hull complained that 'without information the State Department is unable to act intelligently'.[15] The British noticed and were puzzled by the State Department's lack of information. At one point they learned that an American official had asked Massigli to make sure that Murphy was better informed on the situation. The Foreign Office knew that they were better informed on French affairs than was the State Department but had assumed that this was because of the inefficiency of that department. Now they wondered if the French had been keeping information from the Americans.[16] In point of fact, it was not the French who were keeping the United States government uninformed, but the War Department and the White House who were keeping the State Department uninformed. The latter was reduced to begging a foreign official for information. In March 1944 Hull complained bitterly to Bullitt of his position, saying that he wanted to leave the Department. Hull stated that: 'He was trying under terrible difficulties to keep some hand on our larger international policies.' He went on to add that:

He still did not know what had happened at Teheran and that he had no knowledge whatsoever of the constant stream of communications that was being exchanged between the President and Churchill and Stalin. He added that the President seemed to be cut off from advisers of all kinds on international affairs. He certainly was not consulting him, Hull; Hopkins had been ill for some time and he was so ill that he might never come back to work and the President was apparently just making decisions without consulting anyone. He said that while Stettinius was a very decent fellow he was inexperienced in foreign affairs except in the domain of Lend–Lease and could not be expected to advise the President.[17]

Later, on 1 June 1944, Hull went so far as to tell Henri Hoppenot, the then Gaullist representative in Washington that 'all French affairs were decided exclusively by the president' and insisted that he personally knew nothing.[18]

The British do not seem to have understood that they were, at least, part of the reason for the American hostility to de Gaulle. To the British, it was obvious that, given de Gaulle's behaviour towards them, he could not be their tool. Eden insisted that the British were doing all they could to make de Gaulle behave.[19] Furthermore, as Matthews had written, the British were also suspicious of American designs. Oliver Harvey believed that it was the Americans who were thinking of imperial expansion. He was shocked by Roosevelt's talk of making Dakar and the French possessions in the Pacific into postwar Allied bases.[20] Eden himself analysed the American policy towards France in the following way:

> So far as I have been able to piece together the various indications I have received, I would say that they did not wish to see a strong central administration for the French Empire built up in Algiers. They would have preferred if possible to deal separately with each part of the French Empire. They dislike the growth of an independent spirit in any French administration anywhere and consider that any French authority with whom they deal should comply without question with their demands. The fusion of General Giraud's and General de Gaulle's administrations has been unwelcome to them and they would have wished, if this had been possible, to disrupt the Committee of Liberation, to eject de Gaullist members from it, to set up in its place a puppet committee, subservient both to the Allied powers and to General Giraud, with whom alone they would continue to deal on a purely military basis.[21]

Eden went on to suggest that Roosevelt, at least, had evil intentions with regard to the French empire, and that United States policy was to keep the French divided so that the Americans could work their will on the French empire after the war. Eden felt that the Americans did not want to see France restored to great power status but that British interests dictated a strong France in order to assist the British in policing and containing Germany after the war. The negotiations for union between the Giraudists and the Gaullists thus took place against a background of mutual suspicion, with the Americans and British highly suspicious of each other's motives and the French deeply suspicious of both.

Although inevitably much of this was centred on North Africa, a corollary Anglo-American rivalry developed in West Africa. West Africa had rallied to Darlan and, although it had previously been under the Colonial Ministry in Paris, it was now administered by French authorities in North Africa. However, economically it fitted most logically into an arrangement with British West Africa. It so happened that the British had another Resident Minister in West Africa, the extremely energetic Lord Swinton, who was charged with all questions pertaining to that region and he quickly became involved in French West Africa. The Americans had sent as their representative to French West Africa, Admiral Glassford, yet another personal friend of the president. For the Americans, French West Africa was a particularly sensitive subject, because of the strategic importance of Dakar. Glassford soon became alarmed by Swinton's growing influence there. He wrote that Swinton 'has an eye on the assimilation of French West Africa into the British post-war scheme of things'.[22] The British were no less worried about Glassford's influence, and Glassford gave them cause for worry. He arrived once at a meeting of the North African Economic Board's Executive Committee, saying that it was 'American policy that Dakar should be "stemmed" from Algiers,' although he refused to give the reason for this policy. On another occasion, he told Macmillan that he had been appointed 'General Eisenhower's Proconsul in French West Africa'.[23] Such statements could not calm British fears about American intentions in French West Africa.

It is important, therefore, to remember that although the negotiations that led to French unity took place against a background of mutual suspicion, this is not the whole story, for Anglo-American relations in Algiers were dominated in 1943 by Dwight Eisenhower and Harold Macmillan. Eisenhower in many ways symbolised the American dream come true. From a modest background in the Midwest he had risen to become Commander-in-Chief of Allied forces and would eventually become president of the United States. Macmillan, although the great-grandson of a Scottish crofter, had married the daughter of an English duke. He was also one of the heirs of the Macmillan publishing house and half-American. His wealth, Oxford education and marriage qualified him to be a member of the British elite. However, although their backgrounds were widely different, both men were deeply committed to the Anglo-American alliance and to the maintenance of Allied unity. Eisenhower once explained that:

> You are completely right in assuming that the matter of maintaining a firm Anglo-American Partnership for the purpose of winning the war lies close to my heart. There is no single thing that I believe more important to both our countries.[24]

Macmillan felt just as strongly on this question, although his interpretation of the roles of the Americans and the British probably differed from Eisenhower's.

It is said that Macmillan frequently explained to his British colleagues during the Second World War that America was a new Rome to Britain's Greece. One of these colleagues, Richard Crossman, has recorded that Macmillan told him:

We, my dear Crossman, are Greeks in this American empire. You will
find the Americans much as the Greeks found the Romans – great big,
vulgar, bustling people, more vigorous than we are and also more idle,
with more unspoiled virtues but also more corrupt. We must run AFHQ
[Allied Forces Headquarters] as the Greek slaves ran the operations of
the Emperor Claudius.[25]

Macmillan considered himself to be the ideal Greek teacher, working in
the background to educate Americans so as to influence their policy, most
notably towards the French. His ideal Roman is also easy to identify.
Macmillan describes in his memoirs his arrival at the Casablanca Conference of 14–26 January 1943 between Churchill and Roosevelt. He says
that: 'At the head of his [Roosevelt's] bed was sitting Churchill and,
standing to attention like a Roman centurion on the other side, our
Commander-in-Chief, General Eisenhower'.[26] It is a very symbolic scene
(and as we see from the memoirs of Robert Murphy, the other person
present, not entirely correct).[27] The President of the United States is sprawled
on his bed like a Roman emperor with Churchill sitting in attendance and
the centurion standing guard. This is clearly Harold Macmillan's vision of
things, but it is one that would strike a chord with many of his British
colleagues. Most realized – and usually resented – that, in their effort to
maintain British power in the post-war world, they would need the support
of the Americans. Furthermore, like Macmillan, most of them had a similar
sense of superiority before the Americans. What is perhaps unique about
Macmillan is that he did not resent this situation but rather found it ful-
filling to feel that he was working behind the scenes in an almost anonymous
fashion to shape American policy according to British wishes.

Macmillan certainly liked to believe that he had an inordinate amount
of influence over Eisenhower and insists upon this fact throughout his
diary.[28] This fitted in with his theory of the new Greece and Rome. America,
the new Rome, was essentially a military power with little knowledge of
the intricate details of world politics. For this it needed the guidance of
Britain, the new Greece. It is very curious, however, that Eisenhower
hardly mentions Macmillan in his correspondence or in his memoirs and
never once refers to him in his diary. Nor is Macmillan's undue influence
mentioned or even alluded to in American documents. This seems almost
incredible given the State Department's extreme sensitivity both to British
intentions and War Department intrusions in their rightful sphere of action.
Any rumour about Macmillan would almost certainly have reached the
State Department and Cordell Hull. The only conclusion one can come to
is that it is not possible to assess accurately Macmillan's influence on

Eisenhower. It is, however, highly probable that Macmillan had an exaggerated view of his own role. In fact, what the two men shared was a deep commitment to the alliance of their two nations, and it is this fact that allowed the Anglo-American machine to function so smoothly in Algiers.

The first political matter which Macmillan and his American counterpart, Robert Murphy, had to deal with was the thorny one of unity between the French. Roosevelt and Churchill in their correspondence spoke of this unity as a wedding: de Gaulle was the reluctant bride and Giraud the bridegroom. The first step in achieving this unity was to have the two meet. This came about – not without some difficulty as de Gaulle at first refused to come – at the Casablanca Conference. Roosevelt and Churchill forced de Gaulle and Giraud to shake hands and give at least the appearance of friendship. Unity, however, was far from achieved, and during the first half of 1943 negotiations took place between the Gaullists and Giraudists under the watchful supervision of the British and Americans. De Gaulle's intransigence and the desire by former Vichy officials who had attached themselves to Giraud for self-preservation further complicated things. The United States soon realized that replacing Darlan with Giraud was not enough to make the North African regime respectable. North Africa had to liberalise and return to the laws of the Republic. Harry Hopkins felt that a reputable civilian presence was needed in Algiers to bring about such a goal and decided that Jean Monnet was the ideal candidate for such a mission. Monnet had unimpeachable Republican and pro-Allied credentials, having been in the United States since June 1940 where he had worked for the British Supply Council. He could thus also provide desperately needed assistance on economic questions – particularly in the all-important area of supply. His knowledge, position and nationality made it possible for him to tell Giraud that the shortage of shipping meant that the French army could not be immediately completely rearmed and that delays did not mean that the Americans were lukewarm on the idea. Furthermore, Monnet had never been associated with the Gaullists and had many friends in Washington, including Hopkins and Morgenthau, the Secretary of the Treasury.[29]

In early February 1943 Giraud sent a message to Monnet asking for his assistance. Before answering, Monnet consulted Hopkins as to his point of view.[30] Hopkins immediately wrote to both Roosevelt and Hull saying that he thought it would be a very good idea. Hull initially protested on the grounds that Monnet had rather tenuous Gaullist connections, although his real objection may simply have been that such a mission would inevitably be beyond the control and knowledge of the State Department.[31] In any case, Monnet arrived in Algiers in late February and reported on the situation there directly to Hopkins – who then forwarded reports to Hull. He went as a representative of the Combined Munitions Assignments Board, and his ostensible purpose was to work with Giraud on the rearming of the French army through Lend–Lease. In a letter to Eisenhower, Roosevelt hinted that more was involved in Monnet's arrival in Algiers:

> About three weeks ago General Giraud asked Monnet to come to see him. When I learned of this I encouraged the visit; first, because Monnet knows a great deal about the whole problem of supply throughout the world and can, as well as anyone I know, tell Giraud about how the whole business works throughout the world. I am sure also he can be helpful to Murphy and Macmillan as well as Giraud in understanding the whole North African situation as viewed from here. I have discussed all of these matters fully with him and he carries a personal letter from me to you.[32]

The visit, however, was not to be announced by Eisenhower, and, when it did become public knowledge, Roosevelt insisted that any explanation for the visit should be confined to two points: Giraud wanted him to come, and the Americans needed him to work on the supply question. In this way Roosevelt hoped to avoid any accusation of American interference in French domestic affairs.

Soon after his arrival Monnet wrote to Hopkins that people were still very confused in North Africa and that 'certain fundamental principles' needed to be established there. He felt that all ties to Vichy had to be absolutely and completely cut and that some of the personnel from the earlier period had to be replaced. It also had to be clearly shown that the British had no ulterior motives and that they did not wish to take advantage of the weakened condition of France in order to annex French colonies.[33] The first thing that must be done, Monnet felt, was to get rid of all the laws against the Jews. Monnet then stated that he was preparing a speech for Giraud, which the latter gave on 14 March, in which he would announce more liberal policies and would definitely break with Vichy. In this latter concept Monnet closely followed the ideas of René Cassin, holding that French sovereignty had been suspended by the occupation and thus all of Vichy's laws were void. Monnet also showed in this letter that his aims were not terribly different from those of de Gaulle:

> Thus the North African administration with Giraud will take the position of repudiating Vichy and all laws enacted since the armistice – limiting its role to the administration of the territory of North and West Africa and acting as trustees for the French people – guaranteeing to

preserve the full rights of independent and free choice according to the French constitution of the French people, to name their provisional government – building up an army with the assistance of the U.S.A. and sharing in the Allied victories, thus making France one of the victorious nations of the war.

The only major difference between Monnet and de Gaulle was on the question of a provisional government. Monnet held that no provisional government could be established without the express consent of the French people. De Gaulle believed that, given the circumstances, the implied consent was enough, since some kind of government was necessary to avoid direct Allied administration of liberated France, to represent that nation at the peace conference, and to prevent civil war. France could only be one of the victors if she had a government to represent her.

General Catroux, de Gaulle's chief negotiator with Giraud, was quick to understand the significance of what was happening in North Africa. Monnet had written to Hopkins that union between Giraud and de Gaulle could only come about after the situation in North Africa had been transformed. However, this very transformation weakened Giraud. Catroux wrote to de Gaulle:

> General Giraud's situation offers this singularity: it gets weaker as he moves towards us; at the same time as he alienates those elements that are opposed to us, he does not gain our followers. His speech, which is interpreted as, and indeed is, embracing our principles, has provoked some of the resignations that we desire among his collaborators. Would it make sense, at a time when we are gaining ground and when he is becoming dependent on us, to give him back his support? I answer quite firmly in the negative. I advise once more that we should persevere in the patient method that we have adopted. As diminished as his position is, Giraud has been in place for a long time and Algeria will not come to us without his consent and this consent he will give more readily than he will allow it to be taken from him.[34]

In another letter to de Gaulle, Catroux insisted on the positive role of Jean Monnet: 'It is to his influence that we owe the rapprochement of our viewpoints, and, I must add, that he is trying at present to definitely wipe away all divergences that continue.'[35] Catroux found him 'honest, disinterested and understanding'. There is no doubt that Catroux was right, that with every liberalisation of the regime Giraud and Monnet moved inexorably towards the Gaullists who, after all, had been speaking of principles from the very beginning. At the same time, without unity, Giraud was also in a weak position. Murphy explained to Hull that: 'Without this unity, and in some measure because Giraud is still hesitant to eliminate the remnants of Petainism in the Army and Navy, his position is being weakened without an early agreement which would preserve the main lines of his proposal.'[36]

Jean Monnet's mission to Algiers showed that the Americans and the British preferred to act in the background in the negotiations regarding French unity. However, on two occasions they found it necessary to act directly. In both cases it was decided that the best form to give interference was a personal intervention by Eisenhower on the grounds of military necessity. The first time was in early April when Eisenhower (who was absent at the time) sent a telegram (actually written by Macmillan) to de Gaulle asking him to postpone his proposed visit to Algiers for military reasons, as the battle in Tunisia was reaching its most critical point. De Gaulle responded by announcing to the press that Eisenhower did not want him to come to Algiers. In fact, neither the British, Americans, Giraudists, Monnet or even Catroux wanted him to come to Algiers, because they feared disturbances. Monnet described the atmosphere in Algiers to Hopkins:

> While these orderly negotiations were going on, an effort was being made here in Algiers by emissaries and partisans of de Gaulle to create an atmosphere of disturbance. Anonymous circular letters were deposited under every door – rumors were rampant – every action of Giraud was distorted – every delay to act by Giraud, some of which have been unfortunate, were over-emphasized. Attempts to either frighten or to tempt people in Giraud's administration were constantly made. The whole purpose of this was unquestionably to prepare an atmosphere adequate for the arrival of de Gaulle. I do not go as far as to suggest that a 'coup d'état' was planned, but to call it 'psychological pressure' is to put it very mildly indeed.[37]

Catroux himself insisted to de Gaulle: 'You should only appear in Algiers to seal the union and not to either realise it by negotiating or to impose it by the psychological effect of your presence.'[38] In the end de Gaulle did not come, and French unity was achieved. Whether the two facts are connected is impossible to say, but many people certainly believed that they were. Catroux was allowed to conduct leisurely negotiations in a more or less peaceful atmosphere, and Monnet continued reforming Giraud. When de Gaulle finally did arrive in Algiers on 29 May, the basis for unity had been more or less settled, and the French Committee for National Liberation was officially formed on 3 June with Giraud and de Gaulle as co-presidents. With Churchill as 'heavy father' and Eden as 'best man' the wedding finally took place.[39]

Within two weeks another major crisis had broken out between de Gaulle and Giraud over de Gaulle's wish to clearly subordinate the military to a civilian authority – or, in other words, to place Giraud in a subordinate position to himself. Both Roosevelt and Churchill, distrusting de Gaulle as they did, were extremely alarmed by this latest twist in French affairs. After exhausting other possiblities, Macmillan, Murphy and Bedell Smith decided that Eisenhower should talk to the two generals as 'one soldier to other soldiers'.[40] This was Eisenhower's second intervention and once again it was presented as being a purely military one. An agreement was eventually reached that more or less satisfied all parties. De Gaulle was placed in command of his former Free French forces and Giraud over his former North African forces. Everyone knew that the co-presidency and split command were too clumsy to last. But to Macmillan at least, the very fact of agreement having been reached was enough:

If it lasts three months, it will do. For in that time the conception of French union will have become too strong to be overthrown and the Committee itself will (I hope) have developed sufficiently for the civilian elements to be (as they are showing signs) able to stand up to the dictatorial methods of the generals.[41]

These barriers having been more or less successfully hurdled, the next question was of Allied recognition of the French Committee for National Liberation. The British and Russians were initially sympathetic to the idea, but Washington – although it had allowed Martinique and Guadaloupe to rally to the Committee in late June – was opposed to it. Eisenhower, Smith and Murphy wrote a number of telegrams to Washington urging recognition. Their reasoning was often designed to quell Washington's fears about de Gaulle. Murphy argued that:

The civilian members of the Committee are concerned that our delay in recognition implies existency of an American policy of ignoring this body, and consequently that we are supporting an individual in contrast to support for the nearest approach to a representative group which can at present be constituted.
It is believed that Committee will continue to function with an increasing sense of civilian responsibility and that only alternative to such Committee could be assumption of control under de Gaulle in view of Giraud's disinterestedness in political matters. Therefore if we are to avoid giving de Gaulle the means of increasing his personal leadership,

it would seem that an early recognition of the collective nature of Committee is implied.[42]

By the end of July there were definite signs that the State Department was beginning to come round to Murphy's way of thinking. The latter had used an argument that was certain to have an effect on Hull and his department: 'There may be good reasons for creating an impression that the matter of recognition is being left to British initiative but from here it would appear that the American position is being gradually weakened as a result.'[43] Hull was still easily upset by de Gaulle's initiatives, but in late July he agreed to speak to the president in favour of recognition. Dunn felt able to inform Halifax that: 'the more the Department thought about it the less could they see any practical alternative to recognition'.[44] It took a while to convince the president, and much time was wasted in an attempt to find a formula that both the British and Americans could accept and issue jointly. In the end the British and Americans agreed to differ and on 25 August 1943 issued their own mild forms of recognition.

In a sense this is a key moment in the history of American relations with the Free French, because for the first time we see the State Department – reluctantly it is true – coming out in favour of de Gaulle. From now on Hull will be considerably less hostile than will be Roosevelt. To begin with, Hull had never been personally and directly insulted by the Free French in the way Roosevelt had been during his meeting with Philip and Tixier.[45] He had, of course, been attacked in their newspaper, *La Marseillaise*, but, as we have seen, he tended to blame this on the British. Furthermore, two of de Gaulle's worst French enemies, Alexis Léger and Etienne Boegner, were close to Sumner Welles, and they, or their ideas, were often taken to Roosevelt – but never to Hull – by Welles. By instinct Hull was not inclined to support Welles and after his resignation in 1943 the anti-Gaullists lost a powerful friend. Far more important than this, however, was Hull's wish to assert State Department authority over Franco-American relations and to reduce the role of the War Department. This could only be done by establishing proper diplomatic representation in Algiers. Furthermore, when the Committee was formed the British stopped funding the Free French, and this removed one more of Hull's objections to de Gaulle. The growing evidence of Gaullist popularity in metropolitan France further convinced Hull that the Americans needed to show support for the Committee or they would lose some of their influence in France to Britain or Russia. Finally, there was Hull's sensitivy to criticism of him and his department over their Vichy policy. Accepting the Gaullists would end this. By late 1943 a similar situation existed in both Britain and the United

States: the State Department, the War Department and the Foreign Office, as well as British and American representatives in Algiers, all, in differing degrees, looked with favour on the Committee. Opposition to the French Committee of National Liberation (F.C.N.L.) from now on will, with certain important exceptions, come from the top – from Roosevelt and Churchill.

This is true in spite of the fact that the story of the last few months of 1943 is one of constant mistakes by Giraud and of the increasing power of de Gaulle. Giraud's first mistake was to go to Washington in early July. In Giraud's absence, de Gaulle worked hard to strengthen his position and in particular electrified his Algiers audience with his speech on the fourteenth of July. To Giraud, the most important thing was the reconstitution of the French Army. For this reason he went to Washington as soon as he could to push the Americans to rearm the French more quickly. Political questions hardly interested him and even though many people warned him that July was much too early for a trip abroad – that he needed to stay in Algiers and consolidate his position – Giraud disregarded them and left for Washington. More important, those members of the Committee who considered themselves more or less neutral, like Monnet, Maurice Couve de Murville, René Mayer or Henri Bonnet, became more and more irritated at Giraud's lack of political finesse and more and more impressed with de Gaulle. The civilian members of the Committee were certainly troubled by the fact that military power was not subject to civilian control. De Gaulle argued that the commander-in-chief had to be subordinate to governmental authority. After Giraud's return from the United States, de Gaulle succeeded in his purpose. In a series of three decrees on 31 July and 4 August – all signed by Giraud – the co-presidency became a specialised one: Giraud charged with military matters and de Gaulle with political ones. It was also stated that when Giraud took up his functions of commander-in-chief he would no longer be co-president.

The situation remained like this until the autumn. On 8 September Italy signed an armistice with the Allies and, when the news became known, Corsican resistants started an uprising throughout the island. On the eleventh they seized Ajaccio, and Giraud asked the Allies for permission to send troops to assist the resistance. The Allies agreed, and troops were despatched on the thirteenth. The island soon fell to the French. Publicly praised, this action led to fierce debates and recriminations within the Committee. Not only had Giraud not asked for authority from the Committee for such an action, he had failed to even inform them of what was planned. He had only told de Gaulle twelve hours before the attack. Worse than this, Giraud had instituted a state of siege on the island which placed it directly under the authority of the commander-in-chief. Giraud was accused of having exceeded his authority and of having left the military sphere for the political one. Giraud himself refused to take the matter seriously and actually left Algiers for Corsica to take command of the operation. This, of course, only increased the Committee's suspicions.[46] On 2 October de Gaulle became the sole president of the Committee, and Giraud was made commander-in-chief under the authority of a Commissioner for National Defence. The military had been clearly subordinated to a civilian power. A few months later, in April, Giraud would lose even this position and, refusing to take the honorary post of Inspector-General of the army, would go into retirement. It was a strange turn of events for the man who had once been virtually sole master of North Africa. Macmillan said of Giraud:

> I would suppose that never in the whole history of politics has any man frittered away so large a capital in so short a time . . . he has been driven, or rather has voluntarily retreated, from every bastion of his fortress, he has given up every vantage point, he has been exploded by mines of his own making, he has himself dug and opened the trenches that besieged his citadel, and of his decline and fall he has been himself the sole author.[47]

Strangely enough, while Churchill became highly incensed over this change, there was almost no reaction from Washington. For the time being, at least, even Roosevelt seemed reconciled to de Gaulle's growing authority.

As we shall see, Roosevelt became upset with French politics again, not because of the Syrian crisis of November 1943, but because of the arrests of four former officials of Vichy: Pierre Boisson, Marcel Peyrouton, Pierre Pucheu and Pierre-Etienne Flandin, who were to be tried for their roles in the Vichy regime. Churchill and Roosevelt immediately reacted hostilely to this event. Both felt that their honour was engaged, at least in regard to Boisson and Peyrouton who had been actively solicited by the Allies to join them. Churchill wrote to Roosevelt and explained that he felt that they both had an obligation towards the men.[48] This time Roosevelt went along with Churchill's initiative and sent a message to Eisenhower telling him to inform the Committee: 'In view of assistance given to the Allied Armies during the campaign in Africa by Boisson, Peyrouton and Flandin, you are directed to take no action against these individuals at the present time.'[49] The State Department were very much opposed to Churchill and Roosevelt taking action in this case. Not only did they believe it would immensely antagonize the Committee and cause a breach between them and the Allies as well as restart all the old criticisms of America being soft on Vichy, but the Department was even more irritated by the fact that the president had sent an essentially diplomatic communication to Eisenhower, a military commander, without even informing the American representative in Algiers. James Dunn telephoned the American representative to the French Committee, Edwin Wilson and discussed how they could 'hold up' delivery of the message. In typical State Department fashion, Dunn blamed everything on the prime minister. When Roosevelt learned of this, he wrote to Leahy insisting that he felt just as strongly on the question as did the prime minister.[50] Unfortunately for Roosevelt, he and Churchill were alone, and Churchill, typically, after a strong initial response immediately began to weaken on the question. Needless to say, the telegram was held up, and Churchill changed his mind. Roosevelt too was forced to back down. He revoked his ultimatum and left matters in the hands of diplomats.

In fact, it was clear that the Committee was undertaking only a very modest purge of a few important persons. Members of the Committee made it clear to both the British and Americans that these arrests had been made reluctantly and only because pressure from the resistance had become intense. Macmillan pointed out that the Committee had taken no action between September and December which showed that they themselves were not enthusiastic about a purge.[51] De Gaulle himself said as much to Churchill, insisting that 'the Assembly which had been set up as a democratic influence was almost unanimous in demand for severe penalties against collaborationists'.[52] The leader of the resistance group *Combat*, Henri Frenay, felt that de Gaulle would even have liked to have amnestied Pucheu, a former Minister of the Interior who had been responsible for a crackdown on the resistance that had caused many deaths, but that he felt unable to do so.[53]

This debate formed the backdrop to a far more serious question: that of a directive to Eisenhower that would allow him to negotiate a civil affairs agreement with French representatives in preparation for D-Day. This was an issue about which Eisenhower in particular felt strongly. He had been traumatized by the lack of preparation in civil affairs for Operation 'Torch' and did not want to see the same thing repeated on the much greater scale of 'Overlord'. In early 1944 he insisted that:

It is essential that immediate crystallization of plans relating to civil affairs in Metropolitan France be accomplished. This requires conferences with properly accredited French authorities. I assume, of course, that such authorities will be representatives of the Committee of National Liberation.

I therefore request that General de Gaulle be asked to designate an individual or group of individuals with whom I can enter into immediate negotiations in London. The need for prompt action cannot be overemphasized, since we will desire to turn over to French control at the earliest possible date those areas that are not essential to military for operations.[54]

The question of civil affairs in France was a potentially loaded one because it involved handing control to the Committee and ultimately to de Gaulle of administration in an area that would be contiguous to the major battle zone of the European War. We must not forget that de Gaulle had only been allowed into Algiers after fighting had ceased in North Africa. To those who distrusted de Gaulle, granting the Committee authority in France meant not only giving it political legitimation but also implying that it was a real and trustworthy ally. As we have seen, the State Department and the Foreign Office – and in fact most members of both governments – had become convinced that the Committee – and especially de Gaulle – possessed enough popular support in France to give them political legitimacy, and although no one actually liked de Gaulle most were willing to admit that his actions – although not his words – had so far demonstrated him and the Committee to be a trustworthy and democratically minded ally.

Roosevelt, Churchill and a few others took a less charitable view of the situation and felt that France, at least for several months, should have a military administration under American and British officers.[55] In early September the French Committee had set up a special subcommittee to plan for civil affairs in France. The plan which they developed was obviously unacceptable to either the British or Americans because it gave so much power to the Committee. A further complication was that, by now, the Foreign Office had decided that France had to be restored as a Great Power in order to preserve the future balance of power in Europe. Britain by itself could never be an effective counterweight to Germany. It was far from certain that the Americans would remain after the war, and, furthermore, there was the growing threat of the Soviet Union. The Foreign Office did not want Britain to find itself in the position of being the only power policing western Germany, while a potentially hostile and certainly much more powerful Russia controlled the eastern half. The only solution seemed to be to find a powerful, democratic and European ally, and they saw France as the only real possibility for this role. The State Department was rapidly coming to a similar conclusion and, believing de Gaulle to be genuinely popular in France, wished to preserve as much American influence there as possible. The War Department, meanwhile, felt that only the

Committee could gain them the full and coordinated support of the resistance, protect their lines of communication and insure that the Darlan controversy did not repeat itself. The problem was to find a directive that would be acceptable to everyone, that would reassure Churchill and Roosevelt without insulting the French.

A further problem was to determine on what level a civil administration agreement would be negotiated. The Americans all insisted that it had to be negotiated on a military rather than a governmental or diplomatic basis. The British felt that this would be unacceptable to the French, since other agreements for Norway, Belgium and the Netherlands had been negotiated between governments. There was one strong argument for the American viewpoint: a governmental or diplomatic agreement had to be ratified by the Senate, whereas a military one did not. Any such consideration in the Senate would necessarily turn into a debate on American policy towards France in general, past and present, and this Roosevelt would clearly want to avoid at all costs with an election coming in November 1944. Halifax in Washington insisted that the difficulties over the directive came entirely from the president, probably supported by Leahy, and that this attitude had no major support in Washington, either in the State Department, Congress or among the general public. He felt that, given this fact, the British should hold firmly to their viewpoint, since the question of relations with France was so much more important for them than for the Americans.[56] The Foreign Office and the State Department reached agreement on a draft directive by John McCloy, the Under Secretary of War. This was then presented to the president in February 1944. After keeping it on his desk for nearly a month, he finally announced that he disapproved of it and wrote a substitute directive which McCloy felt would be 'definitely insulting' to the French Committee. The War Department and the State Department then decided to rewrite the president's directive in order to change both its form and content.[57] There were further delays on the American side, which Hull explained quite forthrightly to Halifax as being due to the president's unwillingness to give as much power to the French Committee as other parts of the United States government wished.[58] In late March when Roosevelt's directive finally reached the Foreign Office, there was a sense of relief. They discovered that he had adopted most of the re-draft and that it was, therefore, better than expected.[59] Duff Cooper, who was now the British ambassador to the French Committee, still found the directive left much to be desired. He stressed that the Committee had a great deal to offer to the Allies, possessing an empire, army, navy and air force and having the undeniable support of most of the French people. He felt that the Committee deserved more respect.[60]

In a meeting with Roosevelt on the very same day, the American representative to the Committee, Edwin Wilson, tried to reason with Roosevelt on the question. Roosevelt explained how he felt, saying that:

> Eisenhower should have freedom of action to deal with other groups than the Committee, because, for example, the Committee might appoint bad representatives in one region of France, another group might come forward with some worthy representatives who should be considered. I said that it would seem in our interest to have, if possible, a single French authority administer France up to the time of elections for a definitive government, in order to avoid the emergence of competing groups which would tend to fight each other and bring on civil war. If Eisenhower decided to deal with the French Committee and it on the whole was doing a fair job, then if it made bad appointments in some region of France it might be desirable to persuade the Committee to remove those men and appoint better ones rather than to turn to some other French group which would begin to compete with the Committee ... The President said he agreed with this.[61]

Wilson went on to say that he thought that United States interest lay in the re-establishment of a strong, independent and democratic France. Roosevelt said yes, but with certain exceptions such as Dakar, New Caledonia and Indochina. He was especially firm in the case of Indochina, insisting that independence was the trend of the future.

The next step in this drama occurred on 9 April when Cordell Hull gave a major foreign policy speech in which he said that 'the Committee will have every opportunity to undertake civil administration in Metropolitan France, and our co-operation to help in every practical way in making it successful.'[62] Everyone found Cordell Hull's speech encouraging, and Eisenhower began informal discussions with de Gaulle's representative, General Koenig, on the subject. These discussions, however, were stopped by two things. First, Eisenhower discovered that the president did not agree with Hull's speech and, second, the British government, in preparation for D-Day, banned all communications in foreign cypher and all unnecessary travel out of the country. Koenig was cut off from Algiers and furious about it. Hull and the United States government meanwhile were forced to take refuge in the pretence that the president's directive and Hull's speech were the same thing, which was clearly not the case. On the eve of D-Day, there was still no civil affairs arrangement for France. The Allies, however, had clearly achieved their main goal. All French opponents of the Armistice had been united behind the reasonably democratic and undoubtedly popular F.C.N.L. France, furthermore, had come round to almost unanimous support of the Allied cause. In spite of the absence of a civil affairs agreement, it was clear that the events of North Africa would not repeat themselves. What could not be conceded officially would be acknowledged unofficially. The Committee was preparing to administer France, and Eisenhower, for one, had no intention of stopping them.

6 The Anglo-Americans and the Resistance in France

Charles de Gaulle may have been the first resistant, but he was by no means the only one. By June 1944 dozens of resistance movements existed in France and, while most of these had voluntarily announced their allegiance to the alternative French government in Algiers, they still remained largely independent until the arrival of the Allies. It should not surprise us, having seen the slow growth of Free France during the 1940–1942 period, to see the same phenomenon repeated with the interior resistance in France. In 1940 resistance was an isolated act: in Chartres, the prefect, Jean Moulin (later Mercier, Rex or Max) tried to kill himself rather than cover up for the Germans; in Marseille, Henri Frenay-*Charvet* began to recruit army officers; others hid weapons or distributed essays against the Armistice. However, in general, in 1940 the French people were in a state of shock and embraced Pétain as their saviour. They felt grateful that their leaders, unlike those of Belgium or the Netherlands, had stayed with them and were prepared to endure the occupation with them. It must not be forgotten that the defeat of 1940 had profoundly shaken French society. Memories of the hardships of the previous war had provoked a mass exodus in northern France: approximately eight million persons had fled before the German invader and taken to the roads. They were desperately in need of food and housing. Furthermore, over one million French soldiers were taken prisoner by the Germans at this time. Parallel to the collapse and discrediting of the army came the collapse and discrediting of the Third Republic. Finally, the British attack on Oran destroyed for many the ties of alliance with that democracy and provoked a wave of anglophobia. Whether the war continued or not no longer interested most French people, so long as it did not continue on their soil. The greatest desire for most of the French was a return to order and something resembling normalcy. In this frame of mind, de Gaulle's call for resistance was unlikely to provoke a strong response.

However, once it was certain that Britain would resist and that the war, therefore, would be a long, world-wide one involving the United States, it became clear that France could not escape from the war. The growth of the resistance movement is directly related to the number of Allied victories and the severity of the German occupation. By the end of 1940 individuals in favour of resistance were beginning to come together and

form groups. Most of these groups were based on pre-existing organisations, usually political or professional ones.[1] In Lyon a Christian Democrat
group sprang up, while in Dordogne some former members of *Action
française* began to organise as the *Confrérie Notre Dame*. The latter was
one of the first resistance groups to enter into contact with Free France and
enjoyed some of the fastest growth. Henri Frenay-*Charvet* had already
developed plans for a secret army and had formed the first elements of
what would become *Combat* at this time, while in Occupied France the
Musée de l'Homme group, composed essentially of Parisian intellectuals,
was appearing. There were also many socialist groups sprouting at this
time. Given the fact that most of the members of these groups had absolutely
no experience of the demands of clandestine life, it should not surprise us
that most of these early resistants were quickly decimated by the Germans.
Frenay-*Charvet* was one of the few to survive.

De Gaulle was keenly aware of the importance of these movements, and
one of his first actions, on 28 June 1940, was to ask Capt. André Dewavrin-
Passy to organise an intelligence agency, which would later be known as
the BCRAM (*Bureau Central de Renseignements et d'Action militaire*),
which later still was shortened to BCRA. Dewavrin-*Passy* told de Gaulle
that, although he had absolutely no experience of the question, he would
be willing to undertake the task on two conditions: that he would be given
sufficient funds and that the necessary means for transmissions and liaison
with the resistance groups would be found. De Gaulle admitted that he
could provide neither request and suggested that Dewavrin-*Passy* should
speak to British intelligence services.[2] It is important to remember, therefore, that in this early period it was often difficult for the resistance and
Free France to enter into contact with each other and that the Free French
intelligence group was completely dependent on the British. Free France
had few resources, and they needed the British to transmit messages, transport men, distribute weapons and provide other basic services.

At the same time, in true Gaullist fashion, they resented this dependence
and were constantly attacking the British for violating French sovereignty.
De Gaulle and Pleven, for example, complained bitterly that the British
intelligence services constantly tried to steal Free French recruits and turn
them into British agents.[3] Dewavrin-*Passy* was determined to make the
Free French secret services as independent as possible from the British,
and in this he was of course strongly supported by de Gaulle. The personality of Dewavrin-*Passy* is one of the most controversial among the Free
French. There were persistent rumours from many different sources that
he had been closely connected to the *Cagoule* – although to this day he
denies it. He clearly was far to the right in his political views and was not

a great lover of the democratic system. His tenure at the Free French secret services was also a controversial one, with repeated accusations of rather violent interrogation tactics being used on suspected enemy agents.[4] Like so many others, he was tolerated by de Gaulle because he shared the general's sensitivity to questions of French sovereignty. In January 1941 he managed to give the intelligence services some financial independence from the British. In March 1941 he succeeded in getting radio equipment and establishing his own radio links with some members of the resistance. His next project was to establish separate French codes between Carlton Gardens and France. In May 1941 a representative was sent to France to provide agents working with Free France with a code unknown to the British.[5] De Gaulle and Dewavrin-*Passy* were desperately seeking to unite the resistance under them to be the channel between these different organisations and the British, but they tried to do all this without having any independent means. That they succeeded as well as they did shows the extent to which de Gaulle became the symbol of resistance in France.

The early intelligence efforts in France were of extreme interest to the British because they concentrated on finding any information on German preparations to invade Great Britain. Once this immediate threat passed, the resistance took on other tasks: gathering of information on various subjects, propaganda activities and sabotage operations.[6] The British, of course, were convinced of the need to organise resistance in France. They were actually the first to organise networks with the function of undertaking action against the enemy and gathering information. In the summer of 1940 Churchill created the Special Operations Executive (SOE) to develop this activity. In November 1940 the Ministry of Economic Warfare, under whose authority came SOE, held a meeting to discuss the possibilities of resistance. Their aims were extremely limited: passive resistance within French industry used by the Germans, and sabotage of the German war effort in occupied France.[7] As we have seen, these aims were only a small part of those of de Gaulle and Dewavrin-*Passy*, who wished to have France re-enter the war as a unified country. Here is once again, in a different situation, that old conflict between the aims of the Allies who are seeking to win a war, and those of the Free French who want to re-create France as a major power. The essential aim of SOE was military, that of Free France political. It should not surprise us then that the same conflicts that occur on a political level are repeated between the intelligence services.

There was one fact that was of overwhelming importance: the British had sole control over operations until 1944, when Special Force Headquarters (SFHQ) was formed which included the American Office of Strategic Services (OSS). By D-Day, SOE directly controlled about 50 networks and indirectly controlled those that had given allegiance to Free France. They were also responsible, until SFHQ came about, for the parachuting of arms and money to resistance groups – at first primarily to their own networks, then to those of the Free French and even the *maquis*. Until July 1944, the French had almost no part in this machinery. The Free French responded to this situation by trying to play one British intelligence organisation against another. In principle, MI6 was in charge of gathering information and SOE of actual operations, but in reality it was virtually impossible to establish a clearcut division of tasks. SOE was further handicapped by the fact that it did not depend on the War Office but on the Ministry of Economic Warfare. Given the natural jealousy between rival organisations, it is not surprising to discover that the War Office, insisting on the need for security, often refused to give information to SOE, while leading military figures would not meet with that organisation's representatives. There was thus a basic lack of coordination between the military and intelligence services, and this was only partly remedied in 1944 when SFHQ was created.[8]

Unfortunately for the heavily divided French, it was more often than not the SOE and MI6 who took advantage of French differences for their own purposes.[9] In general, the Free French considered their relations with MI6 to be satisfactory but were extremely jealous of the French section of SOE which operated independently of Carlton Gardens and which, given its superior wealth, was able to offer greater means to potential agents. Furthermore, it was to SOE that the Free French had to go for the organisation of their own operations in France and so SOE obviously knew a great deal about Gaullist contacts with the resistance, while Free France could have only indirect knowledge of SOE dealings with those groups directly under SOE's authority. To further complicate the situation, the other Allied nations, notably Poland, Czechoslovakia and Belgium, kept their own agents in the field, although these were almost entirely subordinate to SOE. During the early period, French resistance groups found themselves contacted by different agents, claiming to represent Free France, the SOE, MI6, various American agencies and other Allied governments. Any of these, of course, might in reality be German agents, which made the whole business exceedingly dangerous for both sides. The Free French had a strong argument in insisting that intelligence work should be channelled through one organisation, and the Americans at least saw some justification for this. W.P. Maddox of the OSS branch in London, wrote that:

> Coordination of the will to resistance in France and of plans for eventual insurrection against Vichy, or military combat against Hitler, would

seem in any case a reasonable and desirable procedure. There is good reason to believe that the Free French in London are, at this stage, better prepared to undertake this coordination than any other group . . . To a considerable extent, at least, their purposes coincide with ours, and a basis for joint and collaborative action is therefore provided.[10]

It is noteworthy that the Americans, who started serious intelligence work much later than the British – they did not even possess a central intelligence agency at the time of Pearl Harbor – were considerably more sympathetic towards Free France and that the Free French intelligence services generally preferred to work with them. The Americans realised that the only way they could make up for lost time was to work closely with both the Free French and the British and receive the information that both could give them.

In June 1941 the resistance increased spectacularly in power with the German invasion of the Soviet Union. In one stroke the Communist Party went from being officially indifferent to being the most powerful part of the resistance. Being well organised, highly disciplined and used to some degree of clandestinity, the communists made ideal resistants. Given the turbulent history of pre-war France, their very strength worried Free France, for it aroused the spectre of a communist takeover if the Germans withdrew from key areas, like Paris, before the arrival of Allied troops. However, the very fact that the Communist Party was so disciplined and blindly followed orders from Moscow, in the short term worked to Free France's advantage. The OSS noted that: 'However, while taking into account the importance of the Communist resistance movement, it should be pointed out that, at any rate at the present time, its ready discipline and the orders which have come from Moscow which is Russian rather than Communist have turned it into a submissively Gaullist instrument.'[11] Moscow certainly did not want to hinder the Allied war effort by promoting revolution in France. This would have injured the success of an Anglo-American landing there and would have hurt any advance into Germany. There is no doubt, however, that both Free France and the Anglo-Americans continued to fear the communists. Although they might not distract from the war effort, they still might gather weapons and power in order to act after the war. The Free French also found this a useful way of trying to blackmail the Americans into more overt support for both de Gaulle and the resistance. Catroux, for example, told Murphy in August 1943 that if the rumour grew that the Americans were planning on dealing with the Vichyites when they arrived in France, 'the resistance movements would turn more and more in direction of Russia rather than the Allies for liberation and eventual support

of government.'[12] His point was clear: show support for the Committee or
see a communist ascendency in France.

By the end of 1942 three large movements had developed in the Unoccupied zone: *Combat, Libération* and *Franc-Tireur*. *Combat* had been
founded by Henri Frenay-*Charvet* and was one of the most structured of
the resistance groups – which is not too surprising since much of its
membership was based on army and *Deuxième Bureau* (one of the French
military intelligence services) acquaintances of Frenay. It had clearly been
designed to contain the germs of a secret army. *Libération* was more
clearly political. Its founder, Emmanuel d'Astier de la Vigerie-*Bernard*,
the brother of Henri and François d'Astier whom we have already met in
North Africa, wanted to build a movement that would unite left-wing
elements like trade unions, socialists and communists. D'Astier dreamt of
a national rising that would bring with it a revolution. *Franc-Tireur* was
the most clearly anti-Vichy of these groups and like the others was involved
in propaganda as well as the organisation of armed resistance. In the
northern zone, five major groups emerged during this period: *Ceux de la
résistance* (Those of the Resistance or CDLR), *Ceux de la Libération*
(Those of the Liberation, or CDLL), *l'Organisation civile et militaire* (The
Civil and Military Organisation or OCM), *Libération-Nord*, and the National Front. The OCM was the first to enter into contact with Free France.
The National Front was a communist dominated organisation.

The period from 1942–3 was a profound one for the resistance. As we
have seen, during this period Free France grew in importance and de
Gaulle eventually became the head of an alternative French government
in Algiers. Until 1942 the resistance had developed in a largely isolated
fashion. Beginning in 1942 the various groups started to enter into contact
with each other and with Free France. Inevitably they gave their allegiance
to the Algiers government. The process, however, was a difficult one. In
September 1941 Jean Moulin (*Mercier-Max-Rex*) arrived in London and
informed de Gaulle of his own personal observations on the state of resistance in France. The latter immediately realised that Moulin was the ideal
link between the domestic and the external resistance. A few months later,
in January 1942, he was parachuted into France with the mission of unit-
ing the resistance movements in the unoccupied zone and bringing them
under the authority of Free France. For de Gaulle this was a necessary
development. Until this point Free France had been entirely dependent on
the British. To establish some degree of authority – or even direct contact
– with the resistance movements in France would significantly improve
the bargaining position of Free France and would give them something
very important to offer.

Furthermore, Gaullist political aims demanded the allegiance of the resistance to Free France. The various groups had to acknowledge the authority of Free France in order to make the latter a viable possible government. This, in turn, would increase the Gaullist bargaining power in relation to the Anglo-Americans. Finally, there was the Gaullist obsession with French sovereignty. It was clear to de Gaulle that SOE and MI6 were very active in France and had established their own contacts with the resistance and even their own networks. This situation became even more threatening with the entry of America into the war and the arrival of American intelligence agents in France. These men were also in contact with the resistance and with their superior means could promise almost anything to the under-armed and under-funded French movements. Thus, to increase his own prestige with the Anglo-Americans and to protect French sovereignty, de Gaulle wished to establish Free France as the official channel of communication between the internal resistance and the Anglo-Americans. He was certainly helped toward this goal by the 'Darlan Deal' which outraged the resistance and made them draw rank behind de Gaulle. This in turn certainly aided de Gaulle during his negotiations with Giraud. The resistance movements, of course, resented losing their independence to Carlton Gardens which they felt, with some justification, was totally out of touch with the situation in France. While they could see the need for military coordination, de Gaulle's desire for political control largely irritated them.

Jean Moulin understood and shared de Gaulle's goals. When he returned to France he brought with him a small sum of money, 250 000 francs and several pages of orders to the resistance groups. The secret army was unimpressed. As one member exclaimed: 'Sure, in theory all this is perfect. But in practice it's utterly unfeasible.'[13] This summed up the attitude of the resistance towards Carlton Gardens, and more particularly towards the BCRA. They felt that neither de Gaulle nor Dewavrin-*Passy* had any idea of what the situation in France was like, and they strongly resented Moulin's attempts to bring them to order and discipline. The Free French did, however, have some notable successes. In September 1942, after negotiations in London with Frenay and d'Astier, the three most important movements in the south, *Combat*, *Libération* and *Franc-Tireur*, merged their military sections into one secret army under General Delestraint.[14] In January 1943, the three movements officially united and became MUR (*Mouvements unis de résistance*, United Resistance Movements) with Moulin as president. By this time Moulin had been asked to establish some kind of authority over resistance movements in all of France. In May 1943 a National Resistance Council (CNR) was formed in Paris with Jean

Moulin once again as president, which was a kind of umbrella committee for resistance movements throughout France.

Much to the irritation of Moulin and de Gaulle, independent relations between the resistance and the Anglo-Americans continued. In October 1942 it was discovered that the British had approached Léon Jouhaux, prominent trade unionist and resistant, with the offer of a large sum of money to help in reconstituting the trade union movement in France. Jouhaux, of course, was ecstatic and, in spite of objections from Free France, accepted the offer. D'Astier-*Bernard* felt that the threat was serious and insisted that: 'Our services must be able to substitute themselves for the English services in order to support the French trade union movement.'[15] A more serious case occurred in the very month of the formation of the CNR. Moulin discovered that the NEF (earlier name for MUR) had been in contact with the Americans and the British in Switzerland and had offered to provide them with information in return for funding. When questioned, the NEF admitted that they had deliberately not told Moulin because they were sure he would be against the idea. Their justification was that they desperately needed money and that Carlton Gardens could not provide anywhere near enough. To Moulin, this was a clear attempt at corruption by the Americans, who, by offering 40 million francs a month to the resistance, were trying to buy the movement's support for Giraud. Furthermore, he feared that if these movements began to give information directly to the Allies, de Gaulle's value as an intermediary would decrease substantially. Consequently, Moulin made a series of recommendations to de Gaulle. He admitted that the resistance had a strong argument about funding and urged Carlton Gardens to find some way of quickly sending increased amounts of money to the resistance groups. Moulin wrote that: 'The day we can say that we and not the Allies are financing the fight against deportation [STO], the position of Gaullism in France will be considerably reinforced.' Moulin accepted the fact that it would be practically impossible to force the resistance to give up their contacts with the Anglo-Americans in Switzerland, but he tried to convince them not to provide military intelligence and to have a representative of Free France present during all conversations.[16]

There was, however, also a great deal of resentment against the Anglo-Americans – particularly the British – on the part of the resistance organisations. The American Col. Kittredge discovered this during an interview with E. Petit-*Claudius* of the *Francs-Tireurs et Partisans* (FTP) in November 1943. Petit-*Claudius* explained that the resistance felt that it was ignored by the Anglo-Americans. He complained that many plans had been submitted to London for sabotage of important military targets in

France by the resistance rather than by aerial bombardment, and that these plans had been largely ignored. Resistance leaders felt that it would be less costly in terms of human lives to favour sabotage over bombing. The Anglo-Americans, of course, were afraid that the resistance had been penetrated by the Germans and thus did not wish to entrust them with too many military secrets, but Petit-*Claudius* insisted that it would only be necessary to reveal a tiny part of the general plan to each resistance group. He also expressed resentment that groups under direct British control – and thus not affiliated with the actual French movement – received more money and weapons. He attributed this to a British fear of 'left-wing revolutionary movements', but, if this were the case, they were making a mistake:

> They have in fact been giving at least half the arms sent to France to independent communist groups not definitely associated with the organised French resistance movement. The Communist groups, which constitute less than ten per cent of the resistance effectives now carrying on underground war against the occupying forces, appear to have been willing to serve under British orders in order to obtain arms. They have therefore received at least fifty per cent of the weapons and explosives sent to France by the British.

He thus insisted that the British were achieving the opposite of their own policy.[17] In fact, all elements of the resistance were poorly armed. However, this observation is particularly important because it shows that the French were worrying about what would happen after D-Day, when the Committee would be faced with the Herculean task of establishing order in a country overrun by closely-knit groups of armed young men. The tragedy of the resistance was that – with a few exceptions – it possessed neither the training nor the weapons to confront the Germans, but it was strong enough to threaten unarmed civilians. The resistance might provide the Committee with its most important claim to legitimacy but it was also a threat to that very authority.

The resistance received an important boost in late 1942 when the Germans overran the unoccupied zone and showed that they, at least, had no qualms about breaking the armistice conditions. An even more important event occurred in 1943 with the introduction of STO (*Service du travail obligatoire* or Obligatory Work Service). Germany desperately needed manpower to continue the war effort, and Vichy agreed to provide it. In February all men born between 1 January 1920 and 31 December 1922 were called up for Work Service in Germany for a period of two years.

The reaction in France was overwhelmingly hostile. Large numbers of these young men refused to serve and instead took to the hills. In this way, the *maquis* were born. The resistance did suffer two important setbacks during this period because in June 1943 both General Delestraint, head of the secret army, and Jean Moulin were arrested and eventually killed. No one ever managed to replace Moulin with regard to both the resistance and the Gaullists, and his death was thus a blow to the establishment of Free French control over the movements.

It must always be kept in mind that Jean Moulin was not a glamorous figure. He led no commando raids or sabotage actions nor did he write in the underground press. First and foremost, Jean Moulin was an administrator, and he tried to establish an underground administration to run the various resistance movements. He distributed funds from Free France and was responsible for liaison with London. He also coordinated the distribution of arms. It is not surprising to discover that the various resistance movements strongly resented the presence of Moulin because it infringed on their independence. The resistance was willing to recognise de Gaulle as a symbol – and they certainly were quite pleased to accept any money or weapons that he might be able to offer – but they did not want to give him any real authority over their movements. They wanted to maintain their independence. Moulin on the other hand wanted to establish the resistance as an organised military movement under the political leadership of the French National Committee in London. This was felt to be necessary to satisfy both the long-term goal of preventing civil war and the short-term one of strengthening de Gaulle's bargaining power in relation to Giraud and the Anglo-Americans.

By mid-1943 the British estimated that there were about 150 000 men in the secret army but that only 35 000 of these could be effectively armed. An American report estimated that the resistance could have no more than 200 000 men who were poorly equipped and thus capable of only small-scale activity. This report implied that, to some extent, the lack of weapons was a deliberate policy, particularly with regard to the *maquis*. Arms had only been issued to officers in these units so as 'to enable them to enforce their authority'. There was undeniably a certain suspicion of these poorly disciplined units. The report did, however, come to the conclusion that:

Nevertheless the French secret army, acting in conjunction with other organized elements of resistance, is capable of creating a considerable degree of disruption in the interior of France and of facilitating Allied operations directly as well as indirectly.[18]

The report particularly singled out the area of the Mediterranean coast–Rhone Valley and the Alps as a place where the resistance could be especially useful. This became one of the centre points of Operation 'Anvil', the landings in the south of France, which relied heavily on assistance from the secret army.

One of the most obvious developments in the resistance was the growth of communist units. After the invasion of the Soviet Union the communists had decided to attack the Germans through sabotage, assassinations and other actions. These were at first coordinated by small groups, but in order to increase the efficiency of these groups in 1942 the *Francs-Tireurs et Partisans français* (FTPF and later just FTP) was formed. After a difficult beginning they quickly spread throughout all the Occupied Zone and then into the Unoccupied Zone. The FTP was considerably more active than other resistance organisations, and many non-communists joined it for this reason. However the FTP remained essentially a political movement. Most of its leaders were communists, and some had even fought with the international brigades in Spain. After the introduction of STO the FTP's membership increased even more, particularly among the non-communist rank-and-file. At first the FTP was only supposed to operate in the cities, but STO offered new possibilities because most men took refuge in the countryside. Before STO most units were composed of only seven men and their leader; afterwards companies and even battalions were formed.

By late 1943 the resistance was preparing for D-Day and their role in the liberation. One of the first signs of this was the establishment of Jedburghs in September 1943. A Jedburgh team was usually composed of three officers or noncommissioned officers, French, English or American, who, after receiving intensive training were parachuted in uniform into France. They were sent to train the resistance groups and to prepare them for action when D-Day came. There was also another, perhaps more important, reason for their existence: the Jedburghs were there to help the resistance commanders to establish discipline over their men. It was hoped that the arrival of uniformed Allied officers, bringing secret orders and weapons, would have an impact on the rank-and-file. The Allies too were now convinced of the need to assert discipline over the ever-increasing *maquis*. Commando groups called Operational Groups (OG) were also sent into France. These usually consisted of around thirty men and four officers and could subdivide into much smaller units if necessary. They were well-armed and could communicate with London. Once they had fulfilled their mission, they usually stayed in France for a while in order to assist the *maquis*, and once again, this was believed to have a good effect on discipline.[19]

In December 1943 the resistance was officially given the name of the French Forces of the Interior or FFI. A few days later some of the movements in the north now officially joined the MUR which was renamed the *'Mouvement de libération nationale'* (Movement of National Liberation or MLN). By now the Allies were determined to use any possible assistance from resistance groups to help the landings. In the opinion of SHAEF (Supreme Headquarters Allied Expeditionary Force: Eisenhower's headquarters) the resistance could inflict no serious damage on the Germans. However, they could cause delays, and this in turn might slow down the reinforcement of enemy troops. A SHAEF report came to the conclusion that the cumulative effect of resistance operations might be considerable and 'at a critical stage of operations, not inconceivably decisive'.[20] Algiers, naturally, was delighted by this conclusion as the Committee wanted to involve the French as much as possible in the actual military aspect of the war. De Gaulle himself felt that it was necessary to convince the French that they had largely liberated themselves, and a national uprising of some form was, therefore, of fundamental importance.

Protests continued to be heard, however, about the paucity of arms going to the resistance. In a debate in the Consultative Assembly in January 1944, there were numerous complaints against the United Nations for breaking its promises to arm the resistance and against the Allied military staffs for ignoring underground forces.[21] This debate greatly upset Hull, who immediately began to make requests to Leahy to augment the supply of weapons to the resistance. In March, Hull detailed his reasons for insisting upon the need to increase supplies:

> As the Joint Chiefs of Staff are probably already aware, the question of arming resistance groups has become an important political issue in the eyes of all Frenchmen, wherever located, and the impression seems to have gained general credence that what is being done in this field is being done by the British and that the United States not only played no part in the matter but is even opposed to arming the 'underground' for political reasons.[22]

Hull had returned to his old obsession that the British were trying to hurt America's relationship with the French. He stated this directly to Leahy, who was himself no fan of the British: 'The British are desirous of keeping the matter as much as possible in their own hands, thereby gaining credit in the eyes of the French and lending the appearance of truth to the claim that this Government is indifferent if not actually hostile to the resistance groups in France.' A week later Hull learned that Churchill had established a Special Committee on the Resistance which consisted predominantly of

French and British members, and this confirmed all his suspicions. Soon after this, the Joint Staff Planners, to whom the question had been referred, agreed with Hull and stated that more publicity should be given to the fact that the supplying of resistance groups in northern France was under the direction of Eisenhower.[23] Furthermore, they felt that 'steps should be taken to provide from United States sources equal or greater air lift than that now being provided by the British.' The Gaullists would have been delighted had they known of these reports, and that their policy of playing the British and Americans off against each other was, at least in this case, working.

In April Marshall replied to Hull's letter, saying that:

> During the past twelve months the United States has equipped a French Expeditionary Force comparable in size to our own peacetime army. Our most modern equipment has been made available, at times at the expense of delay in the expansion of our own forces. The British have made substantially no contribution to the French Rearmament Program.[24]

Marshall's answer was quite reasonable. The British and the Americans had essentially divided the task of arming the French: the Americans taking care of the regular army in North Africa while the British tried to help the resistance in metropolitan France. However, Hull also was right, for more important long-term questions were at stake. It was the American army that would provide most of the troops to be used for the liberation of France, and the government, not unnaturally, wanted to be sure that they would be welcomed by the French people. Furthermore, the power centre in the France of the future would return to Paris. In the end, it was what the people of France themselves thought that would really count once the nation had been liberated. Given Hull's feelings of rivalry and suspicion towards the British, it is clear that he would do his best to counteract charges that the Americans were not interested in the resistance. A few days after Marshall's letter, de Gaulle gave a press conference in which he praised British efforts to arm the resistance and implied that the United States was not doing anything on the question. Needless to say, Hull reacted strongly, writing to Marshall: 'This statement is just the sort of thing that we have been hoping to be in a position to combat, and, if I may make a suggestion, it seems to me that some good could be done if use were made in Algiers of such of the information contained in your letter of April 17 as could safely be passed on, even if only orally and informally.'[25] Eisenhower was contacted for his advice on the subject. He explained that the lack of available aircraft on the American side had prevented greater United States involvement in the armament question.

The British had been primarily responsible because their supplies had been on the spot and because the resistance was already familiar with using British weapons. A further problem was the significant lack of qualified personnel in the OSS. He did, however, promise to talk to General Koenig and explain the situation to him.[26]

In May, in an off-the-record interview with the press, de Gaulle showed that he had understood the value of the Anglo-American rivalry. He explained that he did not want 'to give the impression that he wished to criticize the British', but he thought he should mention that British officials had repeatedly said that 'the United States Government was opposed to the arming of members of the French resistance'.[27] The Joint Staff Planners by now had finished a detailed study of the question and made the following pronouncements:

> Any statements are unfounded that because of political reasons the United States is opposed to rearming the French.
> Such statements and lack of knowledge of the facts are detrimental to the interests of the United States, may result in a lack of full cooperation on the part of French resistance groups with United States forces in coming operations, and may hinder the war effort.
> It is desirable that the FCNL be acquainted with the facts of the case.[28]

They went on to suggest that it would be more effective to send a message from the Combined Chiefs of Staff to de Gaulle, because it would force the British to give their support. The British, however, refused to go along with such a plan, and this only served to further increase American suspicions. Hull, of course, had been fairly sure that the British would refuse and had already written to the Acting American representative to the Committee to instruct him to 'lose no opportunity' to emphasise to influential French people that the arming of the resistance was a joint Anglo-American effort.[29]

This consideration, of course, only added to the American insistence on the need for Operation 'Anvil'. This was one of the major Anglo-American strategical debates of World War II, and analyses of the question have inevitably focussed on its relation to the later Cold War. The intention here, however, is simply to consider it in relation to French policy. Basically, the difference was that the Americans wanted to have a second landing in France after the main one in Normandy. This landing would consist predominantly of French troops and would take place in Provence in the south of France. 'Anvil' would require the transfer of large numbers of troops from the Italian theatre and thus would reduce the scope of that campaign. The British wished to continue with a major effort in Italy and to push from there up into central Europe – 'the soft underbelly of Europe' – and on into Germany by a long, circuitous route through Austria. In his memoirs, written during the Cold War, Churchill explained that such an attack would have saved large areas of central Europe from Soviet domination. At the time, however, this does not appear to have been an important consideration. To the Americans, though, the whole plan seemed rather insane, as they preferred to fight the Germans where they were in France and Germany, than where they were nearly absent in Central Europe. They felt that a second landing in France was necessary in support of the earlier one in Normandy: it would distract German troops from the north, and it would provide necessary harbour space for bringing in supplies. Furthermore, such an operation would allow the French to participate in the liberation of their own country, and the Americans had been rearming them precisely for this purpose. It was virtually impossible to arrange for any significant number of French troops to participate in the campaign in the north because of the lack of transport, but this would be much less of a problem in the south because of the closer proximity of North Africa and Italy where most of the French Army was located. 'Anvil' would also give an important role to the resistance which was, as we have seen, particularly strong in these areas. Eisenhower wrote to Marshall:

> It is my view that the contribution to the support of resistance forces should always be in proportion to the ability of resistance to assist planned operations. On this basis we plan to contribute a large part of available air lift and supplies for the Maquis in the south of France to aid ANVIL and thus indirectly assist OVERLORD.[30]

For American policy the situation was ideal: it made possible a large American contribution towards the arming of the resistance, and it made the Americans and French allies against the British. Now it was the British who were not showing sufficient sympathy for the understandable French desire to participate in the liberation of their homeland.

As D-Day neared, Generals Koenig and Cochet were given command of the FFI in the north and south respectively. Both men were attached to the staffs of the supreme Allied commander in his area: Koenig to Eisenhower and Cochet to Wilson. In this way, for practically the first time, the French began to receive a certain amount of military information. Koenig himself was well aware of the difficulties of his position. To begin with, he had been given command over a wide range of resistance movements that had developed largely independently, had differing political aims, were under-armed and under-trained and yet eager to fight the Germans. To complicate his problem, although the FTP was officially part of the FFI they kept their own organisation and refused to reveal their strength. Furthermore they continued their call for a national insurrection and insisted upon having prominent positions on all the resistance and liberation councils. Many non-communists began to worry that the FTP might try to seize power. Therefore it was felt that the resistance had to be quickly disciplined and incorporated into the regular army or, at the least, disarmed. Koenig explained to General Smith:

> No call for calm or prudence will stop the patriots from escaping from the grasp of the enemy and fighting against him. Their action will be effective if it is directed and if they are given the means of fighting; on the other hand, it will be sterile and even have harmful consequences if the Supreme Commander abandons them. Indeed the consequences risk being dramatic not only during operations but also in the later stages of the establishment of peace.[31]

To add to Koenig's difficulties, there was the problem of the chain of command within the FFI. Having operated clandestinely for years, the forces were not really used to taking orders from an outside authority: they were largely self-contained groups and, as in all such organisations, the local leader reigned supreme. We have already seen the hostility that greeted Moulin when he tried to impose some kind of authority from Carlton Gardens. The situation was further complicated by the roles played by BCRA, SOE and the OSS, as well as other intelligence agencies. Koenig was worried that outside interventions by any of these organisations could affect his chain of command. He wanted to exercise his command in a 'normal military manner', and that meant excluding the intelligence organisations from an area in which they had worked for a very long time.[32] If the FFI were to become a disciplined force, two rival command channels could not exist.

When one considers all the evidence, it would appear that the French Committee were far more concerned by the political nature of the resistance than were the Anglo-Americans. It is difficult to find any proof that either the British or the Americans deliberately tried to keep the resistance unarmed because they feared possible revolutionary consequences. On the other hand, there is a great deal of proof that Algiers was deeply concerned by the question, and certain resistance leaders in France were also preoccupied by the strength of the communists. One wrote to de Gaulle in February 1944:

> The communist problem has been slowly but surely getting worse since November. The authority of the FCNL and the CNR is still recognised

by communists in word and in written motions, but they are becoming more and more reserved about practical cooperation in every area. Military coordination is progressing slowly with the FTP, Francs-Tireurs and the Communist Party. The coordination of civil committees and the designation of general secretaries is hindered for the same reason.[33]

In some areas the Free French even complained to the Anglo-Americans that too many arms were going to the communists.[34] Already in July, the Gaullist resistance was worrying about the possibility of a communist takeover in Paris. One Parisian resistance leader wrote to Emmanuel d'Astier de la Vigerie, now Commissaire of the Interior for the FCNL, suggesting that they should form a force of about 15 000 men within the FFI who would be directly under the orders of the Algiers government. He was worried because most of the armed groups in the area were under the orders of a communist leader, Colonel *Rol*-Tanguy, and he, in turn, was under the authority of the Parisian Committee for the Liberation, which was also dominated by the communists. He felt that this special force under the orders of Algiers should be created to seize on the day of the liberation certain buildings in Paris that were significant symbols of authority: the ministries, the Chamber, the Senate, the Elysée, and the Prefecture of Police, for example.[35]

Let us now consider what happened to the FFI after the arrival of the Allies on 6 June. In many areas the FFI certainly did prove to be of assistance. They undertook a large number of guerilla operations: interrupting German communications, clearing airstrips and roads of mines for the Allies, guarding or even destroying bridges. They served as guides and formed reconnaissance patrols. They even saw action against isolated German pockets. In the northern region, the most important area of FFI activity was undoubtedly in Brittany, and unfortunately this resulted in tragedy. Brittany was liberated by an Allied armoured division unsupported by any holding forces. The role of the FFI was therefore an extremely important one, and Marshall, for one, was not dissatisfied with their performance:

> Our reports, however, show that the French resistance troops are fighting well even against regular German forces, and I believe we should make every reasonable effort to get more supplies and equipment to them ... Perhaps the fighting these French resistance troops are now doing indicates that, after our forces open the way to them, they could be formed quickly into combat units and be able soon to engage against the Germans.[36]

In several west-coast ports, the FFI managed to contain three German divisions for a relatively long period of time. However, once the Allies left Avranches, they entered territory that had been largely untouched by war, and villages were quickly liberated. As a general policy, Allied troops disarmed the FFI and then they moved on to the next village. Unfortunately, there remained pockets of German resistance in Brittany and in a number of cases, a few hours after the Allies left a village, the Germans entered it. In many cases they committed atrocities, and the FFI, of course, were now incapable of intervening. The result was that after a few such experiences, the FFI refused to disarm.[37]

The FFI had increased dramatically in strength after D-Day as less idealistic and committed elements rushed to join it. These men now were armed and many roamed the countryside acting in a manner similar to bandits. Another section of the resistance also refused to disarm or enter the regular French army – the FTP which was communist dominated. One SHAEF report concluded:

> At all events, in Brittany there have been roving around the country-side armed bands of reputed communists, the thugs and the worst elements of the country-side, not indigenous to it, committing excesses in the name of the FFI and threatening to bring the whole movement into disrepute. In some areas, it was said that soviets had been proclaimed and that a state of anarchy prevailed.

The situation seemed almost incapable of solution, since the government could not force the FFI to disarm until the German pockets of resistance had been reduced. On the other hand, the destabilisation of the countryside that was occurring was even more dangerous. The situation was aggravated by de Gaulle's decision to appoint Colonel Chevigné to take over military responsibilities in the area. Chevigné followed a policy of promoting former army officers over resistance leaders – even when the former officers had done nothing during the war – and this, naturally, further irritated the resistance, particularly the FTP. Chevigné was following a strictly Gaullist policy: trying to impose military discipline, disarm the FFI and prevent their trying accused traitors. He lacked, however, a certain amount of discretion, having told one FTP officer that the FFI no longer existed after the liberation of an area. Koenig was forced to intervene and to give in to some of the demands of the FFI.[38]

In southern France the situation was even more delicate. According to an SOE report, local FFI commanders emerged as warlords in certain areas after liberation, and the civil administrators were too weak to control them. An equally serious conflict had also developed within the resistance movement itself, between the communist dominated National Front and FTP and non-communist groups. This, in turn, raised the spectre of civil war.[39] With so many Frenchmen armed, the situation seemed particularly dangerous. Any attempt by the government to impose senior commanders over local leaders was deeply resented and rarely obeyed. As in Brittany, some of the poorer elements in the FFI formed into gangs and terrorised the countryside. There were widespread examples of requisitioning and summary justice and even a few isolated cases of bank robbery. A report to de Gaulle found that:

> The French Forces of the Interior are without a definite chain of command. They have leaders at company or battalion level; above that there is no one. Lack of discipline is spreading, often leading to a state of affairs bordering on anarchy. Ringleaders are rising up who see that they have followers. These gangs want bread and fun. The leaders send them into liberated towns to find both. When opportunity arises they try to seize power (for instance in Limoges).[40]

The situation certainly seemed threatening.

For a variety of reasons, however, the revolution did not occur. As we shall see in Chapter 8, the British and Americans increased their support for the Provisional Government. The Russians, furthermore, refused to support any communist uprising in France, because they did not want to distract from the war effort. In fact, once the Germans had left France, the whole reason for the existence of the resistance disappeared. Soon after the liberation, FFI leaders talked of forming a new party from the resistance and contesting elections, but the movement quickly fell apart. This was not really surprising considering how many political tendencies existed within it. As a military force the FFI also disappeared, the best members being incorporated into the French Army. The Provisional Government gradually succeeded in replacing lawlessness with a more orderly situation, and in this they certainly were helped by the presence of large numbers of Allied troops. The government was able to maintain control and eventually to allow the Fourth Republic to come into existence.

7 The Financial Link

Until the union of the French in 1943 Free France did not have enough resources to become self-supporting. Even after its establishment in Algiers the French were dependent on the Anglo-Americans for the rearmament of their military forces, for emergency assistance in liberated areas, for trade, and in fact for almost all of their economic needs. One can safely assert that without this economic assistance in its early days Free France would not have survived and that even in its later days its position would have been precarious. When Charles de Gaulle arrived in London in June 1940, he was not only a man without a country, he was also a man without a salary – and one who had a wife and three children. He was able to become the head of a great movement because the British government, at least at the beginning, paid his salary. Most Free French volunteers were in the same position as de Gaulle, and, while most of them did not have families to support, they all needed to eat. For those Frenchmen who refused the armistice but who did not possess the connections, talents or linguistic skills to integrate into Anglo-American society, there was virtually no choice but to join Free France or to be deported to Vichy. By the same token, most of the colonies that rallied to de Gaulle were either in grave economic crisis or already economically linked to Britain, and they were offered important economic incentives in order to gain their adherence to de Gaulle. When Cordell Hull or William Leahy, or even the Vichy Government, referred to Free France as a British creation, they were basically correct.

In July 1940 the British government agreed that, in general, Free French European personnel would receive basic British rates of pay, while different arrangements would be made for 'non-European and native troops'.[1] The most important financial problem, however, was that of the Free French colonies. Most of these colonies had rallied to de Gaulle primarily because they felt that it would bring economic benefits. A Treasury report on the question claimed that:

> It is scarcely an exaggeration to say that the whole course of the Free French Movement in Africa was economic . . . In fact the unanimity of popular sentiment which made possible the coups d'état at Duala and Brazzaville was very largely due to the fact that French Equatorial Africa and the French Cameroons were at that time faced with economic ruin and were, therefore, swayed by our offers of prompt economic assistance.[2]

British economic policy was based on the idea that they should ensure a reasonable quantity of supplies to the area and that they should buy as much of the produce of these colonies – whether wanted or unwanted – to guarantee an adequate income to the residents. The British blockade, which limited supplies to Vichy Africa, meant that, in general, economic conditions were better in the Free French colonies. This was a major factor in Free France maintaining power.

This was also an enormous task. Previously, these colonies had been almost completely dependent on metropolitan France. Alternative products and markets had to be found, the banking system reorganised to make it independent of Paris, and new sources for vital imports had to be discovered. The choice of trading partners, furthermore, was extremely limited: the British Empire, the United States and the Belgian Congo were the main possibilities. The greatest assistance undeniably came from the British. In March 1941 de Gaulle signed credit and currency agreements with the British Government which set out, among other things, the conditions of British payments to the Free French and covered commercial and economic relations between French Equatorial Africa and the United Kingdom. The first of these provided for advances from the British Treasury to de Gaulle to cover the military expenditure of the Free French Forces – most of which was in the colonies. According to this agreement, payments would not be made directly from the British Treasury to the Free French colonies but via Carlton Gardens. This was logical in that it centralised financing. It also guaranteed de Gaulle's pre-eminence within the Free French since all payments were ultimately determined by him, and it relieved the British of accusations of trying to buy French colonies. It must be emphasised that these advances were only for military expenses and not for civilian ones. Civilian expenses were to be paid for locally from the colony's own income and taxes. The currency agreement established the exchange rate between the pound and the Free French franc as 176.625 francs to the pound and incorporated the Free French colonies into the sterling zone. The colonies could exchange money themselves, of course, but the agreement obliged them to keep Carlton Gardens informed of their transactions.[3]

One of the most important products covered in these accords was cotton. Given wartime circumstances, cotton was a particularly valuable crop and it transformed the economic situation in two of the poorest territories, those of Chad and Oubangui-Chari. Rubber also played a significant role in the economy of French Equatorial Africa, especially once the main sources in the Far East were cut off. Another development was that of trade with neighbouring British colonies. Part of Lord Swinton's role as

Minister Resident in West Africa was to organise commercial relations between British West African colonies, Free French colonies and the Belgian Congo. One of the most remarkable achievements of the war was the growth of regional feeling between these administrations which had previously been involved in an intense rivalry. Under Swinton, a great deal of effort was exerted to plan these economies in relation to war needs and to each other. However, in the end, the British were inevitably the backbone of this system. In 1943 René Pleven, Minister for the Colonies, paid tribute to their role in the economy of Free French Africa:

> We found a comprehension among our Allies for which we will always be grateful. While showing complete respect for our independence and scrupulously avoiding anything that might be viewed as an intrusion into our affairs, Great Britain gave us powerful assistance by guaranteeing the purchase of our products, the ease of our transports and some liberal measures thanks to which the funds that we need for our exports can be converted into sterling.[4]

The British bought coffee, palm seeds, palm oil, sesame seeds, wood, cotton, rubber and other products and all at an extremely favourable exchange rate for the French. Furthermore, payment was made entirely in pounds sterling which meant that the Free French colonies had a constant source of hard currency for the international market. Great care had to be taken to make sure that living standards were maintained at a level similar to that of French West Africa, which still owed allegiance to Vichy, so that no temptation to change sides might take root.

By June 1943, when payments to the French National Committee were stopped because of the formation of the unified French Committee for National Liberation, the British Treasury had advanced nearly 35 million pounds. The French National Committee operated in much the same way as a British government department: it submitted its budget annually to the Treasury which then verified elements of it with relevant British ministries before approving or disapproving particular items. Advances were made at the beginning of each month, and in 1943 these payments averaged one and a half million pounds each. The advances provided for the upkeep of the civil administration in London, for the pay and maintenance of Free French troops (which was estimated at the time as having about 20 000 'white' troops and 'rather more colonial' ones). Munitions and rations for these forces were provided partly by the British and partly by American Lend–Lease. The largest single item was for military expenditure in Syria and Lebanon which totalled roughly six to seven hundred thousand pounds. The intelligence services were also a large item. Until the institution of forced work service in Germany (STO) this had totalled the relatively modest sum of £20 000 a month, but in May 1943 this increased to £70 000 and in June soared to £300 000. De Gaulle himself, although at first given a salary by the British government, soon preferred to have his salary paid from private sources of funding. The British estimated that the private funds of Free France, which consisted mainly of donations from supporters, amounted to about £150 000.[5]

The Free French, of course, had their own sources of income, whether it be selling stamps from their colonial possessions or donations from sympathizers or tax and other income within the colonies. However, the fact remains that they were heavily dependent on the British. The Free French debt towards the British Treasury, on 31 December 1942 came to £24 476 000 sterling. The advances for the second half of 1942 alone came to eight million pounds.[6] All of this at a time when the British economy was overburdened by the cost of war. Indeed, by the end of 1940 it was clear that Britain was rapidly exhausting its financial resources in carrying on the war. The British were forced to throw themselves on the mercy of the Americans and ask for extensive economic assistance. Roosevelt knew that any attempt to loan money would meet with hostility, given the war-debt controversies still remaining from World War I. Instead he devised the ingenious system called Lend–Lease. In one of his most memorable speeches, Roosevelt told the American people that, when a neighbour's house is burning, you do not try to sell him your garden hose, you lend it to him and expect it to be returned when the fire is out. In January 1941 he went to Congress and presented a plan that called for the expenditure of seven billion dollars for war materials that the president could lend, lease, sell, exchange or transfer to any country whose defence was considered to be vital to that of the United States. Two months later Congress voted the law, and the United States became the 'arsenal of democracy'. All aid short of war was to be given to Britain. The Free French and the exiled governments of Europe were allowed to place their own orders under the Lend–Lease system, but only as part of British ones. Although it was only much later that the Free French were given the right to be part of the Lend–Lease system themselves, there is no doubt that they benefited immediately from it. Both Britain and the Free French became largely dependent on the economic bounty of the United States.

In November 1941, as we saw in Chapter 2, Roosevelt announced that the defence of the Free French colonies was vital to that of the United States – the necessary prerequisite to full participation in Lend–Lease. The following September, the two parties signed an agreement admitting Free France to Lend–Lease in its own right. The United States agreed to put the available part of its war production at the disposition of the French National Committee and the French National Committe made the reverse pledge. This was called Reciprocal or Mutual Aid or Reverse Lend–Lease. Of course, Free French war production was tiny in proportion to that of America so Reciprocal Aid usually meant that the French provided free of charge certain facilities and services to Allied troops as a return on what they had already received through Lend-Lease. Under Lend–Lease the United States was the active partner providing supplies to other members of the United Nations; under Reciprocal Aid it was the French or other Allied nations who were the active partners. By the nature of things Lend–Lease was always greater than Reciprocal Aid, but the French greatly valued the fact that the agreement was reciprocal because it showed 'the growing importance of French participation in the common war effort'.[7] The most advantageous thing for the French was that raw materials were not included as part of Reciprocal Aid, and American purchases of products like chrome and nickel assured the French National Committee of an important income in dollars which could be used to buy civilian supplies for the colonies.[8]

In November 1942 the Allies invaded North Africa, and the United States gained a French problem of its own. One of the most important elements in maintaining the stability of North Africa – and particularly that of the native population – was the economic situation. North Africa produced mainly either agricultural or mineral products, and most of these were sold to metropolitan France. Furthermore, it was also largely dependent on imports from mainland France of various necessities like clothes, petroleum products, coal, milk, sugar, soap and medical supplies. All of this was broken by the invasion, and furthermore, a serious and unusual wheat shortage also threatened the area at that time. In trying to deal with the situation, the Americans were hampered by serious shortages in shipping – which for obvious reasons was oriented towards wartime activities. In fact, throughout the war, the most serious handicap in supplying the civilian populations in liberated areas would not be that of finding the necessary supplies but of shipping them to the area in which they were needed. However, even when ships were found this was not the end of the problem, for the North African transport system was quite poor which meant that there were almost insurmountable difficulties in distribution. Finally the arrival of large amounts of American currency, brought in by the soldiers stationed there, only intensified the crisis by devaluing the local currency. To the American military, all of these economic problems meant that civil disturbances and even serious unrest were likely to occur at any time and would certainly detract from the war effort.[9] Rapid economic assistance was thus absolutely necessary but under conditions that made it virtually impossible.

On 17 November Robert Murphy wrote to Hull to emphasise the need for economic assistance:

> Study and execution of a program of economic supply for French North Africa is a matter of urgent necessity . . . The mere arrival here of our Armed Forces will by itself reduce the supply of consumers' goods. A grave and immediate problem is presented by the fact that North Africa is separated from France, its principal source of supply. It is extremely necessary that the civil departments of the United States and the United Kingdom take immediate action . . . We have skeleton organisation to deal with these matters. A senior Foreign Office officer who is experienced in financial matters would be of great use . . . It would be wise to assign a representative of Lend–Lease and no more than two persons from the Board of Economic Warfare at once.[10]

Hull wrote to Murphy at the same time, informing him that they were sending over 8000 tons of supplies that had been ordered by French officials before the invasion. He also told Murphy that the State Department and the Lend–Lease Administration had been given responsibility for ensuring that North Africa would receive adequate supplies. The United States would replace Europe as North Africa's chief source of supplies.[11] The State Department began preparing a comprehensive economic programme for North Africa and recruited a fairly large staff to assist Murphy on these matters. They were given a large number of duties: to ensure that essential products were available for the population and for vital utilities and industries; to purchase materials from North Africa; to handle currency and financial problems; to deal with the maintenance and repair of the transport system; the maintenance of public health; and the expansion of the production of food and other vital materials.[12] It was a remarkably comprehensive programme and one which established American dominance in virtually every area of North African economic life. From 8 November 1942 to 31 March 1943 the Lend–Lease authorities shipped 26 million dollars worth of civilian goods – not including transport and insurance charges – from the United States to North Africa. This was only a fraction of the effort, for it does not include either military assistance or civilian goods which were shipped from Great Britain.[13]

Of course, the British also wanted to be involved in economic questions in North Africa. Even before the landings they sent a report to the Combined Chiefs of Staff on economic measures to be taken upon occupation. While the State Department was developing its own programme of aid, the

Secretary of the Combined Chiefs of Staff, General Deane, wrote to Hull, suggesting that economic policies must be considered on a combined basis and that, therefore, the State Department should begin conversations with representatives of the British Ministry of Economic Warfare.[14] The North African Economic Board was set up to deal with these matters, and its membership was Anglo-American. For the Political Warfare Executive of the British government, the Allies' priorities were clear: 'Anglo-American interest lies in satisfying first and foremost the needs of the natives of French North Africa.' They felt that this should take priority even over the Free French.[15] The Political Warfare Executive found that three products were particularly needed by the natives of North Africa: green tea, sugar and cotton textiles. Coincidentally, the British Empire was a major producer of the first and third of these products. It was strongly recommended that the British government should make every effort to supply these needs, particularly that of clothing, to the native inhabitants on the theory that: 'Native feeling in favour of Britain can be consolidated if shipments of cotton textiles are made in the near future'. It was also felt that it would be advantageous to make sure that the origin of the shipments was known.[16] Clearly, an Anglo-American rivalry was developing over supplying the economic needs of North Africa – and this quickly spread over into West Africa too – and just as clearly the situation was certain to alarm the French. The French response to this, particularly after the formation of the FCNL, was to try to develop trade within the French colonial empire. This, of course, irritated the Allies who felt that the French, like the Anglo-Americans, should make their supplies available to the Combined Boards for distribution among all the United Nations on the basis of need. To the French, however, the vital question of national sovereignty was involved.[17]

The currency situation was another bone of contention between the Allies and the French in North Africa. On 14 November 1942 the rate of exchange was set at 75 francs to the dollar and 300 francs to the pound. Since the exchange rate in Free French Africa was 176 francs to the pound, the North Africans were obviously not pleased with this decision and protested that they should receive the same rate as de Gaulle. The British were inclined to make concessions and suggested a rate of 50 francs to the dollar and 200 to the pound. However, the Treasury, State and War Departments insisted on the aforementioned rate. The Americans felt that, since the beginning of the war, the purchasing power of North African francs had declined tremendously. Inflation had soared, while currency reserves had been depleted. This had led to the development of a black market in North Africa where the franc sold for 125 to 150 francs to the dollar. The American government insisted that the official exchange rate should not be too outrageously different from the black market rate. They felt also that American soldiers should not feel robbed when buying products. In effect, one of the results of the Allied invasion was to link the North African franc to the American dollar, which, of course, greatly stabilized the former currency. A relatively high exchange rate also, it was suggested, benefited the French because American soldiers then spent more – thus increasing North Africa's dollar reserves. It also benefited North African exports and a decrease in the rate could be expected to have a deflationary effect on exports.[18] Giraud and the North African French, however, clearly felt that they were being exploited by the high rate and wished it to be the same as that for the Free French. The United States government could hardly continue to refuse such a request, especially after it had agreed to a policy of promoting union between the two French factions. This was certainly one of the necessary steps in that direction. At the Casablanca Conference, therefore, an agreement was reached to revise the exchange rate which was later set at 50 francs to the dollar in both North and Free French Africa.

Perhaps the most important initiative taken by the Allies in North Africa, however, was the decision to rearm the French.[19] As we have seen, from the very beginning the Allies had hoped that the invasion of North Africa would cause the French to re-enter the war on their side. After the 'Darlan Deal' this result was obtained. However the French forces, under the terms of the armistice, had been reduced both in manpower and equipment. The fighting in Tunisia quickly showed that the French were too poorly armed to effectively combat the Germans. As we have seen, by December 1942 the decision was made to rearm the French. Eisenhower was an enthusiastic supporter of this policy, writing to the Combined Chiefs of Staff that 'the enthusiastic and effective cooperation of French forces is a vital factor in all our calculations'.[20] Marshall, certainly, could see the advantages of such a plan:

> General Marshall said that he was in favor of proceeding with a definite programme for re-equipping the French forces. This would, of course, imply French acceptance of our organisation and training methods, and would inevitably delay the progress of equipping our own forces. He thought, however, that we should do the thing wholeheartedly, and he was prepared, subject to General Eisenhower's views, to modify the United States programme in order to equip French forces up to a strength of 250 000. All the equipment provided for the French would be at the expense of United States troops forming in America.[21]

Marshall felt justified in making such a recommendation because the French Army was already constituted – its units existed, its troops had received training and there was a great deal of officer and non-commissioned officer talent available. From the point of view of speed and financing, it was thus in theory considerably more advantageous to arm trained French soldiers already in units than to save the weapons for American men who still needed to be trained and organised.[22] Furthermore, there were fears of a manpower shortage developing in the United States and Britain, and the addition of French troops would solve this problem.[23] It would also increase the effectiveness of French cooperation, which Eisenhower so strongly advocated, and unite them even more closely to the Allies. From every angle the policy seemed sound.

At the Casablanca Conference, in a private meeting with Giraud, Roosevelt officially committed the United States to a policy of rearming the French. At the meeting Giraud had handed the president a list of equipment the French needed. According to this memorandum the United States would provide the French with enough equipment for three armoured divisions, eight motorized divisions, and an air force of 500 fighter planes, 300 bombers and 200 transport planes. A shipping allocation of 65 000 tons of space would be alloted monthly which would mean that the material would be delivered by summer.[24] The problem was that the president had not consulted any of his advisers before writing on the paper, 'Yes, in principle'. Giraud was convinced that he had won. Marshall only learned of the agreement a few days later when General Béthouart, now military attaché in Washington, handed him a copy of it. Hull felt that Roosevelt had signed it over a drink, and the president virtually admitted as much to Stimson, the Secretary of War.[25] Needless to say, nothing was done at first to implement this agreement, mainly because it was practically impossible to find the necessary shipping. The delay did not mean that Marshall and the rest of the American military establishment were not committed to rearming the French. It just meant that Giraud's plan was impractical. In fact, little material reached the French before May – after the fighting in Tunisia had stopped.

It is important to remember that this decision was entirely made by the Americans and that the programme was completely funded by them. Although they agreed with the general idea, the British, in fact, had objections to several elements in the plan. To begin with, they felt the programme was too large. The British representative to the Combined Chiefs of Staff, Sir John Dill, doubted that eleven French divisions could ever be used in Tunisia, and that in any case they would not be ready before the end of fighting in North Africa.[26] The British also felt that the

Americans were trying to do it too quickly – particularly in view of the serious shortage of shipping – and that this might endanger other, more important, operations. At one point the British Chiefs of Staff went so far as to suggest that it might be necessary to stop ships carrying supplies to the French Army and divert them to other uses.[27] The French, however, were clearly demoralised and impatient. Eisenhower felt that no unnecessary delay could be tolerated:

> He [Giraud] is now gravely concerned that long delay in the delivery of new equipment may actually result in weakening his hold on the army and may react on morale to the point where the French forces can no longer be relied on even for second line service and maintenance of internal order. We have had some local reverses and we now more than ever depend upon the French to garrison areas where the native population is known to be disaffected.[28]

Murphy supported Eisenhower, writing on the same day that:

> This disillusionment [of the French with regard to rearmament plans] is giving rise to a belief both in the Administration and the Army here that the United Nations have no intention of supporting a French army except as a defensive force; that the military effort here is being held back, as a matter of policy; and that as a result French troops will have no share in the conquest of France and France will not be present at the victory. This belief is having its effect on the morale of the French army.[29]

Roosevelt was angered by these complaints and insisted that he had never given any definite dates for the arrival of supplies to Giraud. He had simply agreed to the principle of rearmament and that the rest depended on the shipping situation – which depended upon events in Tunisia. He commented that: 'I wish our good friends in North Africa would get their feet on the ground' and qualified the whole outcry as '*une bêtise*'.[30] However, in general, the British were content to sit back and watch. They certainly found it an immense economic relief to stop funding de Gaulle and the Free French Army, after the formation of the FCNL. The United States then assumed the burden of providing weapons for the combined French forces.

There was another reason behind the American decision to rearm the French – it could be used as a form of political blackmail. John McCloy discovered how important this question was to the French when he visited North Africa:

He said that it became clear upon his arrival in North Africa that the key issue in North Africa affairs was the rearmament of the French troops. The French were anxious and apprehensive about our intentions in this regard, and rumours of all kinds were circulating, including the rumor that the French would not be armed for combat, but would be used to guard lines of communication. Before consulting General Giraud, Mr. McCloy discussed the question with Mr. Murphy and asked him whether he wished Mr. McCloy to link his discussions of re-armament with the major unsettled political issues, restoration of the laws of the French Republic and union between the forces of General Giraud and General de Gaulle. Mr. Murphy was eager that Mr. McCloy should undertake this step, indicating that he had found General Giraud slow to carry out his expressed intentions in this sphere.[31]

The rearming of the French was thus to be contingent on the French showing themselves to be worthwhile and stable allies. It was another form of pressure on Giraud – who was absolutely obsessed with recreating the French Army – to force him to liberalise the regime and reach an agreement with de Gaulle. It is not too much to say that this was not the only time when the threat was used, for the Americans found it a very useful lever with the French. When Hull or Roosevelt were angry at the French, their instinctive response was to threaten to stop the rearmament process. An agreement was usually reached, however, and the threats rarely got beyond the stage of vague menacings. In only one case did the United States go so far as to cut off the supply of weapons to the French and that was in the spring of 1945 when the French occupied the Val d'Aosta in Italy against Allied orders and appeared to be on the verge of annexing it. This had an immediate effect, and the French withdrew.

As this example illustrates, the rearmament programme did not stop with the North African Army, which eventually became the First French Army under General de Lattre de Tassigny and formed the bulk of Allied forces that landed in the south of France. Even after the liberation the question remained an important one. At first, Eisenhower had thought only of forming liberated Frenchmen into units to provide needed labour and ensure the security of communications. This idea, however, did not please the French, who had to pacify the resistance. The French Forces of the Interior, as we have seen, seemed a definite danger to the stability of France, and de Gaulle wished to incorporate them into the regular army structure in order to place them more firmly under government control. At first Eisenhower was not very enthused by the project, but in November 1944 he changed his mind:

Hesitancy in considering the rearming of additional divisions was based on the idea that there would not be time to equip and train those units prior to the end of the war in Western Europe. Recent events have caused me to review that question, and it now appears that some additional combat units can be made ready for combat in time to be of use provided the equipment and shipping can be made available and cleared through our presently congested ports.[32]

The advantages, to Eisenhower, were obvious: the French had already fought well both in Italy and France, and it would save American and British lives.

The resistance movements within France were also largely funded by the Anglo-Americans, although in this case the British were the main providers. In mid-1943 the budget of the resistance was estimated at 40 million francs a month for normal expenses, plus 50 million francs more each month which were used to fight against the deportation of French workers (STO). The Free French intelligence service, BCRA, insisted to Lord Selborne, Minister for Economic Warfare into whose department fell the SOE, that these payments had to be made regularly as the number of Frenchmen who were sent to work in Germany was directly related to the size and regularity of payments.[33] The report presents as evidence for this statement that certain groups of *maquis* saw their membership drop in two months from 30 000 to 9500 men because of insufficient funding. The money provided to the resistance was a joint Anglo-Franco-American venture, with the British and Americans contributing about the same amount – although most of the arms came from the British.[34] The most difficult part was not convincing the Anglo-Americans to make large donations, but actually transforming their money into French francs and sending it to the resistance in France. A supply of francs did exist in Algiers, but often pounds or dollars were simply sent to France and exchanged there secretly. The worst problem was one of distribution. The preferred method had the virtue of simplicity: the money was placed in a crate and parachuted to some place in the middle of nowhere. Normally members of the resistance would be waiting nearby to receive the package. Of course this was not always the case, and large sums of money, not infrequently, simply disappeared. The French, for this reason, were extremely dissatisfied with the system and sought to find another, surer method of sending funds to France.

BCRA thought that it would be safer to launder money through Switzerland and suggested as much to the English. This, of course, caused other – and probably more serious problems. Much of the market in Allied currency in Switzerland was indirectly controlled by the Germans, who were only too pleased, for the purposes of their own economic warfare, to get their hands on large quantities of pounds or dollars.[35] Such transactions, therefore, could only involve relatively small sums of money. A further problem was that British wartime legislation was very strict in regard to the exportation of capital, and the French, therefore, would have to get special authorisation from the Treasury for any such action. To the great surprise of BCRA, its members discovered that the British Treasury was totally unfamiliar with such transactions through Switzerland and was rather disgusted at the idea. One official described it as a 'stinky business', which seemed to apply less to speculators in France than to the Swiss intermediaries, and to the profits they hoped to make on the deal. The British banks that the French contacted were equally opposed to such transactions, and it was only with great difficulty that the Treasury managed to convince one to undertake a small transfer to provide emergency funds.[36] In the end, faced with British disapproval, the French exchanged only a small amount of currency through Switzerland and were forced to rely primarily on the clumsy method of parachuting funds.

Anglo-American aid to the French did not stop with the Liberation and went far beyond the military sphere. In late 1943 Monnet returned to Washington to negotiate a relief programme for liberated France. Under an agreement signed in Algiers in September 1943, military supplies were to be provided to the French as part of Lend–Lease, while civilian supplies would be paid for in dollars. At the time this was considered to be a reasonable decision because of the large numbers of American troops in North Africa who were spending dollars there. However, as the centre of war activity shifted to other spheres, large numbers of troops were transferred and the dollar holdings naturally decreased. Reciprocal Aid also came into effect. The Lend–Lease agreement negotiated in North Africa was considerably less advantageous to the French than the earlier one with the French National Committee – which still applied in the former Free French colonies. Under the North African agreement, Reciprocal Aid was defined far more broadly so that it included not only aid to American troops but also the provision of raw materials. This was not such a disadvantage in North Africa which had relatively few large mineral deposits, but if the agreement was extended to the rest of the empire it would mean a serious shortage in dollars, and these in turn were desperately needed to buy civilian supplies.[37] Furthermore, Lend–Lease had been automatically applied to North Africa with the arrival of American troops, but Reciprocal Aid only came into effect with the signing of the agreement. When it did take effect it meant that the United States paid for fewer things directly in dollars and consequently diminished the dollar reserves in Algiers.

By early 1944 it was clear that the Committee no longer had the necessary supply of dollars to pay all its bills. In January, Monnet requested a renegotiation of the Lend–Lease agreement for North Africa – in view of this situation – in order to make it more general.[38] The United States expressed sympathy with French financial problems and agreed to provide some aid but insisted upon maintaining the principle that civilian goods should be paid for in dollars. The Department of State explained in a memorandum that Lend–Lease was only used for civilian supplies in areas of active military operations. Instead, they agreed to try to purchase more products in French colonies so as to increase the supply of dollars, and suggested that if the Committee no longer had enough dollars they could make payments in gold.[39] The British took a similar position in regard to their own supplies to the French.

It was now time to negotiate a Lend–Lease agreement for metropolitan France since Allied troops would soon be landing there. The French, of course, wanted as broad an agreement as possible. The main point of debate was over long-life industrial articles, which Monnet wanted to have delivered on credit terms so as to get French production restarted to meet the needs of the civil population. In a memorandum of 15 July the United States essentially rejected this approach, saying that only long-life industrial articles that were vital to the war effort or to the support of Allied troops would be provided under Lend–Lease. The question was further complicated by policy differences within the United States government between the Treasury Department and the Foreign Economic Administration (FEA). The latter preferred a broader approach to Lend–Lease than did the Treasury, which advocated the narrow one of 15 July.[40] Hull himself, although approving the 15 July memorandum, inclined towards the broader view. He wrote to Roosevelt in September that:

> Viewed as of the present date and position of the war, the memorandum of July 15th means, in effect, a rejection of Monnet's program and would require the French to pay cash currently for all items not required as necessary military aid. I do not think you intended, nor would I recommend, so flat a position. On the other hand, you would not wish to approve at this stage the French program, amounting as it does to something over a billion dollars of industrial items to be paid for on credit terms.[41]

On 15 September, however, the president decided to postpone indefinitely any negotiations on the question – much to Hull's annoyance. The negotiations continued to drag on throughout 1944.

By January 1945, however, de Gaulle was clearly getting impatient with the situation and, at a meeting of the Economic Committee, insisted that it was necessary rapidly to conclude a Lend–Lease agreement with the United States. He felt that if it was not signed by 1 February, France should reconsider its contribution to Reciprocal Aid which took away from national resources, and a statement to this effect was sent to the Americans.[42] In February, in fact, an agreement was reached, and Monnet returned to Paris to present it to the Committee. A French analysis of the document was generally positive. It admitted that the United States could hardly be expected to promote an agreement that would be highly unfavourable to them and acknowledged that the Americans, therefore, wished to see an equalisation of Lend–Lease and Reciprocal Aid. To the French this seemed impossible, since they benefited from two billion dollars worth of free arms. Whatever happened, the French were certain to remain in debt to the United States, although they felt that the question of French contributions should be considered more broadly. The French argued that World War II was part of a thirty years war, and that their earlier, and more important role, during World War I, should also be taken into account. On the whole however, the agreement was felt to offer a substantial aid to the French economy in spite of the poor state of the nation's Treasury.[43]

Monnet emphasised that the agreement was identical to that reached with the Russians and British, and he detailed its most important advantages. The credit conditions were satisfactory, with an interest rate of $2\frac{3}{8}$ per cent payable over 30 years. The French reserved the right to revise the programmes and to cancel orders if they thought necessary. The agreement also guaranteed that the French would pay the lowest possible price for any items. It called for the purchase of 1675 million dollars of raw materials and industrial tools under conditions of pure Lend–Lease and 900 million dollars of material needed for the industrial recovery in France. These latter purchases were payable 20 per cent on delivery and 80 per cent on long-term credit. For Monnet, the major problem was that the Lend–Lease agreement was not retroactive and that, therefore, the French had to pay about 50 million dollars worth of bills for previous imports. However, the Committee concurred that the agreement was a significant improvement over the current situation and approved it.[44] Accords for both Mutual Aid and Lend–Lease were signed in Washington on 28 February of that year.

In the end, the financial assistance that the French received from the Anglo-Americans was as vital for the recovery of France as the political and military help. From the moment Britain decided to assist the establishment of de Gaulle in some French territory their economic aid became necessary and without it the Gaullist movement could not have developed. However, this was a considerable strain on a nation that was fighting for its own survival, and it is not surprising that the Americans began to contribute more and more to Free France. Thanks to Anglo-American assistance the French army was recreated, and de Gaulle could realise his dream of having France present among the victors of the war.

8 The Provisional Government of France, 1944–45

On 6 June, 1944, D-Day, Allied forces began the invasion of France. De Gaulle had been invited to London a few days before and had arrived on 4 June. He came trailing clouds of disagreement. To begin with, on 3 June the French Committee of National Liberation officially changed its name to the Provisional Government of France – a change which the British wanted to recognize but which both Churchill and Roosevelt refused to even consider. Furthermore, there was still no civil affairs agreement for France, and, although the British had offered to begin negotiations, de Gaulle refused unless the Americans participated. The third disagreement was over the issue of supplementary francs for Allied troops which had been printed in the United States and which had not been fully approved by the FCNL. Finally, de Gaulle had been expected to come with some of his ministers in order to make at least some kind of start on an agreement but in a fit of temper had come alone, stating that he was there only in his military capacity. From there, the situation continued to deteriorate. When de Gaulle arrived in London he was taken out to the prime minister's private railway car near Southhampton. Churchill and de Gaulle immediately started their usual quarrelling and pouting. The group, which included Eden and Ernest Bevin of the Labour Party, then proceeded to a less than jubilant lunch:

> The luncheon party in the train was deplorable, since de G[aulle] refused to have political talks with us or respond to the President's invitation to visit Washington. The P.M. fulminated in his execrable French, and Ernie Bevin made things worse by saying that the Labour Party would be 'hurt' if de G. refused to have political talks with us. This remark, when translated, provoked an outburst from de G. 'Blessés!' said he, 'vous dites que vous serez blessés.' Had it not occurred to them that France was blessée? Had we no thought of French feelings? Ernie Bevin, understanding no word of de G.'s tirade, urgently demanded a translation, but was cut short by the P.M., who wanted to have another go at de G. himself. He was gracious and threatening by turns; neither gambit had the slightest effect on de G.[1]

131

From there, de Gaulle was taken to Eisenhower's headquarters and shown the Supreme Commander's proclamation for D-Day. De Gaulle had apparently understood that he could suggest changes. He presented these suggestions the next day only to discover that 20 million copies of the text had already been printed and that, therefore, it was too late to change anything. De Gaulle was so angry over this that he refused to allow special French liaison officers, whose training had been paid for by the British government, to accompany Allied troops into France. He also refused to broadcast with Eisenhower and the heads of state of the Netherlands, Belgium and Norway and threatened to denounce the supplemetary francs as counterfeit. Roosevelt, meanwhile, was coyly trying to arrange for a visit by de Gaulle to the United States without actually inviting him. All of this led Cadogan to write in his diary:

> We endured the usual passionate anti-de G[aulle] harangue from P.M. On this subject, we get away from politics and diplomacy and even common sense. It's a girls' school. Roosevelt, P.M. and – it must be admitted de G. – all behave like girls approaching the age of puberty. Nothing to be done.[2]

In the end, however, de Gaulle relented slightly and did broadcast (although at a separate time from the others) and did allow a few of the liaison officers to go.

Events in France, however, were soon to force everyone together. It was obvious to all that in order to successfully fight the Germans someone had to maintain order in France, and that this could not be done by Allied troops without a serious and perhaps catastrophic loss of manpower. In the absence of a directive, almost by default, Eisenhower was forced to allow the Committee to administer France. On 14 June de Gaulle set foot in metropolitan France for the first time in four years and received a warm reception in Bayeux. He took with him François Coulet and Colonel de Chevigné, and these last two remained in France in order to begin the administration of liberated territories. Coulet was responsible for the civil aspect of administration and Chevigné for the military part. Allied commanders were at first unsure of how to respond to their presence. On 16 June the chief Allied Civil Affairs officer, General Lewis told Coulet that he would provisionally accept their presence while awaiting instructions from his government. Coulet indignantly responded:

> It did not matter whether he accepted my presence or not because my presence was a fact and no instruction from his government could change this fact. I had been sent to France by the Provisional Government in

order to affirm and maintain French sovereignty and that, furthermore, I was not stupid enough not to recognise the existence and the value in the region I was charged with administering of basic military necessities and that I never would do anything that would injure military necessities.[3]

The Allies appear to have been reassured by Coulet's response and agreed to cooperate with him.

One of Coulet's most difficult problems was that of the controversy over the supplementary francs. Negotiations on the question had been held with Monnet since December 1943, and apparently there had been misunderstandings on both sides. The FCNL had requested that the Allies should not use American or British currency in France because it would inevitably devalue the franc. Since large supplies of French francs could not be obtained from France, the only solution seemed to be to print a special issue of supplementary francs. It was agreed with Monnet that these notes would be printed by the Bureau of Engraving and Printing in the United States. Pierre Mendès-France, the Commissioner for Finance, during a visit to Washington reviewed and approved these decisions.[4] It is then unclear what happened but apparently these agreements had not been properly debated in the FCNL, and the Committee claimed that it had been presented with a *fait accompli*. Massigli insisted to the Americans that the Committee had not given their approval and that he did not believe Monnet had done so either and that if he had 'he had exceeded his authority'.[5] The British tended to side with the French interpretation of events. Eden argued that:

It was not altogether reasonable for the President to suggest that the French representatives in Washington had acquiesced in the issue of the special currency. M. Monnet had argued strongly in favour of a 'French National Currency' and in the end had only acquiesced in the preparation of this special currency on the express condition that a separate issue of French national currency should be printed concurrently and should be used to redeem the Allied military currency 'very promptly'.[6]

The British felt there were very serious problems with the supplementary notes: there was no indication on the notes as to who was the issuing authority; the United Kingdom and the United States would be 'morally responsible' for honouring the notes if no agreement was reached with the French; and this would make them liable to expenses which rightfully should be borne by the French under Reciprocal Aid.

The French were in a dilemma over the question too. On 8 June the FCNL had written a memorandum to the American and British governments on the currency, saying that:

The right to issue money having belonged traditionally to the national authority in France, and to it alone, the provisional Government of the Republic cannot recognize as of any legal value notes put in circulation without its consent. It therefore reserves its judgment as to the financial, moral and political results of this action which has been brought to its notice.[7]

The basic problem for the French, however, was that everywhere in France people had accepted the notes. When François Coulet arrived, the local banks asked him what attitude they should adopt towards the money. Coulet wanted neither to do anything that could be interpreted as recognising the currency nor as hindering military operations. He therefore told the banks to accept the money but to put it in a special account. By 27 June the four banks in Bayeux had received 170 000 francs of this money. Coulet was alarmed to discover that local French citizens showed a notable tendency to pay their taxes in supplementary francs rather than in Bank of France notes. From 16–26 June 54 000 francs of supplementary currency had been received out of 128 000 francs of taxes paid. Coulet decided to tell the local tax administration to refuse to accept the money but before doing so warned Allied commanders. Needless to say, Allied authorities were extremely upset over Coulet's decision and asked him to suspend the payment of taxes until an agreement could be reached on the governmental level. Coulet finally agreed to make no announcement for the moment but only on the condition that the Allies would assure the exchange of the supplementary currency with notes from the Bank of France. This accord was kept secret from fear it would discredit the supplementary francs.[8] The situation remained like this until de Gaulle's visit to the United States.

As this example illustrates, relations were generally good between the Allied military and French civilians. Allied officers, in general, behaved very well and were particularly solicitous of French leaders. In Cherbourg, for example, the American commander addressed the town leaders in French, explaining that he was there to help them and 'not to administer Cherbourg'. After four years of Nazi domination, the effect on the French was electric, and they actively undertook their jobs with increasing efficiency. The Allies were extremely pleased, noting: 'Such successful results have certainly justified the insistence in the training of civil affairs officers that in liberated territory the first requisite was to keep constantly in mind how you would feel if your country was being liberated by foreign allies.' The same report expressed real pleasure over the Gaullist administration:

Moderation had been the keynote of the policy and attitude adopted by de Gaulle's appointees and the men they named to subordinate posts.

They had shown a readiness to respect the wishes of the Allies, the Resistance and general public opinion.[9]

This does not mean that there was no Allied interference in French domestic questions. Coulet noted at least two cases when the Americans had relieved the mayor of his functions and held a new election. Although he protested against such violations of French sovereignty, he found himself forced to accept both cases because of the attitude of the two mayors and because the local population had wholeheartedly supported the American actions.

There were also cases when, before the arrival of Gaullist administrators, the Allies had made arrests based on information from the local population. This too had to be accepted, but an agreement was soon reached that allowed all these suspects to be turned over to French officials except in the case of espionage activities.[10] The Allies understandably wished to assure the security of their bridgehead and could not wait until the arrival of French administrators before dealing with suspected German spies. The French authorities could understand this and were satisfied to have the prisoners handed over to them later.[11] In spite of the absence of a civil affairs agreement, the Committee thus came to administer France, almost by default. They simply walked in and with the tacit acceptance of the Allied High Command began administering liberated territory. By the time de Gaulle arrived in the United States for an official visit on 6 July, the civil affairs question had been effectively settled and an agreement was easily reached. Months of haggling had been ended by simple military necessity. However, Roosevelt refused to give way on the question of the level on which the agreement would be signed. In the end the civil affairs agreements were signed on the governmental level between the British and the French and on the military level between the Americans and the French.

On the whole, throughout the period of occupation, relations continued to be good between the Allies and the French. This was true in spite of the fact that the French authorities were of course extremely sensitive to any offence against French sovereignty. There were particularly strong objections to any direct Allied approach to local industries and companies as the French suspected the Americans especially of using their position to prepare the way for their domination of the French postwar economy. There were also certain major grievances that the French in all walks of life held against the Anglo-Americans. First and foremost of these was their treatment of German prisoners. After having suffered four years of German occupation and numerous atrocities at their conquerors' hands – particularly as the tide was turning in favour of the Allies – the French clearly wanted revenge. The Americans, on the other hand, felt they had to respect the Geneva

Convention, if only to guarantee that their own men taken prisoner in Germany would be decently treated. The situation was so bad that convoys of German prisoners had to travel with large numbers of Allied soldiers, not because they feared the Germans might try to escape but from fear of what the French would do to them. Patton, for example, tormented one SS officer by threatening to turn him over to the French.[12]

In fact, it could hardly be otherwise given the scope of the economic crisis in France. Shortages of food and coal made the winter of 1944–5 worse in many ways than the previous ones under occupation. Due to military needs public transport was virtually halted. French people seeing German prisoners – some of them known to have committed atrocities – provided with good food and clothing, heat and truck or train transport, all of which were denied to them, could not help but feel bitterness. It was frequently stated that the Americans kept German and Italian prisoners of war fed but not French civilians. In the south of France there were also numerous complaints about Italian prisoners of war because, Italy now being a co-belligerent, they were allowed to circulate freely and go to cinemas and cafés. The French could not forget how the Italians had shamefully declared war in June 1940 when the nation was already reeling from the German invasion. The Americans were a good scapegoat for all economic problems. People constantly complained that they had not delivered promised weapons to the French Army or badly needed machine tools to industry or consumer goods to civilians. Jefferson Caffery, the American ambassador in Paris, noted in early 1945 that the Allies could not win because, even if they managed to provide the French with a certain amount of transport, the government would have to choose between military, industrial and civilian needs and whichever was chosen the losers would continue to complain that it was the failure of the Americans that caused their problems.

Another cause of bitterness was requisitioning, which had not infrequently got out of hand especially in the provinces. The requisitioning of buildings was a particular problem as, because of repeated bombings, large numbers of French people were without any place to live. The frequent requisitioning of transport – given the crisis in that domain – was also a valid cause of complaint. However, it must be stated that Allied commanding officers did make real efforts to deal with the problem, and Caffery, after investigating the problem, believed that many of these complaints were imaginary. Furthermore, there was no denying that the members of the resistance abused the system of requisitioning far more than did the Allies. Most Allied observers found the French to be in a psychologically delicate condition. Allied victories made their earlier defeat even more humiliating, and there was a collective desire to forget that it had even occurred. An OSS report declared that:

> Whether the French over the future will want this man who apparently considers himself today as the male incarnation of Joan of Arc as their future leader, I do not know, but I do feel that, short of an accident, the first government of liberated France will be headed by de Gaulle. There is no other choice, and also he will be chosen, because, by doing so, the French, in some subtle way which is hard to explain, can fulfill what is almost a psychic impulse – a soul craving – to be able to tell their children that France was never defeated, that it kept fighting on till victory. I do not know what the answer to this riddle may be, but I am persuaded that we may have to meet unreasonableness – almost hysteria – with calm and almost more than understanding; that the strong partner will have to go far more than half-way to meet the weaker partner, and that we will have to find some means more effective than any heretofore found to convince the French people that we have no ulterior aims.[13]

Caffery insisted that: 'Physical privations and moral humiliation have left a mark on French mentality.' One of the saddest examples of this was the panic which ensued in the Rouen region when British soldiers were replaced by black American soldiers. There were numerous and completely unsubstantiated reports of rapes, murders and thefts and frantic calls for the Allies to transfer all black soldiers out of the region.

A further problem was that a state of virtual lawlessness reigned throughout much of France. As we have seen, much of this was caused by the former resistance, now called the French Forces of the Interior (FFI). Some groups were often little more than gangs that roamed the countryside preying on the weak. There was, of course, a concentrated effort by the Provisional Government to absorb the resistance into the regular army, but many, especially among the communists, refused to join. The case was particularly critical in Rennes and in the south of France. One American diplomat described the situation in Marseilles as follows:

> The over-all political situation in the Marseille Region is volcanic in character. People are seething with unrest and dissatisfaction . . . If civil strife should break out in France, it is more than likely to have its origin in the Marseille Region. The political and economic stage is set for it. An open break may be avoided, however, by the Regional Commissioner, who has thus far shown ability to maintain some semblance of law and order, particularly in the event there should be some improvement in the economic situation.[14]

Fears of a communist attempt to seize power arose both within the government and among the Allies. Eisenhower found that:

> The fact of the matter is that in two areas, one Toulouse and the other Limoges, the Communists were so strong and so well armed that there was no control over them whatsoever. They refused to obey the orders of the appointed authorities and are doing exactly as they please. He [Juin] regards the situation with very considerable trepidation. I explained to him that we were all in favor of maintaining order and that we wanted the French to do it, not ourselves.[15]

Eisenhower insisted to General Wilson, the Supreme Commander in the Mediterranean, that more French troops had to be sent from Africa so that order could be preserved in France.

Needless to say, the unrest in France had a profound effect on Anglo-American policy. Both Roosevelt and Churchill were forced to give way before the insistent demands to strengthen the French government. Marshall, King and Arnold insisted to the president that military needs required an agreement:

> The issue from the point of view purely of military operations is that General Eisenhower finds himself as an Allied Commander without specific directive and with the two governments he serves in effect in disagreement. The Prime Minister's support of your position is understood, but in this matter he dominates neither the Cabinet nor the Foreign Office. The situation is serious and its effect on military operations unhappy at best, and may be dangerous in view of possible reactions of the French Underground and resistance groups, who have generally expressed their allegiance to de Gaulle.[16]

On 7 July 1944 the Secretaries of State, War and Treasury wrote a memorandum to the president that suggested a 'new approach' in dealing with the Committee. The latter would now be called the 'Civil Authority', 'Administrative Authority', 'De Facto Authority' or 'French Authority', and civil affairs agreements would be signed. The FCNL would also become the issuing authority for the supplementary francs. Roosevelt gave his accord and chose 'De Facto Authority' as the title to be given to the Committee.[17] At a press conference on 14 July, during de Gaulle's visit, Roosevelt announced this form of recognition and also stated his acceptance of the British texts of agreement on civil affairs. The Allies were forced to adapt their policy to the needs of France once again later in that month. On 15 August the Parisian police went on strike; three days later the trade unions called for a general strike. The next day an insurrection started in Paris and the insurgents occupied the prefecture of police. The situation was extremely serious in Paris for the metro and bus strike meant that large numbers of people were constantly on the streets. Gas had been completely turned off, and there was no electricity at night. It was practically impossible to bring supplies into Paris, and, once the Germans as a reprisal had burnt the mills at Pantin, there was only enough flour left for seven days. To add to the tenseness of the situation, trucks were constantly pulling up to German headquarters and carrying things away. Many people felt that the Germans were preparing to flee Paris and take with them all the booty they could find.[18] The next day, a resistance leader reported that both the resistance and the general population in Paris would be humiliated if German troops left the city without a fight from the local FFI. He also announced that a scenario had been decided between resistance leaders in which the Republic would be proclaimed at the Hôtel de Ville and General de Gaulle and the Provisional Government acclaimed.[19]

From the very beginning of the Paris insurrection the Algiers government and its representatives showed signs of barely controlled panic. On the 15th Leclerc had already approached Patton, threatening to resign if he were not authorised to advance on Paris. Patton told him he was a baby. On the 17th he approached Patton again and was once again refused permission.[20] On 16 August Supreme Headquarters (SHAEF) learned that de Gaulle was to leave Algiers the next day. They informed the War Department that: 'It is our understanding that this is not merely a visit but that General de Gaulle in France intends to stay.'[21] On the 20th, however, the situation improved slightly as the resistance and the Germans negotiated a controversial truce. The situation remained tight though, and on the same day an emissary of Colonel *Rol*-Tanguy, a communist and leader of the Parisian resistance, reached Allied headquarters. On 20 August de Gaulle arrived in France, accompanied by André Le Troquer, who had been appointed Minister for the Liberated Territories, and went directly to see Eisenhower. According to Oliver Harvey of the Foreign Office:

He [Eisenhower] had at once taken the initiative with de G[aulle]., told him that the Leclerc Division should go first into Paris as a token of the Allies, that Gen. de G. should go in too and that he would make Gen. Koenig military governor. General de G. was evidently quite overcome by this and when Gen. Eisenhower followed it up by saying that de G. in turn must help him by explaining to the French that they would only get little food to begin with because all transport must be kept for the advancing armies, he took it quite well.[22]

The next day de Gaulle wrote to Eisenhower: 'Information received today from Paris leads me to believe that in view of the almost total disappearance of police, and of German forces in Paris, and of the extreme scarcity of supplies there, serious trouble may shortly be expected in the capital.'[23] He insisted that it was essential to occupy the city as quickly as possible.

Eisenhower had originally hoped to defer the capture of Paris as long as possible for several reasons of which the most important was the problem of supplying the population, which the Supreme Commander feared would be too great for the Allies' limited means. He did not, however, really think that it would be possible to wait long before capturing Paris. He reasoned that: 'If the enemy tries to hold Paris with any real strength he would be a constant menace to our flank. If he largely evacuates the place, it falls into our hands whether we like it or not.'[24] In the same letter Eisenhower informed Marshall that:

> When Paris is entered it is my intention to employ the French division for occupation. In entering the city it will be accompanied by token units of British and American forces. Some days thereafter General de Gaulle will be allowed to make his formal entry into the city.

What Eisenhower had not taken into account was the possibility of an uprising in Paris that would lead either to a massive slaughter of the resistance or a communist takeover of the city.

On 21 August the CNR decided to end the truce, and Paris was called to resistance. Massigli explained to the State Department why this had been done:

> The decision to call upon the people to rise was made at the end of last week. Massigli said that this may have been premature from a military point of view but it was occasioned by a move on the part of the Communists to assume complete control of the situation in Paris. They had even gone so far as to name their own Prefect of Police. Once the decision to take unified action had been made the Communists however cooperated fully with the Resistance Council and withdrew the appointment. De Gaulle has now appointed Luizet as Prefect of Police.[25]

On the 22nd fighting restarted in Paris, and Eisenhower and Bradley decided that they would have to intervene. The next day the Leclerc division and other forces started for Paris, and the first Allied troops reached it on 24 August. On the 25th, the military commander of Paris, General von Choltitz surrendered, and Charles de Gaulle arrived in the city. On the following day the Parisian crowds turned out to cheer de Gaulle on his walk from the Arc de Triumphe to a *Te Deum* at Notre Dame. Paris was liberated, and she had chosen de Gaulle as her ruler.

This does not mean, however, that de Gaulle felt himself to be absolutely secure. According to Eisenhower's memoirs, on the morning of the 27th, de Gaulle asked the Americans to send two divisions to prevent any further trouble in the city. Eisenhower found something rather bittersweet in the whole affair:

> My memory flashed back almost two years, to Africa and our political problems of that time. There we had accepted the governmental organization already in existence and never during our entire stay had one of the French officials asked for Allied troops in order to establish or affirm his position as a local administrative authority. Here there seemed a touch of the sardonic in the picture of France's symbol of liberation having to ask for Allied forces to establish and maintain a similar position in the heart of the freed capital.

Eisenhower could not spare any men for long, but he agreed to allow some to parade through the city on their way to active duty. When Eisenhower's memoirs appeared in 1948, de Gaulle immediately denied the story and said that he had had no need of American assistance to subdue Paris for Paris was entirely his. He insisted that he had never asked for the troops.[26] There is no doubt, however, that the situation was very tense in Paris for a while after the liberation with pockets of Germans and Vichy *miliciens* continuing to resist, and bands of armed FFI – many of them having joined at the last minute – roaming the city.

There is also no doubt that throughout this period de Gaulle exploited the communist threat to his own advantage with the Allies. Just after the Normandy landings, the OSS learned of a memorandum sent by General Revers to de Gaulle about the threat of communist control of the resistance. In this report, General Revers stated that: 'The Communist Party is trying to obtain a leading position in the Resistance Movement, keeping its eye on the chaotic period which will ensue upon France's liberation.' Both the National Front and the FTP, which had substantial non-communist membership, were dominated by the communists, and resistance movements in Paris, Rennes and Lille had communists in key positions. The report further claimed that:

> The war against Germany is only of secondary importance to them since they are looking ahead to mass activity, preparing general strikes and the like. The Communist Party is counting on the fact that the bourgeois elements will have undergone graver suffering than they,

which will allow the Communists to seize power during the period after the Nazis leave and before the Allies and the French come in.[27]

De Gaulle himself told James Forrestal, the American Secretary of the Navy, in August 1944 that:

> . . . It must not be forgotten to what extent he had stood alone in 1940 and how many Frenchmen had been willing to follow Marshal Pétain. Unless the Democracies will make effective guarantees of peace in Europe, who can tell what protection the French people will seek in 5, 10, or 15 years time in order to avoid another war.[28]

De Gaulle was certainly careful to enlist communist support, including them in his government and visiting Moscow in December 1944. During this visit the American Ambassador, Averell Harriman wrote: 'The Soviet agressive policy will, de Gaulle believes, create fear among the smaller nations in Western Europe and they will look to France to lead and cement Western European opinion in order to offset Russian domination of Europe.'[29] De Gaulle clearly used the communist threat to gain American assistance. In May 1945 de Gaulle informed Jefferson Caffery that after the war there would be only two major powers in the world: the United States and the Soviet Union. Britain, he felt, would not remain an important power, and he insisted that he would much prefer to work with the United States, but: 'If I cannot work with you I must work with the Soviets in order to survive even if it is only for a while and even if in the long run they gobble us up too.'[30] He then went on to state his grievances against the Allies: their failure to supply coal, weapons and industrial supplies and their refusal to invite France to Yalta. De Gaulle may quite legitimately have feared communist influence in France, but it is clear that he also tried to use that threat to his own advantage, particularly when dealing with the Americans. It is also obvious that the Americans were receptive to this tactic. One American report stated that: 'While recognizing the difficulties of dealing with the present French Government, the continued failure to recognize the French Nation as an equal ally and to take militant action to assist her in settlement of her problems can lead to chaos through which the Soviet influence will prevail.' The same report insisted that: 'France is the pivotal state if we are to check Soviet influence on the continent, the effort must be made there.'[31] It is difficult to assess to what extent this threat was real. De Gaulle and Free French leaders clearly had believed that there was a danger of communist take-over in Paris if Allied troops did not arrive quickly enough. On the other hand, it seems evident that it was not Soviet policy to encourage a communist uprising in France.

Stalin wanted to defeat Germany as quickly as possible and for this he needed American and British assistance. A civil war in France would certainly have seriously retarded the Allied war effort. What would happen after the war was another matter.

By September de Gaulle had formed a new government that included members of the resistance, and it was present in Paris, trying to re-establish order throughout the country. On 15 August the Americans and French had landed in the south of France and were now pushing north-wards at lightning speed to join up with Eisenhower's men. By September much of France had been liberated, but the very swiftness of the liberation had left a state of lawlessness in its wake. The Allied troops were gener-ally unable to remain behind to maintain order and, as we have seen, pockets of German resistance remained and bands of renegade FFI roamed the countryside. Needless to say, such an unstable situation on his lines of communication and supply and on the flank of his army worried Eisen-hower. He wrote to Washington, insisting that the Provisional Government must be strengthened as much as possible:

> From the military point of view the existence of a strong central author-ity in France is essential, particularly in view of the difficult economic and supply situation which faces us this winter. The only French authority with whom we can deal is the present Council of Ministers and we urge that every support be given to it including formal recognition as the Provisional Government of France.[32]

Eisenhower suggested that recognition should occur simultaneously with the announcement of the creation of a Zone of the Interior – that is an area under civilian control.

Hull, in fact, had been lobbying the president for complete recognition since mid-September. The Secretary of State himself took action to open the French embassy to the Gaullist representative. A few days later he wrote to Roosevelt: 'In my opinion the time has come to give serious consideration to the question of announcing this Government's recognition of the *de facto* French authority as the Provisional Government of France.' Among the many reasons he gave was: 'Lack of recognition will make it more difficult for the Committee to maintain the internal stability neces-sary for the prosecution of the war and orderly rehabilitation of the country.'[33] Hull repeated his request on 21 September, this time using his familiar argument about British jockeying for position:

> What I fear is a repetition of our experience with the North African situation in which Mr. Churchill consistently supported our policy, while

all other British Services, from the Foreign Office down, fought tooth and nail against it. In other words, I fully expect that in innumerable ways it will be represented to the French that the British Government is willing, and even eager, to extend recognition but that the United States remains adamant in its opposition.[34]

Hull feared that American influence in France would be undermined if recognition were withheld much longer. On 14 October Churchill wrote to Roosevelt announcing that he too had changed his mind and was now in favour of recognition.[35] Eisenhower's recommendation arrived on the 20th and by the next day, when Roosevelt met with Stettinius who had replaced Sumner Welles as Under Secretary of State, the president realized that he was now completely isolated on the question. He gave his agreement. On 23 October, the British, Americans and Soviets officially recognised the Committee as the provisional Government of France. The British, however, were furious over the short notice they had received.

This does not mean that de Gaulle was now satisfied with the position he had reached. Quite the contrary, for he continued to push for an ever greater role for France. By late 1944 he had convinced all major Anglo-American officials except Roosevelt and Churchill that it was in their interests to see a strong France. This was enough to achieve a large part of de Gaulle's goals. French soldiers were allowed to participate in the campaign in Germany and took Stuttgart; France became part of the European Advisory Commission and one of the occupying powers of Germany with its own sector; and finally, France was given a permanent seat on the United Nations Security Council and the veto that went with it. American policy was clearly directed towards respecting 'the psychological factor in the French mind' and treating France not in accordance with her present weakness but with a view to her future potential strength and importance.[36] The French were present at both the surrender of Germany and of Japan. The defeated France of June 1940 had become one of the victors. This does not mean that de Gaulle received all he wanted, for his dearest wish, that of French participation in the peace conferences, was denied to him. Roosevelt and Churchill's personal hostility ensured that he would not be invited to Yalta or to Potsdam.

Friction between the Allies and the Free French was also by no means over. A series of controversies occurred even after the recognition of the Provisional Government that nearly brought Franco-Allied relations to a breaking point. The first of these involved Eisenhower's plans to abandon Strasbourg. In November 1944 Generals Patton and Devers had been sent into Alsace-Lorraine in order to secure the Rhine. Wishing to push into

Germany as quickly as possible, Devers had turned northwards to assist
Patton and left the French First Army under de Lattre in charge of reducing
the German pocket around Colmar. By mid-December Leclerc, who was
now under de Lattre's command, was asking to be transferred to the
American Seventh Army because he was unhappy over operations against
the Colmar pocket. In fact, the French First Army had not only allowed
the pocket to stabilize, but the Germans had even been able to reinforce
it with men and weapons. By the end of the year it was clear that this
posed a serious problem to the Allies. When the Germans began a major
thrust through the Ardennes, the Allies, instead of having behind them the
strong easily defendable Rhine, found large numbers of Germans threatening to erupt from the Colmar pocket. Eisenhower's natural reaction was
to withdraw and regroup troops so as to secure a better defensive position.
This, however, would mean abandoning Strasbourg – the city for which
the French and Germans had fought so many wars and an ultimate symbol
of French power. De Gaulle reacted in a fury, ordering de Lattre to secure
the defence of Strasbourg himself, if necessary. On 3 January he met with
Eisenhower – with Churchill coincidentally present – and informed him
that:

> Retreat in Alsace would yield French territory to the enemy. In the
> realm of strategy, this would be only a maneuver. But for France, it
> would be a national disaster. For Alsace is sacred ground.[37]

Eisenhower became extremely alarmed by the strength of the French reaction and wrote to Marshall that: 'They became so agitated that we here
became convinced that the actual fear of De Gaulle and his administration
was that they would lose control of the entire French situation and that we
would have a state bordering upon anarchy in the whole country.'[38] Needless
to say, the Allies did not withdraw from Alsace. Instead they invested
large numbers of troops in trying to eliminate the Colmar pocket – much
to Patton's disgust, who felt that it was removing troops from a vital area
to one of secondary importance.[39]

After Strasbourg, de Gaulle seems almost to have been provoking con-
frontations in order to dramatise his grievances against the Allies and, it
must be said, to utilise a form of blackmail. In February he refused to meet
with Roosevelt who was passing through Algiers on his return from the
Yalta Conference. It must be said that Roosevelt had given very short
notice of this meeting and that it was not entirely reasonable of the American
president to summon a French leader to meet with him on French territory,
especially when it was no longer a war zone and particularly when refusing an invitation to Paris at the same time. The main purpose of de Gaulle's

refusal, however, was to protest his exclusion from Yalta. Another major controversy occurred over Allied orders to de Lattre, who by now had crossed the Rhine, to evacuate Stuttgart to the American Seventh Army which needed it to serve as a link in its communications and supply system for current operations. On de Gaulle's instructions, de Lattre refused to evacuate. There is no question here of the famous personality conflict with Roosevelt, for Truman was now president and he was completely impartial towards de Gaulle. In any case, this action infuriated Eisenhower, who wrote to de Gaulle:

> Under the circumstances, I must of course accept the situation, as I myself am unwilling to take any action which would reduce the effectiveness of the military effort against Germany, either by withholding supplies from the First French Army or by any other measures which would affect their fighting strength. Moreover, I will never personally be a party to initiating any type of struggle or quarrel between your government and troops under my command, which could result only in weakening bonds of national friendship as well as the exemplary spirit of cooperation that has characterized the actions of French and American forces in the battle line.[40]

Eisenhower went on to reply to de Gaulle's blackmail with his own. He told the French president that he would tell the Combined Chiefs of Staff that he could no longer count on being able to use French forces that they were planning on equipping. The threat was clear: unless the French got out of Stuttgart, the Allies might stop rearming the French.

In fact, de Gaulle was jockeying for position, trying to ensure as large a French zone of occupation in Germany as possible. Germany had originally been divided into three zones, British, American and Russian, that were more or less equally divided according to population and economic assets. When it was decided to allot a zone to the French this area had to be taken from the American and British zones – Stalin was not willing to sacrifice any of the Soviet zone – and carved in such a way that it would not cut off American and British supply lines but would give the French a substantial area. The resulting problem was thus very delicate. The question was decided at Yalta, at which de Gaulle was not present, and he, like many other French people, naturally resented that a question vital to their security – much more vital to them, in fact than to the Anglo-Americans, since they had been invaded three times within living memory by Germany – had been decided in their absence. The French continually pressed their own desires in regard to the occupation zone and endlessly asserted their own security needs. One of their major requests was to incorporate part of the left bank of the Rhine into France. Impatient over, as he saw it, the lack of comprehension exhibited by the Anglo-Americans, de Gaulle took matters into his own hands over Stuttgart. The military question did of course interest him, because he wanted to be able to tell the French that their army had taken and held a major German city. This was important for a French sense of grandeur. But his main interest was political, as he made clear to Eisenhower:

> The difficulty we have just come up against stems from a situation which has nothing to do with you, but is the fault of the lack of agreement and consequently of liaison between the American and British Governments on the one hand, and the French Government on the other, on the policy of the war in general and the occupation of enemy territories in particular . . . since the French Government has not succeeded in reaching a common agreement, it is obviously driven to act on its own initiative.[41]

De Gaulle went on to repeat the usual complaints. He made the point even clearer in a letter to Truman:

> As matters now stand and in the same spirit of frankness with which you were pleased to address me, I believe it my duty to express the wish that such unfortunate incidents may be avoided. To that end the Allies of France need only recognize that questions so closely touching France as the occupation of German territory should be discussed and decided with her. As you know, this unfortunately has not been the case thus far, in spite of my repeated requests.[42]

The French were allowed to stay in Stuttgart for the time being.

At the same time a far more serious incident was occurring in Italy. To assist Field Marshall Alexander who was in charge of operations in Italy, French troops on the border had carried out operations against two German divisions there. These operations had been a success, but during them some French troops had crossed into Italy. Rumours had been flying for months that the French wished to occupy part of the Val d'Aosta and were only looking for a suitable occasion to do so. The Anglo-Americans were greatly disturbed by this situation. In early May Devers issued orders to the French to withdraw across the border, but they were ignored. The problem was further complicated by the attitude of these French forces. Alexander reported that: 'Meanwhile the French since their entry into the country have adopted a truculent and provocative attitude towards the Italians and in consequence Italian Partisans have not surrendered their arms and I consider an immediate clash between French and Italians very likely.' He also discovered that the French were constructing road blocks in order to slow down Allied advances in the region.[43] Eisenhower felt that the French would not withdraw until an agreement on their zones of occupation in Germany had been reached. He told Murphy that the French were using the same tactics against the Allies as the Allies were using against Russia: all troops would hold their ground until various outstanding matters had been settled.[44]

This case was, however, considerably more explosive than the one in Stuttgart. Lawlessness was rampant in that part of Italy with bands of armed Germans and Italian fascists still terrorizing the population. Furthermore, the local Italian government in Aosta resigned to protest the French interference. But perhaps the most important fact to the Allies was that they were engaged in a similar dispute at the same time with Tito and the Yugoslavs in the Venezia Giulia in north-east Italy. Giving in to the French here would significantly strengthen Tito in his demands. The French complained that it was a matter of honour since they had been invaded through these valleys in 1940. By early June it was clear that no amount of oral representations would get the French to withdraw. At the same time, a crisis had re-exploded in Syria and Lebanon between the British and the French. The Allies decided that serious measures would have to be taken in the Val d'Aosta, particularly after a letter from General Doyen, commander of the French army in the Alps, stated: 'General de Gaulle has instructed me to make as clear as possible to the Allied Command that I have received the order to prevent the setting up of Allied Military Government in territories occupied by our troops and administered by us by all necessary means without exception.' Truman wrote to de Gaulle insisting that it was 'almost unbelievable' that the French, who had been armed by the Americans, should threaten to attack Allied soldiers who had recently sacrificed so much to aid in the liberation of France. Significantly Truman wrote the letter on 6 June 1945, the first anniversary of the Normandy landings. Truman proceeded to ask de Gaulle to reconsider his position and concluded by saying:

> While this threat by the French Government is outstanding against American soldiers, I regret that I have no alternative but to issue instructions that no further issues of military equipment or munitions can be made to French troops. Rations will continue to be supplied.[45]

Three days later General Juin, Chief of Staff of the French Army, met with Alexander to discuss the problem. Juin stated that he could not immediately withdraw all the troops because of the effect it would have on French *amour propre* and suggested that withdrawal might take place gradually over a month. Alexander replied that he personally would be willing to accept such an arrangement if it began immediately and was finished by the end of June.[46] An agreement was soon reached with the French, and the United States resumed its supplies.

The final major conflict between the French and the Allies was over French participation in the Pacific War primarily in the liberation of Indochina. The situation there was particularly delicate for after the collapse of the Vichy government in 1944 Indochina, although occupied by the Japanese, was in a kind of administrative limbo. This question quickly developed into a significant policy difference between the British and Americans. The first controversy was the rather basic one of in whose command Indochina belonged. Both the China Command, under Chiang Kai Shek and General Wedemeyer (American) and the South East Asian Command under Admiral Mountbatten (British) claimed Indochina. The American/British split was thus already evident from the very beginning. From there the situation only became more complicated. The French Colonial Army in Indochina was estimated to contain around 54 000 men of which approximately 15 000 were Europeans. After the Japanese occupation began, their main duty was to guard the Chinese–Indochinese border. The area thus contained a potentially large and well-trained resistance organisation near Allied territory, and both the British and French felt it was worth developing. The Americans were officially undecided in their policy towards Indochina, but in reality Roosevelt wanted it put under an international trusteeship that would lead to independence in the near future. In early January 1944 he expressed his point of view on the subject to the British ambassador:

> I saw Halifax last week and told him quite frankly that it was perfectly true that I had, for over a year, expressed the opinion that Indo-China should not go back to France but that it should be administered by an international trusteeship. France has had the country – thirty million inhabitants for nearly one hundred years, and the people are worse off than they were at the beginning.[47]

The problem was further complicated by the existence of the nationalist Annamese Viet Minh organisation, and it was widely believed that their organisation had been strengthened by Japanese military personnel who assisted their opposition to the French.[48] However, dislike of the French could not compare with the hatred most people in Indochina felt towards their traditional enemy, China. It was known that many Chinese still clung to the idea of 'Greater China' which included Indochina. Roosevelt frequently played upon this idea:

He [Roosevelt] said that at his conference at Cairo he had turned to Chiang-Kai-Shek in the presence of Churchill and had asked 'Do you want Indo-China?' Chiang-Kai-Shek had replied that he did not, but felt that Indo-China should be given independence. The President said that Churchill was not in agreement with him on this point, since Churchill obviously had fears regarding Burma. The Russians, however, were in agreement.[49]

Of course Chiang had enough problems already in China, but this did not dampen Indochinese suspicions as to Chinese intentions.

It should not, however, be assumed that Roosevelt's views represented a consensus in the American Government. Far from it. It is true that there was an obvious concern in Washington that a controversy could break in the United States over French use of Lend–Lease equipment to recover colonial territories, especially since other imperial powers would follow suit.[50] It might be stated in certain liberal quarters that the Americans were arming imperialists to recapture their possessions in order to continue their exploitation of colonial peoples. However, this did not seem to trouble Washington greatly. The State Department maintained that it was in America's interest to develop a strong France and that, therefore, Indochina had to be returned to France. Furthermore, they supported the British demands for assisting the French resistance movements and allowing the French Army to participate in the liberation of Indochina. Edward Stettinius, then Under Secretary of State, wrote to Roosevelt:

> Subject to your approval, the State Department will proceed on the assumption that French armed forces will be employed to at least some extent in the military operations, and that in the administration of Indo-China it will be desirable to employ French nationals who have an intimate knowledge of the country and its problems.[51]

General Donovan and the OSS also supported the British, wishing to participate themselves in work with the resistance groups in Indochina. Donovan wrote to Hull asking for his support, which Hull was inclined to give:

> Subject to your [Roosevelt's] approval, the Department will reply to General Donovan that it has no objection to furnishing supplies and equipment to resistance groups, both French and native, actually within Indochina, nor to American collaboration with the French Military Mission at Chungking or to her French officers or officials in furtherance of the contemplated operations or any other military operations in Indochina for the defeat of Japan.[52]

Needless to say, Roosevelt did not agree. It is, in general, an oversimplification to see a Eurocentric State Department in conflict with an anti-imperialist president. The State Department had supported the Lebanese and Syrians in all their conflicts with the French, and Roosevelt's anti-imperialism was far from consistent. However, in the case of Indochina this is not an inaccurate description of the situation.

The War Department on the other hand expressed little interest in either aiding the resistance movements or in allowing the French Army to reconquer Indochina. This, however, does not seem to have come from their agreement with Roosevelt's ideas so much as from the belief that Indochina had little strategic importance in the Pacific War. They viewed the British insistence on Indochina in the same way as they did Churchill's insistence on pushing through Italy into the Balkans and the 'soft underbelly of Europe'. Such campaigns, the War Department felt, would absorb massive numbers of Allied troops to no real useful purpose. It was better to attack Germany and Japan directly. The American Joint Staff Planners were quite clear on this point: 'The Indo-Chinese area is of relatively minor military significance. Activities of resistance groups in Indo-China are not of great military benefit to the United States.'[53] Once this policy was decided, the Americans simply did not have the resources to organise a side-campaign in Indochina in order to please the French. They simply did not have the shipping and equipment that the French would need there.[54] There were signs, however, that as time went on British and French insistence on the question began to alarm the War Department. In early 1945 the State–War–Navy Coordinating Committee argued that:

> A continued policy of (1) declining to utilize offered French assistance in this area and (2) of failing to take action in this area with United States forces may lead to a situation where inaction by the United States has the practical effect of indicating lack of United States interest in this area. Such a policy might lead eventually to strong British representations that Indo-China should form part of the Southeast Asia Command rather than of the Indo-Chinese theater. If this view should be adopted, the British and French acting together, would be in a position to exercise greater influence than the United States, not only in determining the operations to be undertaken with respect to Indo-China but also as to the disposition of that area after it is liberated.[55]

This shows obvious State Department influence, referring to the old State Department obsession with preserving American influence against the British. However, even the Planners exhibited these suspicions sometimes, writing that:

By acquiescing to French desires rather than United States policy regarding Indo-China, the British are successfully creating an over-all situation, based on a series of seemingly minor requests by the British and French, intended to commit the United States to a position whereby Indo-China should logically be considered in a British rather than a U.S. sphere of primary strategic interest.[56]

Furthermore, one American official warned of the danger that Admiral Fénard, the French naval attaché in Washington, was, by submitting a series of questions on Indochina to various United States Government agencies and obtaining answers to them, writing American policy. He urged that some kind of coherent policy on Indochina should be developed and agreed to among these agencies.[57]

The British, of course, were quite insistent that action should take place in Indochina, if only among the resistance groups, and that this action should be under British control. For their part, the British strongly suspected American designs on Indochina. The British felt that the Americans would like to establish naval bases in Indochina, particularly in Camranh Bay which would be ideal for the Pacific Fleet. It was felt that Roosevelt's flirtations with the Chinese over Indochina was part of a larger design. An SOE report claimed that:

> In addition, their apparent support of the Chinese cause was believed to be due to the fact that China, being unable to develop further territory, the Americans would almost certainly be able to take the leading part in any so-called 'Chinese development'. The British view was that if the French were kicked out of F[rench] I[ndo] C[hina], this might be used as a precedent to get us out of some of our possessions in the Far East. It was therefore decided to give the French such support as we were able.[58]

British policy towards the French was thus once again based on British desires to protect their own empire. Mountbatten insisted that: 'Siam and Indo-China are of vital importance to S[outh] E[ast] A[sian] C[ommand] because through them lies the enemy land and air reinforcements route to Burma and Malaya.' He felt that revolt should be organized in Indochina in coordination with the reconquest of Burma.[59] To do this the British needed the cooperation of the French.

The controversy over what command Indochina belonged to was finally settled at Potsdam in a decision that would later have tragic repercussions. Indochina was divided into two parts that were north and south of the 16th Parallel (latitude 16° North). The China Command became responsible for the northern part and the South East Asian Command for the southern part. After Japanese surrender, the Chinese refused to leave the northern part and insisted, with American support, that they and not the French were responsible for disarming the Japanese in that area and exercising control there. Most of the French resistance was in the northern part, and they too were disarmed by the Chinese occupiers. An SOE report on the situation ended with the ominous phrase: 'The only people to benefit by this lack of co-ordination on the part of the Allies were the Annamese revolutionaries who took full advantage of the chaos.'[60]

The period from June 1944 marked the triumph of Gaullism in World War II. A small band of dissidents without resources had set out to erase the Armistice and recreate France as a Republic fighting wholeheartedly beside the Allies. De Gaulle had insisted that his movement was the real soul of France, and on the Champs-Elysées he received his vindication. However, it was one thing to be a symbol and quite another to be a leader participating in the everyday give and take of political life especially at a time when the nation was in complete upheaval. De Gaulle and his government were under new pressures, but they continued to use the methods of the weak and to be obsessed with questions of French sovereignty – particularly when national security was involved. Anglo-American friction also continued both with the French and with each other. On the fundamental question of metropolitan France, however, the Americans and British were united: the Provisional Government had to be strengthened in order to prevent serious disorder in France. De Gaulle and his movement although not loved were necessary.

9 'Our Mutual Headache': Churchill, Roosevelt and de Gaulle

Perhaps the most fascinating topic for a student of Anglo-American policy towards the French during World War II is that of the role of personal relations between Churchill, Roosevelt and de Gaulle. It is well-known that de Gaulle deeply distrusted the 'Anglo-Saxons', as the French prefer to call the Anglo-Americans. It is equally well-known that Roosevelt intensely disliked de Gaulle, although he was not incapable of charming him if American policy dictated such a course.[1] The attitude of Churchill is less clear, seeming to be a mixture of admiration and detestation. Henry Wallace, the American vice-president, described Churchill's freely expressed views on de Gaulle: 'Churchill spoke very contemptuously of the vanity, pettiness, and discourtesy of de Gaulle, saying he had raised him from a pup but that he still barked a bit.'[2] There is no doubt, though, that he respected and even felt a sense of gratitude for de Gaulle's stand in 1940. One thing is certain, that while a large number of pages has been devoted to the personal relationships of these men, few of these studies have seriously studied the body of archival material on the subject. In this chapter, we will try to use this information to establish the truth – as much as possible – about Churchill's and Roosevelt's feelings about de Gaulle and then to consider to what extent this influenced Anglo-American policy.

Churchill's attitude towards France and the French has been a frequent subject of analysis, and therefore we will not comment on it in any great detail here.[3] When Churchill invited de Gaulle to Britain in June 1944 for the Normandy Landings, he told him that:

> Ever since 1907, I have in good times and bad times been a sincere friend of France, as my words and actions show, and it is to me an intense pain that barriers have been raised to an association which to me was very dear. Here in this visit of yours, which I personally arranged, I had the hope that there was a chance of putting things right. Now I have only the hope that it may not be the last chance.[4]

The extent of Churchill's Francophilia is, in fact, debatable. Most of Churchill's writings were based on the Whig interpretation of history: that is, that Britain – and more particularly England – was a unique nation that bore no resemblance to her continental neighbours. In his life of Marlborough he saw a clear distinction between the historical liberty of England and the despotism of France. Of course, Marlborough's world was not that of the twentieth century, but Churchill remained convinced that England, and in fact all of the English-speaking world, were in many ways a chosen people, apart from and above all others. As Douglas Johnson has pointed out, he spoke against an Anglo-French alliance in 1925, insisting that Britain could stand alone. In June 1940 Churchill was in a certain sense relieved by being released from the Anglo-French alliance. Britain could now act on her own and not be hampered by the half-heartedness and even incompetence of French authorities. He became almost heady, giving some of the greatest speeches of his life, as he summoned the British to live 'their finest hour'.

What is really remarkable about this earlier quotation is not that Churchill claims to be a Francophile but that it makes the prime minister's relationship and feelings for France dependent on his personal relationship with de Gaulle. It is undeniably a statement of the importance of personal diplomacy for Churchill – a fact which de Gaulle could never understand. At first, there is no doubt that Churchill felt quite positively towards the Frenchman. In his memoirs, Churchill claims to have recognised de Gaulle almost instantly as *'l'homme du destin'*, but this may indeed simply be an exaggeration.[5] However, there is no doubt that Churchill was personally in favour of the effort to create a Free French movement and of de Gaulle's leadership of that movement. On 24 June 1940 he wrote to General Ismay:

It seems most important to establish now before the trap closes an organisation for enabling French officers and soldiers, as well as important technicians, who wish to fight to make their way to various ports. A sort of 'underground railway' as in the olden days of slavery should be established and a Scarlet Pimpernel organisation set up. I have no doubt that there will be a steady flow of determined men and we need all we can get for the defence of the French colonies. The Admiralty and Air Force must co-operate. General de Gaulle and his committee would of course be the operative authority.[6]

The idea of Free France appealed to Churchill's romantic nature as did General de Gaulle himself: the only member of that last government to remain faithful to the Republic; the only man willing to break rank with defeatism and proclaim to the world that the Allies would win. De Gaulle's act showed that he believed, like Churchill, in the ability of the English race to stand alone and win glory – and, more importantly, final victory – in doing so.

We must remember that the de Gaulle of 1940 was not yet an Anglophobe and even showed a few small signs of Americanophilia. He was virtually the only member of Paul Reynaud's government who repeatedly argued that this was not the end of a European war but the beginning of a world war – the British would resist and the United States would fight and win. His desperation to keep France in the war had led him on 15 June 1940 to support an idea by Jean Monnet for Franco-British Union. De Gaulle, who was in London on a mission for Reynaud, convinced Churchill and secured his approval. Thus de Gaulle made his first real impact on Churchill as the champion of the Franco-British alliance. When this plan was rejected by the French government, de Gaulle fled to London and threw in his lot with the English. He refused to condemn – nor it must be admitted to actually sanction – the British attack on Oran nor did he utter any criticism of the British over Dakar. He frequently praised the spirit of resistance of the English people and, in a major speech at Oxford University, emphasized the need for the Franco-British alliance:

> For centuries, France and England have been the source and the champions of human liberty. Liberty will perish if these sources are not combined and if these champions are not united. All the resources of intelligence and will power, which have for such a long time sprung up separately from your country and mine in favour of the same cause, that of civilisation, is it not necessary to put them together since the adversaries of our ideal have united to destroy them?[7]

Such a statement could only appeal to Churchill who, like de Gaulle, insisted that they were involved in a battle for civilisation and that with failure a new 'more sinister' Dark Ages would emerge.[8] Churchill was undoubtedly sincere when he stated that de Gaulle took with him in that airplane from Bordeaux 'the honour of France'.[9] It is safe to say that no member of the British government ever forgot the supreme act of faith in Britain that de Gaulle's stand signified: there was always an element of the irrational in British support for the man who had stood by them in 1940. We might even go so far as to say that Churchill was the chief major supporter of de Gaulle during this early period. Most other important personalities could not see the need for de Gaulle, who after all had almost nothing to offer – at least not until August 1940 when parts of the empire began to rally to him – and whose patronage risked offending Vichy.

The problem was that while Churchill and de Gaulle – at least at the beginning – spoke the same language, they did not have the same aims and, what was perhaps worse from a personal point of view, de Gaulle was not really grateful to Churchill for all he had done. To de Gaulle, Churchill whatever his faults was always the leader who had stood alone against Hitler, and had by so doing made possible the restoration of France. To de Gaulle, Churchill was '*l'homme de la guerre*', and he told General Catroux that: 'The game is being played between Hitler and him.'[10] It is in this capacity that de Gaulle liked to pay tribute to the British prime minister:

> The harsh and painful incidents that often arose between us, because of the friction of our two characters, of the opposition of some of the interests of our two countries, and of the unfair advantage taken by England of wounded France, have influenced my attitude towards the Prime Minister, but not my judgment. Winston Churchill appeared to me, from one end of the drama to the other, as the great champion of a great enterprise and the great artist of a great history.[11]

This quotation is extremely interesting because de Gaulle talks of Britain's negative role in the development of Free France but does not mention its greater, positive role. As we have seen, Free France was almost entirely funded by the British Government, and many people viewed it as a British creation. This de Gaulle would never admit. Instead he created the myth of himself, the man who starting from literally nothing but a few devoted followers created not an alternative French government but the real French government, and by his refusal to bend, forced the Allies to accept it. Psychologically, probably, this was the best interpretation for defeated France which needed to re-establish its pride and belief in itself. It was in this spirit that de Gaulle, when about to leave for Algiers in May 1943, told Eden: 'The English people have been marvellous' – a remark that led Oliver Harvey to comment: 'No compliments to H[is] M[ajesty's] G[overnment].'[12] De Gaulle carried his lack of gratitude beyond the realm of politics and into that of his personal relationships – and it is here that we must seek the root of Churchill's hostility to de Gaulle. De Gaulle admitted that Churchill was a great man. He even admitted that Churchill was the man who symbolized resistance to Hitler, but he could not bring himself to thank Churchill for all his support in the early days of Free France.[13]

Relations between the two men only seriously deteriorated, however, after the Anglo-Free French attack on Syria. De Gaulle felt betrayed by the conditions of armistice signed by the British military and Vichy representatives, which ignored the demands of Free France. His temper tantrum in the office of Oliver Lyttelton, British Minister in the Middle East, shocked many, including Spears, who had previously been de Gaulle's greatest supporter. De Gaulle's behaviour during various visits to the Middle East, led Churchill to exclaim that 'de Gaulle was completely subservient with him but what was odious was his insufferable rudeness to anyone on a lower level.'[14] This did not remain the case, for by the end of the war de Gaulle had treated Churchill as rudely as he had treated anyone else. The 'pup' would, indeed, not only bark but bite the hand that fed him. In particular, in January 1943 he had at first refused an invitation to the Casablanca Conference and was only obliged to come when Churchill sent him a threatening note. Among other things, Churchill insisted that: 'arrangements must be made for North Africa'. There was nothing that could be more calculated to irritate de Gaulle than the suggestion that two foreign leaders were meeting on French territory to decide the future of French possessions. De Gaulle's acceptance letter detailed his grievances and spoke of the Allies in rather sarcastic terms:

> The decisions that have been taken without the knowledge of Fighting France concerning North and West Africa as well as the upholding in these regions of an authority stemming from Vichy, have led to an internal situation which does not, it seems, entirely satisfy the Allies and which quite definitely does not satisfy France.
>
> At the moment, President Roosevelt and you ask me to take part, without warning, in discussions of which I know neither the programme nor the conditions, and in which you expect me to discuss with you, suddenly, problems which embrace the whole future of the French Empire and of France itself.[15]

Here de Gaulle was expressing his anger and distrust of the Allies. They had made an agreement with Admiral Darlan, in order to facilitate their landings in North Africa and had found themselves criticized throughout the world for keeping quislings in power. Now they were calling in de Gaulle in order to give legitimacy to their North African arrangements, and de Gaulle mocked them for this. At the same time he was furious because France was reduced to such a state that Roosevelt and Churchill could meet on what de Gaulle considered to be her soil, without having to demand the authorisation of a central French power, and, what is worse, could summon French leaders to pay them court. De Gaulle concluded his letter with an admission of weakness that must have hurt him terribly: 'I acknowledge, however, despite these questions of form, grave though they may be, that the general situation of the war and the position in which France is situated at the moment, cannot allow me to refuse to meet the President of the United States and His Britannic Majesty's Prime Minister.' De Gaulle was coming because Churchill had threatened to withdraw his support, but he made it clear that he did not want to do so.

De Gaulle repeatedly claimed that his aims were not the same as those of the British, and that, in fact, every one of the major Allied nations had a different war aim. He had seen Darlan's assassination as a warning of the chaos into which France would be plunged if some kind of legitimate French government was not re-established. In a letter to Giraud he wrote of his belief in the need for a 'Central French authority based on the National Union for war'. De Gaulle felt that this was the only way to protect French sovereignty.[16] He was trying to erase the armistice, to re-establish a central French government based on republican legitimacy and to place France among the victors. This obviously could only be a corollary to British and American war aims. He explained this to the American ambassador in London: ' "This war . . . is not just one war. Against Germany there is Russia's war, France's war, Great Britain's war. There is also, now, the United States' war. Everything would have been all right from the beginning, all would be all right today, if there had been only one war." '[17] The Armistice had separated France from its allies and placed it in a weakened and subordinate position. His considerations, therefore, could not be the same as those of the British or Americans.

It is important to keep in mind that de Gaulle was ultrasensitive to the weakness of France and thus to any real or imagined assault on French sovereignty. In other words, he saw France as a victim not only of the Germans but also of the Anglo-Americans and reacted sharply to anything which confirmed this view. His words and actions then provoked hostility in Churchill and to a lesser extent Roosevelt. Their response in turn confirmed de Gaulle's often unfounded suspicions and made him feel personally hurt. Often de Gaulle did not understand why someone was angry with him and so interpreted any expression of such feelings as further evidence of sinister designs. Harold Macmillan, who, as we have seen, worked very closely with de Gaulle during the war, said of him:

Nobody could deny – even his worst enemy – that the General is filled with an intense and patriotic fervour. This takes the form of that peculiar *orgueil* for which there is no real English equivalent. This arrogance makes him from time to time almost impossible to deal with; but it is, as no doubt modern psychologists would agree, the reverse side of an extreme sensibility. I have never known a man at once so ungracious and so sentimental . . . At the same time, he would immensely like to be liked, and the smallest act of courtesy or special kindness touches him with a deep emotion. No Frenchman could at the same time be so unlike the majority of Frenchmen and yet so representative of the present spirit of France. The terrible mixture of inferiority complex and spiritual pride are characteristic of the sad situation into which France has fallen.

I have often felt that the solutions here could not be dealt with by politicians. They are rather problems for the professional psychiatrist.[18]

The key word here is 'inferiority complex' and it is often repeated by both British and American commentators. The French were operating with an inferiority complex throughout the war, which started with the military defeat of France in 1940 and was made worse by Britain's determined resistance – which although wished for made France's Armistice look even more shabby than it actually was – and by the overwhelmingly superior economic and military might of the United States.

This led to confused feelings on the part of the French. They felt anxious over whether the Anglo-Americans would win and knew that France's only hope for reconstitution as a powerful and independent nation depended on that victory. At the same time they felt resentment at being so dependent on these other nations. In their weakness they were reduced to insisting constantly that France really was a great nation. To quote Macmillan again: 'They entertain the pathetic belief that by insisting verbally upon France's greatness they can make her in fact great again.' This led de Gaulle to be unbending on any questions of French sovereignty and to suspect the worst of his allies, and this in turn Churchill and Roosevelt found immensely irritating. Eden commented in his diary that de Gaulle was convinced that being 'politically stiff' was the only way to get concessions from the Anglo-Americans but in regard to Churchill 'the tactics could not be worse'.[19] And so de Gaulle went on, provoking the personal antagonism of Churchill and Roosevelt – two men who were used to being catered to and not to being treated rudely – without, at least at first, meaning to and almost without realising it.

The origins of Roosevelt's hostility are considerably more difficult to find than those of Churchill's. To begin with, he met de Gaulle only twice, briefly at the Casablanca Conference and then during de Gaulle's visit to Washington in July 1944 – during which by all accounts, de Gaulle behaved perfectly. During the first major crisis in Free French–American relations, that of St Pierre and Miquelon, Roosevelt played only a very small role and clearly thought that Hull was being rather silly in insisting on such a question. In his early correspondence with Churchill, until the invasion of North Africa in November 1942, Roosevelt speaks little of de Gaulle. The Americans did refuse to allow the Free French to participate in the attack, but this was because they feared a renewal of the fratricidal strife in Syria and thought that the North African French would be almost certain to resist an Allied landing that included the Free French. It is also true that Roosevelt insisted that de Gaulle should not be told of the impending invasion, but this stemmed not from personal hostility but from fears – which dated from the unfortunate Anglo-Free French expedition to Dakar – that the Free French were leaky. There is no real evidence of any personal feeling, however.

Roosevelt, unlike Churchill and de Gaulle, never wrote his memoirs. In fact he did not like to write about his policies and viewpoints. While Churchill compulsively wrote dozens of pages on tactics or war aims or some foreign policy question, Roosevelt preferred to keep everyone – including his closest aides – guessing. The essence of his foreign policy, as Warren Kimball has so brilliantly shown, was to juggle.[20] He tried never to let his right hand know what his left hand was doing. The classic example of this was with his messages to Churchill: he sent them out through the Navy Department and received his answers through the War Department. Almost none of them were even seen by the State Department, and no one but himself saw all the messages. It is certain, however, that one thing that Roosevelt had observed about French political life throughout his long presidency was that it was essentially unstable. Governments came and went, leading Roosevelt to comment to de Gaulle that on some days even he, the president of the United States, had not been sure who the prime minister of France had been.[21] Roosevelt saw this pattern repeated in Free France, which was constantly shedding members – sometimes for good reasons, sometimes for not so good reasons. He also saw this with the French Committee for National Liberation, which was formed in June 1943 and which had major cabinet reshuffles in November 1943 and again in September 1944. Thus we can safely say that for Roosevelt, French politics meant instability.

This observation led him to his oft-repeated conclusion that everything must be subordinated to the military situation and that no government should be imposed on France. He explained to the American representative to the French Committee that his French policy was based on 'two fundamental principles':

> The first is that military considerations in the prosecution of the war against Germany are and must remain paramount . . . The second basic principle which has guided this Government is that sovereignty resides in the people and that as long as over 90 per cent of the French people are not free to exercise their political rights, no individual or group will be recognized by the United States as the Government of France or the French Empire.[22]

On this question there is absolutely no difference in his treatment of de Gaulle or Giraud or Darlan. At the time of the controversy over the 'Darlan

Deal' he insisted that: 'The future French government will be established – not by any individual in metropolitan France or overseas – but by the French people themselves after they have been set free by the victory of the United Nations.'[23] Furthermore, far from being the inveterate supporter of Giraud as he is often portrayed, Roosevelt wrote to Churchill on 1 January 1943, when Giraud had just assumed power in North Africa:

> I feel very strongly that we have a military occupation in North Africa and as such our Commanding General has complete charge of all matters civil as well as military. We must not let any of our French friends forget this for a moment. By the same token I don't want any of them to think that we are going to recognize anyone or any committee or group as representing the French Government or the French Empire. The people of France will settle their own affairs after we have won this war. Until then we can deal with local Frenchmen on a local basis wherever our armies occupy former French territory and if these local officials won't play ball we will have to replace them.[24]

This quote is frequently cited by historians, but it is less frequently made clear that it refers to North Africa under Giraud, not under de Gaulle. There is no doubt, furthermore, that he never seriously considered the North African enterprise to be one of 'military occupation'. In September 1942 he wrote to Admiral Leahy about 'the general objective of leaving civilian administration as far as possible in French hands' and stated that 'every effort [must] be made to obtain either cooperation or at least neutrality in the interest of military success'.[25] United States policy towards Vichy had been based on the hope of securing French cooperation and assistance. Furthermore, in January 1944 Roosevelt wrote a detailed analysis of his French policy for the new representative to the French Committee of National Liberation, Edwin Wilson. There was no talk of 'military occupation' here. He explained to Wilson that:

> It should likewise be emphasized that our forces were sent to North Africa as friends and liberators, and not for the purpose of occupying the territory of an ally. Consequently, questions of local security, administration and the protection of our long and vital lines of communication were largely left in the hands of French officials, who had to deal with a problem of unusual difficulty.[26]

It is noticeable that Roosevelt's use of the term 'military occupation' only occurred when he felt particularly irritated at the French for some reason. In this letter to Churchill we see a Roosevelt who is disgusted with the fury of the French infighting and instability that had directly resulted in the assassination of Admiral Darlan a few days before. It is in this context that his statement about 'military occupation' must be taken. Recognizing only local leaders, Roosevelt felt, would discourage this rivalry. It would also serve to develop separate administrations throughout the French Empire and thus encourage the independence of these areas. In this way, his aim of decolonisation would be pursued. This statement represents a very harsh assessment of the French and confirms that Roosevelt felt that all of France's leaders had failed the nation.

It is not surprising, therefore, that he spoke of all these leaders with equal sarcasm. In November 1942, Roosevelt wrote to Churchill that:

> In regard to de Gaulle, I have hitherto enjoyed a quiet satisfaction in leaving him in your hands – apparently I have now acquired a similar problem in brother Giraud.
>
> I wholly agree that we must prevent rivalry between the French émigré factions and I have no objection to a de Gaulle emissary visiting Kingpin [codename for Giraud] in Algiers. We must remember that there is also a cat fight in progress between Kingpin and Darlan, each claiming full military command of French forces in North and West Africa.
>
> The principal thought to be driven home to all three of these prima donnas is that the situation is today solely in the military field and that any decision by any one of them, or by all of them, is subject to review and approval of Eisenhower.[27]

Clearly Roosevelt did not think highly of any of the three. There is no moral judgment passed here – all three men are simply 'prima donnas' – and it is here that Roosevelt differs most clearly from Churchill and, in fact, from most public opinion in Britain and the United States. In popular judgement, François Darlan was a quisling while Charles de Gaulle was the symbol of republican legitimacy. Even Churchill shared this view. To equate the two men could only degrade de Gaulle. Roosevelt's letter expressed a sharp disgust with French politics, which is little more than a 'cat fight'. Given such leaders and such behaviour, he can only hope that the French people themselves will find better ones – although, given their record during the Third Republic, this may seem unlikely to him. In any case, even if they do not, he will not be responsible for it.

From this point on, the Churchill/Roosevelt correspondence shows a growing hatred of de Gaulle. The two men excited each other in their detestation. The origins of Churchill's feelings are obvious. However, it is more difficult to understand why Roosevelt felt personally hostile to a man he would only meet briefly in late January 1943. The answer must obviously lie in the Free French organisation in the United States which, as we have seen, was riddled with problems and had already alienated Cordell Hull and the State Department. However, once the United States had established bases in Free French territory the two sides were forced to work together. The controversy over the 'Darlan Deal' threatened American relations with the Free French and a concerted effort was made in Washington to show the Gaullists that they were not being cast aside. Hull received both André Philip, a resistance leader who had come out of France to work with de Gaulle, and Admiral d'Argenlieu, who only a few months before had behaved in a rather remarkable fashion in New Caledonia. Roosevelt, with Sumner Welles present, even agreed to meet with Philip and Tixier, the Free French representative in Washington. The result was a fiasco. The account of this conversation, which was written by Sumner Welles and published in *Foreign Relations of the United States, 1942*, says the following:

> It is noteworthy that throughout the entire conversation which lasted some fifty minutes, neither one of them expressed the slightest gratitude or recognition of the liberation of North Africa by American forces, but insisted over and over again in almost exactly the same words that the administration of North Africa must be in their own hands 'not later than two or three weeks from now which will give you time to occupy Tunisia.'

Here again we come up against that old problem of gratitude. The Americans were quite simply hurt that the French expressed no gratitude for the numbers of their own men who had died or been wounded and for the effort they had made to liberate North Africa. Of course, the Gaullists did not think that North Africa was really 'liberated' as long as Darlan remained in power. If we examine the manuscript account of this meeting, we see that the published account is incomplete. The following paragraph is missing:

> It would be quite impossible to attempt to report the latter part of the conversation held by these two individuals with the President. They both of them howled at the top of their lungs and spoke at the same time, and paid not the slightest attention to what the President was saying to them.[28]

How unused must Roosevelt, probably the most powerful man in the world, have been to such treatment. There is no doubt that he hated both men afterwards, especially Philip, and that he detested de Gaulle for putting them in positions of power. He frequently mentioned Tixier and Philip's membership of the later French Committee of National Liberation in a very disapproving tone.[29] When this was combined with de Gaulle's, as Roosevelt saw it, rude behaviour over the Casablanca Conference, it became certain that Roosevelt would not become a supporter of Gaullism.

In his essay to Wilson, Roosevelt set out his views on de Gaulle and the Gaullists. Not even Roosevelt denied that de Gaulle had done a great thing in June 1940, and the president spoke of the 'dark days when General de Gaulle inspired universal admiration by raising the banner of resistance'. However, there was a great deal that Roosevelt found objectionable about Gaullism. To begin with, Roosevelt felt that de Gaulle was more concerned with advancing his own political interests than in fighting the war:

> It was our sincere hope that the discussions which took place last summer in Algiers would lead to real unity among Frenchmen. What the world witnessed instead was an unrelenting struggle for political power which at the risk of seriously effecting the war effort was even carried to the point of including efforts to encourage desertions from French naval and merchant ships, thereby threatening to immobilize them at a time when every ton of shipping was urgently needed.[30]

Roosevelt also objected to the Gaullists' anti-American propaganda and the frequent French refusal to recognise the American role in the liberation of their nation – gratitude once again. The president was also angered by French efforts to play off Britain and the United States against each other and both of these against the Soviet Union. De Gaulle was trying to trouble Allied unity at a time when it was absolutely necessary to the war effort. There is no doubt that some of the Free French antics did hinder the war effort, although never very seriously. The Gaullists were, in their opinion, fighting for the soul of France. They felt they had to use any reasonable methods to discredit Vichyism or neo-Vichyism in order to show that such ideas did not really represent France. The problem was that de Gaulle's definition of 'reasonable' and that of his Allies did not always agree.

At bottom, Roosevelt's criticisms of the Free French are almost as emotional as Churchill's – or as de Gaulle's unreasoning suspicions of the Anglo-Americans. It became a frequent joke, not only between Roosevelt and Churchill but also among their subordinates, to speak of French unity as a wedding with de Gaulle as the shy and reluctant bride and Giraud as the groom. But even as unity was progressing, the two men would sometimes cook up schemes to be rid of de Gaulle – and these plans, although probably only formulated in anger and not seriously meant, would have justified de Gaulle's worst fears if he had known about them. In May 1943, for example, Roosevelt was so irritated by repeated attacks on

Allied (and particularly American) policy by de Gaulle and his followers,
that he wrote to Churchill: 'I think we might talk over the formation of an
entirely new French Committee subject in its membership to the approval
of you and me.' In another letter, Roosevelt described de Gaulle to Churchill
as 'our mutual headache'.[31] Later, after the formation of the Committee,
Roosevelt gave full vent to his feelings in another letter to Churchill:

> I am fed up with de Gaulle, and the secret personal and political machi-
> nations of that Committee in the last few days indicate that there is no
> possibility of our working with de Gaulle. If these were peace times it
> wouldn't make so much difference but I am absolutely convinced that
> he has been and is now injuring our war effort and that he is a very
> dangerous threat to us. I agree with you that he likes neither the British
> nor the Americans and that he would double-cross both of us at the first
> opportunity. I agree with you that the time has arrived when we must
> break with him. It is an intolerable situation.[32]

This letter was Roosevelt's immediate response to the discovery that the
original Committee of seven, which included Philip, had been increased to
fourteen, incorporating, among others, the equally detested Tixier. Surprisingly enough, Churchill sent a soothing response:

> Some of my colleagues have questioned your sentence 'I agree with you
> that the time has arrived when we must break with him.' As you will
> remember, I sent a telegram from the White House when we were
> together, but, as I told you at the time, the Cabinet did not accept this
> view because, inter alia, this was a new fact to me and we were all
> inclined to give the meeting a fair chance. Since then we have been
> watching their manoeuvres with growing dissatisfaction. It would not,
> however, be right to say that we have decided 'That the time has arrived
> when we must break with him.' This may come but it would come as
> the result of his refusing to accept the necessary military conditions to
> ensure that the French Army remains in trustworthy hands on which full
> agreement exists between our two Governments.[33]

Churchill was subordinating his personal feelings to the British Cabinet's
point of view and forcing Roosevelt to do the same.

Churchill, however, was just as given to emotional outbursts as Roosevelt.
In a letter to Duff Cooper, who had recently been appointed British representative to the French Committee, Churchill said of de Gaulle: 'He is
a man Fascist-minded, opportunist, unscrupulous, ambitious to the last
degree and his coming into power in the new France would lead to great
schisms there and also to a considerable estrangement between France and

the Western Democracies.'[34] The only difference here between Churchill and Roosevelt's opinion is that Churchill uses considerably more violent language. After the Committee arrested several former officials of Vichy in December 1943, Churchill reacted in a very hostile fashion, telephoning Macmillan to complain and, as the latter described it 'roaring like an excited bull down the telephone'.[35] Churchill seems to have derived a certain enjoyment from keeping Spears in Syria, even though he knew that the French detested the British minister. He was also certainly more than willing to side with Roosevelt in blocking for several months both a civil affairs agreement with the French and recognition of the Committee in 1944. Churchill frequently said that he considered himself to be Roosevelt's lieutenant, and many historians have deduced from this that he slavishly followed Roosevelt's French policy. As we have seen, Churchill felt quite passionately about de Gaulle and hardly needed Roosevelt to increase his hostility. Furthermore, it was frequently Churchill who egged on Roosevelt. When the Committee ended the co-presidency in November 1943, it was Churchill who protested not Roosevelt. During the Lebanese constitutional crisis, it was Churchill who wrote to Roosevelt suggesting that if de Gaulle did not meet their demands, 'we should withdraw our recognition from the French National Committee and stop the process of arming troops in North Africa.'[36] Roosevelt, not wanting to get involved in a struggle between imperialist powers, did not even respond. Furthermore, it was Churchill who was first thrown into a rage about the arrests of three former Vichy officials, Boisson, Peyrouton and Flandin, and it was he who encouraged Roosevelt to take a firm stand on the question – much to the State Department's horror. Finally, it is certain that Churchill never slavishly followed Roosevelt on any other question. On questions involving Italy or British imperial policy, Churchill frequently disagreed with Roosevelt or simply ignored him. Therefore, it is safe to say that when Churchill agreed with Roosevelt on French questions, he did so because he wanted to, because he himself was angry at de Gaulle. He considered that the British Cabinet would be more influenced by Roosevelt's anger – the American president was, after all, a more remote figure – than by his own. One of his letters to Eden is particularly instructive of this tactic. The letter was written in July 1943 when the Foreign Office was pressing for some degree of recognition of the French Committee. Churchill insisted that there was no need to rush such a decision:

> Indeed, I think that a certain delay is salutary. It must be remembered that de Gaulle has been bitterly attacking the American policy, that he has gained many successes against the wish of the President, the most

notable being the overthrow of Boisson. All this will cost him and the Committee dear. It is often easier to offend potentates than to placate them. For this I consider time and proofs of good will are needed.[37]

It is tempting to wonder which potentate Churchill is referring to and why he is so worried about the personal feelings of Franklin Roosevelt. It seems more likely that he is transferring his own feelings to the American president – who, it was known, generally shared them about de Gaulle – in the hope that this would have more influence with the British Cabinet.

It quickly became clear to the American, however, that Churchill was not supported by anyone else in the British government. General Marshall, Admiral King and General Arnold were quite convinced of this, telling Roosevelt: 'The Prime Minister's support of your position is understood, but in this matter he dominates neither the Cabinet nor the Foreign Office.'[38] In fact, Churchill's rages against de Gaulle generally followed the same pattern: he would be spectacularly furious for several days and then begin to calm down. Soon he would start listening to the cabinet and his other advisers and soften his demands. Eventually, he would forget his anger and put the needs of British policy first. Thus it quickly became clear that however emotional Churchill might become on the subject and however extraordinary his rages might be, he rightly would not allow his feelings to determine British policy. He might enjoy irritating de Gaulle in relatively minor ways – such as delaying recognition or leaving Spears in Syria – but he was not going to 'break' de Gaulle. Furthermore, as time went on, it became clear that de Gaulle was not the dangerous demagogue that the Americans imagined and, as he showed his ability to govern and his capacity to accept democratic methods, American hostility began to evaporate. Roosevelt, like Churchill, could be reasoned with, and both men were willing to forget their personal animosities to further a stable Europe after the war. After the summer of 1943 Roosevelt was generally satisfied with de Gaulle's performance and, except for the Boisson, Peyrouton and Flandin case – which admittedly involved American guarantees – he rarely showed any signs of anger with the French. He was even quite capable of turning on all his charm for de Gaulle when the latter visited Washington in July 1944. This does not mean that he or Churchill liked de Gaulle: they simply realized that he was probably the best leader that France had produced during the war, and that however drastic his words he was wholeheartedly on the Allied side. However, Roosevelt still was not willing to invite him to the Yalta Conference.

It would certainly have been beneficial to de Gaulle if, in his dealings with the British and Americans, he had been charming. Churchill and

Roosevelt certainly did not like him and did not enjoy his company. There is no escaping the conclusion that had he been less unbending, had he been willing to cultivate and flatter Churchill and Roosevelt, they would have been far more receptive to his demands and far more willing to include him in conferences. However, this is only part of the question. By being a genial personality, de Gaulle might have gained something from the Anglo-Americans, but he would almost certainly have lost more in France. The fact of the matter is that the French applauded de Gaulle's behaviour to the Allies. To a defeated and occupied nation, de Gaulle's insistence on French sovereignty struck a chord and gave the French a sense of pride. In those tragic and peculiar times, de Gaulle gave voice to millions of Frenchmen who wanted simply to erase the defeat of 1940 and to affirm to the world that they were still a great power. De Gaulle's personality may have irritated Churchill and Roosevelt, but it won him France.

Notes

1 De Gaulle in London and the Formation of Free France, 1940–42

1. Edward Spears, *Assignment to Catastrophe*, I (London, 1954), 254.
2. On 18 June 1940 Pétain authorised the transfer of part of the government to North Africa. In the end this was not done. Only 26 deputies and one senator left on 21 June with official authorisation from the government. Included in that number were most major opponents to the Armistice. Upon arrival in Casablanca, once again by order of the government, they were placed under virtual house arrest. In one stroke Pétain had neutralised most of his opposition.
3. For more on the de Gaulle/Pétain relationship see Marc Ferro, *Pétain* (Paris, 1987) and René Rémond, 'Two Destinies: Pétain and De Gaulle' in Hugh Gough and John Horne (eds) *De Gaulle and Twentieth Century France* (London, 1994).
4. Generally called by the French 'Mers-el-Kebir'.
5. René Cassin, *Des hommes partis de rien* (Paris, 1974) 77.
6. Cassin to René Pleven, 25 Sept 1940, 382AP/31, Cassin Papers, *Archives Nationales*, Paris (henceforth cited as AN).
7. This quotation is from de Gaulle, *War Memoirs, I: The Call to Honour, 1940–42* (Paris, 1954, Eng. trans. London, 1955).
8. Speech given at the White City, London, 27 July 1940, in Philippe de Gaulle (ed.), *Lettres, notes et carnets, juin 1940–juillet 1941* (Paris, 1981) 60 (henceforth cited as *Lettres . . .*).
9. Cassin Diary, entry for 26 June 1940, 382AP/27, Cassin Papers, AN.
10. Henceforth, persons who assumed aliases will be listed under both their assumed name and their real name. The alias will be placed in italics (for example, Capt. *Passy*-Dewavrin). The main exception to this rule will be for Philippe *Leclerc*-de Hautecloque, who was – and still is – universally known simply as Leclerc.
11. This will be considered in more detail in Chapter 8, where Indochina is discussed.
12. Report on Free French forces in Great Britain, FO892/7, Public Record Office, Kew (henceforth cited as PRO).
13. The standard history is A. J. Marder, *Operation Menace* (Oxford, 1976).
14. See, for example, de Gaulle to Churchill, 7 Aug 1940, *Lettres . . . , juin 1940–juillet 1941*, 73–4. In fact, part of de Gaulle's agreement with the British Government in August 1940 was that Parliament would enact a law that would allow members of the Free French to acquire British nationality. See Halifax to Sir John Anderson, 30 Sept 1940, Prem 4/14/5, PRO.
15. For more on this see René Cassin to Adrien Tixier, 16 Feb 1942, 382AP/59, Cassin Papers, AN.
16. Cassin to Pleven, 25 Sept 1940, 382AP/31, Cassin Papers, AN.
17. Meeting, 17 June 1940, War Cabinet conclusions, Cab 65/7, PRO.

18. Entry, 18 June 1940, in John Colville, *The Fringes of Power: Downing Street Diaries 1939–1955* (London, 1985) 164.
19. Entry, 18 February 1941, David Dilks (ed.), *The Cadogan Diaries 1938–1945* (London, 1971) 355.
20. Parr to Eden, 26 July 1941, FO 892/78, PRO.
21. Cabinet conclusions, 28 June 1940; Cab 65/7, PRO.
22. The debate on this question is in the conclusions of the War Cabinet meetings of 13 July 1940 and 15 July 1940, Cab 65/8.
23. Memorandum by the Foreign Office on relations with General de Gaulle, dated 7 Aug 1943, in WP (44) 288, 1 June 1944, Cab 66/50, PRO.
24. Entry, 3 Jan 1941, Dilks, 346. Cadogan went so far as to ring up a friend at the Home Office to ask him to make Muselier as comfortable as possible.
25. Record of conversation between the Prime Minister and General de Gaulle, 9 Jan 1941, FO 954/8, Eden Papers, PRO.
26. All of this correspondence is contained in Prem 3/120/4, PRO.
27. Entry for 26 Sept 1941, Dilks (ed.) 407. Although his name is not given in the published text, Cadogan was obviously referring to Bessborough.
28. Eden to Churchill, 26 Sept 1941, Prem 3/120/4, PRO.
29. Desmond Morton to Prime Minister, 10 July 1940, Prem 7/2, PRO.

2 Free France and the United States, 1940–42

1. Leahy to Roosevelt, 22 Nov 1941, printed in Leahy, *I Was There* (New York, 1950) 470.
2. Leahy to Roosevelt, 26 Aug 1941, Leahy, 463.
3. The 'shield' theory of Vichy was for a long time the generally accepted one amongst French historians. This concept was exploded by the American Robert Paxton in his book *Vichy France: Old Guard and New Order* (New York, 1972).
4. Roosevelt to Edwin Wilson, American representative to the French Committee, 5 Jan 1944, President's Secretary's File, France 1944–45, Franklin D. Roosevelt Library, Hyde Park, New York (henceforth cited as FDRL).
5. Leahy, 27.
6. Unofficial conversation between Baudet and Matthews, 8 June 1942, Guerre 1939–45, Londres, CNF, file no. 209, Ministère des Affaires Étrangères, Paris (henceforth cited as MAE).
7. N.a., 4 Nov 1942, 851.01/748, State Dept Papers, National Archives, Washington, D.C. (henceforth cited as NA).
8. See, for example, Tixier's reports to the National Commissary of Foreign Affairs, 10 June 1942, vol. 11 and 21 Nov 1942, vol. 210, MAE.
9. See reports from early 1941 in FO 371/28319, PRO.
10. Interrogatoire N° 3975, 31 July 1941, 382/AP/63, Cassin Papers, AN.
11. This correspondence is in FO 371/28319, PRO.
12. De Gaulle to Siéyès, N° 3722, 15 May 1941, FO 371/28320, PRO.
13. De Gaulle to Jacques de Sièyes, N° 3958, 24 May 1941, FO 371/28321, PRO.
14. Somerville Smith to Mack, 7 June 1941, FO 371/28321, PRO.
15. Ibid.

16. See memorandum by Somerville Smith to Desmond Morton, 16 May 1941, and attached minutes by Foreign Office officials, FO 371/28320.
17. De Gaulle to de Siéyès, 2 June 1941, *Lettres . . . , juin 1940–juillet 1941*, 346.
18. De Gaulle to Pleven, 20 May 1941, N° 150, Guerre 1939–45, Londres/ Alger, CNF, vol. 211, MAE.
19. This correspondence is contained in FO 371/28323, PRO.
20. See Pleven to de Gaulle, 2 Aug 1941, 382/AP/51, Cassin Papers, AN.
21. Report by Harold Mack on a conversation with Anthony Biddle, 28 May 1941, FO 371/28321; for Biddle's reports to the State Department, see, among others, 740.0011 EW1939/13148, 15460, 15921, and 23039, State Department Papers, NA; For the Burman/Biddle correspondence and British commentaries on it, see FO 371/28320, PRO.
22. Mallon to Hull, 20 Oct 1941, N° 251, *Foreign Relations of the United States, 1941, II, Europe* (Washington, 1959) 580–1 (henceforth all volumes of this series will be cited as FRUS).
23. Cunningham to de Gaulle, 25 Nov 1941, 382/AP/60/1, AN.
24. De Gaulle to Halifax for Free French delegation, 22 Jan 1942, Londres/ Alger, vol. 109, MAE.
25. De Gaulle to Muselier and Colonel Fontaine, 18 Sept 1940, Spears Papers 2/6, Churchill College Cambridge (henceforth cited as CCAC); Morton to Prime Minister, 29 Nov 1940, Prem 7/3, PRO. The standard study is Douglas Anglin, *The St Pierre and Miquelon Affaire* (Toronto, 1966).
26. Hull, *The Memoirs of Cordell Hull* (New York, 1948) 1135–6.
27. Hopkins in a private memorandum, Robert Sherwood, *Roosevelt and Hopkins: An Intimate History* (New York, 1948) 484.
28. The best analysis of the events in New Caledonia is Kim Mulholland, 'The Trials of the Free French in New Caledonia, 1940–1942', in *French Historical Studies* (Fall, 1986).
29. Minutes of 7th Meeting of Combined Chiefs of Staff, 21 Feb 1942, RG 165, ABC 336 New Caledonia, Box 246, National Archives, Washington, D.C.
30. Patch to Marshall, 21 April 1942, N° NR-9, Ibid.
31. De Gaulle to d'Argenlieu, 8 April 1942, *Lettres . . . , juillet 1941–juin 1943*, 243.
32. Patch to Marshall, 6 and 7 May 1942 in RG 165, ABC 336 New Caledonia, Box 246, NA.
33. De Gaulle to Contre-Amiral Cabanier, 9 May 1942, *Lettres . . . , juillet 1941– juin 1943*, 260–61 and British Air Ministry to Joint Staff Mission, Washington, 9 May 1942, WO 193/129, PRO.
34. De Gaulle to d'Argenlieu, 11 May 1942, *Lettres . . . , juillet 1941–juin 1943*, 261.
35. Memorandum of a conversation with Tixier by Berle, 30 April 1942, 851.00/ 3039, State Department Papers, NA.
36. See Hoover's reports in the State Department files: 851.00 and 851.01 at the National Archives in Washington.
37. No author, 29 May 1942, 851.01/558, State Department Papers, NA. See also Raoul Aglion, *Roosevelt and de Gaulle: Allies in Conflict* (NY, 1988).
38. Sumner Welles hated Tixier so much that he actually asked Roosevelt to request the Free French to transfer him. Fortunately, he was dissuaded from

this idea and instead asked Halifax to ask Eden to talk to Massigli. This correspondence is contained in the Hopkins Papers, Sherwood Collection, Box 330, Book 7, Post-Casablanca Files.

39. Berle to Dunn, 30 April 1942, 851.00/3040, State Department Papers, NA.
40. Report by Division of Near Eastern Affairs, State Department, 5 Sept 1942, RG 218, US Joint Chiefs of Staff Geographical File 1942–45, 000.1 Free French (9 May 1942), NA.
41. De Gaulle to Cassin, 8 July 1941, *Lettres . . . , juin 1940–juillet 1941*, 384–5.
42. Memorandum by the French National Committee, 15 June 1942 and memorandum of a conversation with Adrien Tixier by Adolf Berle, both in 851.01/8501/2, State Department Papers, NA. When de Gaulle, at the Hôtel de Ville on 26 August 1944, gave his famous reply to Georges Bidault's request that he proclaim the Fourth Republic ('No, the Republic has never ceased to exist'), he meant exactly what he said. The Republic had simply gone with him to London.
43. De Gaulle to Roosevelt, *War Memoirs, II, Documents*, 66–71.
44. Atherton to Welles, 26 Oct 1942, *FRUS 1942, II, Europe* (Washington, 1962) 544.

3 Lebanon and Syria

1. Needless to say, this had provoked a sharp response from de Gaulle, who agreed that the decision was a good one, but resented that Churchill had made it during his absence and that he (de Gaulle) had not actually given the order. It was a case of not respecting French sovereignty. See de Gaulle to Catroux, 22 Sept 1940, *Lettres . . . juin 1940–juillet 1941*, 119.
2. Catroux to de Larminat, 19 March 1941, AJ/72/428/A, Catroux Papers, AN.
3. Catroux to de Gaulle, 19 March 1941, Ibid.
4. The text of Catroux's declaration, in the original French, and the British declaration supporting it is given in Annex 1 to Woodward, *British Foreign Policy during World War II, I* (London, 1971) 584–6.
5. Catroux to Eden, 29 May 1941, AJ/72/428/A, Catroux Papers, AN.
6. O-in-C Middle East to War Office, 16 July 1941, Spears Papers, Box 1, Middle East Centre, St Antony's College, Oxford (henceforth cited as MECSAC).
7. De Gaulle to Spears, 13 July 1941, *Lettres . . . juillet 1941–mai 1943*, 389.
8. For an account of this meeting see Spears diary, 21 July 1941, Spears Papers, Box 1, Ibid., and de Gaulle, *War Memoirs, I*, 190–6.
9. De Gaulle to Cassin, 2 Aug 1941, *Lettres, juillet 1941–mai 1943*, 35.
10. Spears to Somerville Smith, 17 July 1941, Spears Papers, Box 1, MECSAC.
11. The Lyttelton–de Gaulle correspondence and accords are published in Woodward, I, 586–93.
12. C-in-C Middle East to War Office, op cit.
13. See, for example, de Gaulle, 'Note sans indication d'utilisation', 5 Aug 1941, *Lettres . . . , juillet 1941–mai 1943*, 41–2, in which he says, among other things: 'The Free French cannot accept that their effort in Syria and the Lebanon in cooperation with the British should end in the usurpation of France's rights by her own ally.'

14. De Gaulle to Cassin, 1 Aug 1941, Ibid., 34.
15. Despatch from Beyrouth, 17 April 1942, 382 AP/60/1, Cassin Papers, AN.
16. Spears Diary, 2 Aug 1941, Spears Papers, Box 1, MECSAC & de Gaulle to Lyttelton, 2 Aug 1941, *Lettres . . . juillet 1941–mai 1943*, 35–6.
17. Catroux to Lyttelton, 1 Aug 1941, AJ/72/428/C, Catroux Papers, AN.
18. Spears to Churchill, n.d., Spears Papers, 1/134 CCAC.
19. Spears Mission Diary, 12 Oct 1940, Spears Papers 2/6, CCAC.
20. For Catroux's side of things see his memoirs, *Dans la bataille* (Paris, 1949).
21. Spears Diary, 23 Aug 1942, Spears Papers, Box 1, MECSAC.
22. De Gaulle to Pleven, 14 Aug 1942, *War Memoirs, II Documents*, 39.
23. Entry, 10 June 1945, Harvey diary, 383.
24. Edwin Wilson, 'Memorandum of a Conversation with President Roosevelt', 24 March 1944, 851.00/3185 1/2, State Department Papers, NA.
25. Catroux to Carlton Gardens, 7 June 1942, 72 AJ/429, Catroux Papers, AN.
26. Catroux to Carlton Gardens, 20 May 1942, Ibid.
27. Wallace Murray to Wadsworth, 7 April 1943, 740.0011 EW/28083, State Department Papers, NA.
28. Catroux to Carlton Gardens, 7 Aug 1942, op cit.
29. For Gwynn's reports to Washington, see the series 740.0011EW, State Department Papers, NA. Some are published in FRUS.
30. De Gaulle to Pleven and Dejean, 16 Aug 1942, *War Memoirs, II, Documents*, 39–40.
31. Catroux on a meeting with the Consul-General of the United States in Kabul, 2 May 1942, 72AJ/429, Catroux Papers, AN.
32. Division of European Affairs, State Department, 7 Sept 1942, RG 218, Joint Chiefs of Staff, Geographic File, 1942–5, 000.1 Free French (9 May 1942).
33. West European and African Sections, OSS, 8 Sept 1942, Ibid.
34. De Gaulle to Pleven and Dejean, 11 Aug 1942, *War Memoirs, II, Documents*, 35.
35. See, in particular, Halifax's despatch to the Foreign Office during the Lebanese crisis of November 1943, in which he warns that: 'Display of indignation by us at the arrest of Lebanese leaders would meet with very little sympathy in the U.S. press which, however unjustifiably, would draw analogy with the imprisonment of Gandhi and Nehru.' 16 Nov 1943, FO 660/38, PRO.
36. See Wallace Murray to Wadsworth, 7 April 1943, op cit.
37. Memorandum by Lt Col Harold Hoskins, 9 Oct 1943, *FRUS 1943, IV: Near East and Africa* (Washington, 1964) 996.
38. Department of State to British Embassy, 25 Oct 1943, Ibid., 999.
39. The correspondence between Churchill and de Gaulle is published in de Gaulle, *War Memoirs, II, Documents*.
40. 'Minutes of a meeting with Wendell Wilkie', 10 Sept 1942, *Lettres . . . juillet 1941–mai 1943*, 382.
41. Spears to Foreign Office, 28 July 1943, FO 660/35, PRO.
42. Lord Duncannon?, 'Anglo-French Relations in Syria and Lebanon, April–October 1943', FO 660/36, PRO.
43. Foreign Office to Spears, 6 Nov 1943, FO 660/37, PRO.
44. See Wadsworth to Secretary of State, 24 Oct 1943, *FRUS 1943, IV, Near East and Africa*, 998.
45. Foreign Office to Resmin, 11 Nov 1943, FO 660/37, PRO.

46.   Eden to Minister of State Cairo, 11 Nov 1943, Ibid.
47.   Eden to Resmin, 14 Nov 1943, Ibid.
48.   The text of this communication is printed in de Gaulle, *War Memoirs, II, Documents*, 291–2.
49.   Kimball, II, C-504, 13 Nov 1943, 599.
50.   De Gaulle to Catroux, 13 Nov 1943, *War Memoirs, II, Documents*, 291.
51.   De Gaulle to Helleu, 13 Nov 1943, Ibid., 292–3.
52.   Makins to Foreign Office, 12 Nov 1943, FO 660/37, PRO.
53.   Casey to Foreign Office, 14 Nov 1943, Ibid.
54.   Casey to Foreign Office, 15 Nov 1943, Ibid.
55.   Macmillan, 'Record of a Conversation with Palewski', 18 Nov 1943, FO 660/38.
56.   Minister of State to Resmin, 18 Nov 1943, FO 660/38, PRO.
57.   Macmillan, 'Record of a Conversation with Catroux', 1 Dec 1943, FO 660/40, PRO.
58.   Resmin to Foreign Office, 23 Nov 1943, FO 660/40, PRO.
59.   Chataigneau to Massigli, 10 Jan 1944, F60/826, AN.
60.   Report by Sûreté aux Armes de Beyrouth, 1 July 1944, F60/824, AN.
61.   Beynet to Bidault, 3 Nov 1944, Ibid. Most of his reports are contained in this series.
62.   'Foreign Office Memorandum on Spears's Conduct in the Arming of Gendarmerie', 23 July 1944, E4423/217/819, FO 371/40314, PRO. This file also contains other correspondence relative to this affair, including Eden's memorandum giving the history of the dispute, 23 July 1944, E4425.
63.   See Woodward, IV, 239 and Ralph Smith, Military Attaché Paris to Bissell, War Department, 1 June 1945, RG 218, Joint Chiefs of Staff, Chariman's file, Leahy, 1942–48, Box 4, Folder 18, NA.
64.   Entry, 20 Oct 1944, Harvey diary, 364.
65.   Memorandum by Wadsworth, 16 Oct 1944, RG 226, OSS Papers, entry 17, 106015.
66.   Woodward, IV, 335.
67.   Churchill to de Gaulle, 31 May 1945, *FRUS 1945, VIII, Near East and Africa* (Washington, 1969) 1124

4 North Africa, 1940–42

1.   Robert Murphy, *Diplomat Among Warriors* (Garden City, New York, 1964) 68. In his memoirs Leahy insists that: 'The idea of an invasion of Africa was not new. Roosevelt had had it in mind for a long time, and, by his direction, some advance preparation had been made before I returned from France.' Leahy goes on to insist that: 'It has been said that Roosevelt ordered "Operation Torch" in the face of opposition from his senior advisers. I never opposed the North African invasion.' He claims that only Marshall was really opposed to the idea. Leahy, 111.
2.   For more information on this, the memoirs of one of these vice-consuls, Kenneth Pendar, *Adventure in Diplomacy: Our French Dilemma* (New York, 1945) is particularly interesting, although seriously flawed by the author's excessive detestation of de Gaulle.

3.   Murphy, 97–8.
4.   Dwight Eisenhower, *Crusade in Europe* (Garden City, 1948) 88.
5.   See Foreign Office to Washington Embassy, N° 2597; 15 May 1941, T 160/
     1106/F17672, PRO.
6.   Report dated 3 Feb 1941, FO 892/105, PRO.
7.   The excellent biography of Darlan by Hervé Coutau-Bégarie and Claude
     Huan (Paris, 1989) has done much to show Darlan as a more sympathetic
     and consistent personality than his popular image. It is difficult, however, to
     do away with the label of opportunist.
8.   27 May 1942, 382AP/31, Cassin Papers, AN.
9.   Cole (Murphy) to War Department, ? Oct 1942, *FRUS 1942, II Europe*
     (Washington D.C., 1962) 392.
10. Ibid., 15 Oct 1942, 394.
11. Entry, 8 Nov 1942, Harry Butcher, *My Three Years with Eisenhower* (New
     York, 1946) 178.
12. Entry, 2 Sept 1942, Robert H. Ferrell (ed.), *The Eisenhower Diaries* (Lon-
     don, 1981) 76–7.
13. 'Note on a conversation with General Eisenhower', 13 Aug 1942, in Bullitt,
     560.
14. At Churchill's urging. See Churchill to Roosevelt, 1 Sept 1942, C-142,
     Kimball, I, 585.
15. 'Mr. Robert Murphy', Elsey Papers, HSTL. Cordell Hull says as much in
     his memoirs, 1196–7.
16. Roosevelt to Churchill, 2 Sept 1942, N° 182, Kimball, I, 589.
17. Churchill to Roosevelt, 14 Sept 1942, Ibid., I, 594.
18. Entry, 7 Nov 1942, Butcher, 171.
19. Eisenhower to Combined Chiefs of Staff, 8 Nov 1942, in Alfred Chandler,
     et al. (eds) *The Papers of Dwight David Eisenhower: The War Years, II*
     (London, 1970) 670–1.
20. Eisenhower to Smith, 9 Nov 1942, Chandler, II, 677.
21. 'Note sur les evenements d'Alger dans la nuit du 29–30 décembre', 8 June
     1943, F/1a/3732, AN.
22. Eisenhower to Smith, 9 Nov 1942, op cit.
23. 'Record of Events and Documents from the Date that Lieutenant General
     Mark W. Clark entered into Negotiations with Admiral Jean François Darlan
     until Darlan was assassinated on Christmas Eve, 1942, p. 4, Box 35, folder
     1, Mark Clark Papers, the Citadel, Charleston, South Carolina.
24. Ibid., 10.
25. Eisenhower to Clark, 10 Nov 1942, Chandler, II, 683.
26. Eisenhower to Combined Chiefs of Staff, 14 Nov 1942, Chandler, II, 707.
27. Which was apparently real. Hervé Coutau-Bégarie and Claude Huan found
     and published (*Darlan*, Paris, 1989) a telegram from Pétain giving his ben-
     ediction to Darlan's action. See *Darlan*, 619.
28. *The New York Times* was among the most charitable, saying on 17 Nov
     1942: 'we do not for a moment believe that the course our Government is
     following means that we have mistaken our enemies for friends, or lost
     interest in the real cause for which our friends are fighting – namely, the life
     of the French Republic . . . The French Republic never had a better friend
     than the President who directs our policy in this crisis.'

29. 12 Nov 1942, col. 137, *Parliamentary Debates*, House of Commons, vol. 385.
30. See Charles Eade (ed.), *Winston Churchill's Secret Session Speeches* (London, 1946) 98–9. The complete text of Churchill's speech is not printed here, as certain derogatory references to General de Gaulle have been deleted. The complete speech can be found in 'France and the Free French, 1942–45' (3), Map Room Papers, FDRL.
31. Report of a telephone conversation between the President and Cordell Hull on Hull's meeting with Tixier and Philip, 14 Nov 1942, Reel 35, France General 1937–44, Hull Papers, Library of Congress (henceforth cited as LC).
32. Memorandum of a conversation between Hull, Tixier, d'Argenlieu and Atherton by Ray Atherton, 8 Dec 1942, reel 29, Free French groups, Hull Papers, LC.
33. Hull to Algiers, 25 Nov 1942, 851R.00/108A, State Department Papers, N.A.; to Algiers, 30 Nov 1942, Hull Papers, LC.
34. Churchill to Roosevelt, 17 Nov 1942, C-193, Kimball, II, 7.
35. Entries, 15 and 19 Nov 1942, Dilks, 493–495.
36. British Chiefs of Staff to Eisenhower, 2 Jan 1943, FO 660/11, PRO.
37. De Gaulle to Catroux, Eboué, etc., 10 Nov 1942, de Gaulle, *War Memoirs, II, Documents*, 80.
38. Donovan to General Deane, 22 Dec 1942, RG 218, Joint Chiefs of Staff, Central Decimal File 1942–5, CCS 385.7 (10 Oct 1942) NA.
39. 12 Nov 1942, col. 136, *Parliamentary Debates, House of Commons*, vol. 385.
40. Record of an interview between de Gaulle and Churchill, 16 Nov 1942, *War Memoirs, II, Documents*, 91.
41. War Cabinet 165 (42), 7 Dec 1942, Cabinet 65/28, PRO.
42. War Cabinet 171 (42), 21 Dec 1942, Ibid.
43. T. S. Kittredge, 'Record of a Conversation of Gen. de Lattre de Tassigny and Ambassador Winant, 10 Nov 43, 11 Nov 43,' F/la/3735, AN.
44. Entry, 27 Dec 1942, Dilks, 500.
45. The best account of Darlan's work by far in North Africa is the biography by Coutau-Bégarie and Huan. I have followed them closely.
46. 'North Africa: Summary of Proposed Course of Action', 24 Dec 1942, Hopkins Papers, Sherwood Collection, Box 330, Book 7, Post-Casablanca Files, FDRL.
47. 'Report on . . .', 82, Clark Papers, the Citadel.
48. Entry, 29 Nov 1942, Butcher, 207.
49. Matthews to Secretary of State, 26 Dec 1942, 851R.00/125, State Department Papers, NA.
50. Ibid., 90.
51. Murphy, 143.
52. 'Report on . . .', 91, Clark Papers, the Citadel.
53. 'Note sur les Evénements d'Alger dans la nuit du 29–30 décembre', 8 June 1943, F/1a/3732, AN. The other reports cited are also contained in this box.
54. J. C. Holmes to Chief of Staff (Smith), 10 Jan 1943, FO 660/12, PRO.
55. Hull and Marshall to Eisenhower and Murphy, 9 Jan 1943, Torch 1, Section 5, Map Room Papers, FDRL.

56. PD (P. J. Dixon?) 'Political Situation in North Africa, 11 Jan 1943, FO 660/
     12, PRO.
57. Resmin to Foreign Office, 9 Feb 1943, Z1984, FO 371/36118, PRO.
58. Memorandum by Carvell, British Consulate General, 8 Jan 1943, FO 660/
     14, PRO.
59. Memorandum by Harold Macmillan?, 8 Jan 1943, FO 660/14, PRO.
60. Political and Economic Council Meeting, 12 Jan 1943, 851.00/242, State
     Department Papers, NA.
61. Murphy to Combined Chiefs of Staff, 13 Jan 1943, Torch 1, Sec 5, Map
     Room Papers, FDRL.

5 Unity? 1943–44

1.   This fact was not lost on the French, who wrote in Document N° 18, from
     the Centre d'Information et de documentation. 'One must distinguish be-
     tween the policy of the United States and of England. The imperial policy
     of England in the present situation is conservative and defensive. That of the
     United States is expansionist.' 15 Dec 1943, F/1a/3790, AN.
2.   Although Roosevelt's anti-imperialism could be a bit selective. He was
     quite vocal about India, which, after all, thanks to Gandhi's nonviolent
     campaign for independence, had captured the popular imagination. On other
     countries, such as Burma, he was much less anti-imperialist.
3.   Murphy, 54.
4.   Leahy, 167. Although it must be admitted that Admiral Leahy, because of
     the traditional rivalry between the British and American navies, was more
     likely to be suspicious of the British.
5.   Entry, 31 Dec 1942, Blum, Wallace Diary, 159.
6.   Peake to Mack, 7 Aug 1943, FO 660/22, PRO.
7.   Entry, 31 March 1943, Leahy Diary, LC.
8.   Matthews to Hull, 1 Jan 1943, *FRUS, 1943, II, Europe* (Washington, 1964)
     24.
9.   Matthews to Leahy, 10 Dec 1942, Leahy Papers, LC.
10. See the chapter on 'Lend Lease and the Open Door'.
11. Eden to Halifax, 22 Feb 1943, FO 954/8, Avon Papers, PRO.
12. Entry, 1 Feb 1942, H. G. Nicholas (ed.), *Washington Despatches 1941–45,
     Weekly Political Reports from the British Embassy* (London, 1981), 143.
13. Leahy, 112–13.
14. The best analysis of Roosevelt's conduct of foreign policy is without ques-
     tion, Warren Kimball's *The Juggler: Franklin D. Roosevelt as Wartime
     Statesman* (Princeton, 1991).
15. Entry, 7 June 1943, Leahy Diary, LC.
16. Michael Wright to Mack, 12 Aug 1943, FO 660/21, PRO.
17. Memorandum by Bullitt, 11 March 1944, Bullitt, 604.
18. Hoppenot to F.C.N.L., 1 June 1944, de Gaulle, *War Memoirs, II, Docu-
     ments,* 336.
19. Eden to Halifax, 8 Jan 1943, FO 954/8, Avon Papers, PRO.
20. Entry, 8 Feb 1943, Harvey diary, 218.
21. Anthony Eden, draft Cabinet memorandum 'United States Policy towards

France', 12? July 1943, Z8225/8, FO 371/36301, PRO. Much of this was actually written by Strang.

22. Glassford, 'French West Africa', 27 Feb 1943, Map Room Papers, France and the Free French, 1942–45 (3) FDRL.
23. Resident Minister's Office, Algiers to Foreign Office, N° 1289, 24 July 1943, and Harold Macmillan, 'Record of a conversation with Glassford on 28 July 1943', 30 July 1943, Lord Swinton Papers 270/5/8, CCAC.
24. Eisenhower to Maxwell Taylor, 24 Jan 1944, Chandler, III, 1683.
25. *Sunday Telegraph*, 9 Feb 1964, quoted in Alister Horne, *Harold Macmillan, 1: 1894–1956* (London, 1988) 160.
26. Harold Macmillan, *The Blast of War* (London, 1967) 245.
27. See the chapter 'Celebrity Conference in Casablanca' in Murphy.
28. See, for example, entries for 18 June 1943 and 18 Oct 1943, 125 & 259.
29. The standard work on Monnet's role is André Kaspi, *La mission de Jean Monnet à Alger* (Paris, 1971).
30. Monnet to Hopkins, 4 Feb 1943, Hopkins Papers, Sherwood Collection, Book 7: Post Casablanca Files, FDRL.
31. Robert Sherwood, *Roosevelt and Hopkins: An Intimate History* (New York, 1948) 679.
32. President to Eisenhower, 22 Feb 1943, Hopkins Papers, Sherwood Collection, op cit.
33. Monnet to Hopkins, 8 March 1943, Ibid.
34. Catroux to de Gaulle, N° 7 CAB, 28 March 1943, F/1a/3715, AN.
35. Catroux to de Gaulle, 15 May 1943, N° 500 Cab 900, F/1a/3715, AN.
36. Murphy to Hull, 24 April 1943, *FRUS, 1943, II Europe*, 100.
37. Monnet to Hopkins, 6 May 1943, Hopkins Papers, Sherwood Collection, op cit.
38. Catroux to de Gaulle, 28 March 1943, F/1a/3715, AN.
39. Churchill to Roosevelt, C-298, 31 May 1943, Kimball, II, 228.
40. Entry, 16 June 1943, Macmillan, *War Diaries*, 124. For de Gaulle's rather sarcastic account of this meeting see the *War Memoirs, II*, 129–31.
41. Entry, 22 June 1943, *War Diaries*, 131.
42. Murphy to Hull and Welles, 17 July 1943, *FRUS, 1943, II, Europe*, 172–3.
43. Murphy to Under Secretary, 31 July 1943, Ibid, 179.
44. Halifax to Foreign Office, N° 3328, 21 July 1943, Z8146/G, FO 371/36301, PRO.
45. For more on this see pp. 164–5.
46. See Murphy's summary of the situation in Roosevelt to Churchill, R-359, 25 Sept 1943, Kimball, II, 465.
47. Harold Macmillan, 'Memorandum on recognition', 3 Jan 1944, Prem 3/182/6, PRO.
48. Churchill to Roosevelt, C-513, 21 Dec 1943, Kimball, II, 625.
49. In Roosevelt to Churchill, R-423, 22 Dec 1943, Kimball, II, 626.
50. George M. Elsey Papers, notes used to prepare briefings for President Truman, Truman Library, Independence, Missouri (henceforth cited as HSTL).
51. Macmillan to Foreign Office, N° 2871, 1 Jan 1944, Prem 3/182/3, PRO.
52. Chapin, Acting U.S. representative to the Committee to Hull, 17 Jan 1944, *FRUS, 1944, III: Europe*, 645. De Gaulle is obviously taunting Churchill when he says 'democratic influence'. In effect he is saying that the Allies

had insisted on democratizing the Committee, and the Consultative Assembly, whose creation was decided on 17 September 1943, was the result. Unfortunately, it did not always behave as the Anglo-Americans wished.

53. Henri Frenay, *The Night Will End* (Eng. trans. New York, 1976), 321.
54. Eisenhower to Combined Chiefs of Staff and Combined Civil Affairs Committee, 19 Jan 1944, Chandler, III, 1667.
55. Quoted in Woodward, *III*, 10.
56. Halifax to Foreign Office, 5 Dec 1943, Prem 3/177/6, PRO.
57. Halifax to Foreign Office, 2 March 1944, U1745/G, FO 371/40362, PRO.
58. Halifax to Foreign Office, 11 March 1944, U2006, Ibid.
59. Minute by Mack, 21 March 1944, U2385, Ibid.
60. Duff Cooper to Foreign Office, N° 377, 24 March 1944, U2492, Ibid.
61. Edwin Wilson, 'Memorandum of a Conversation with the President', 24 March 1944, 851.00/31851/2, State Department Papers, NA.
62. Hull, 1429.

6 The Anglo-Americans and the Resistance in France

1. This is what H. R. Kedward has shown in his book *Resistance in Vichy France* (London, 1988).
2. Passy, 'Relations entre le BCRAM et les services secrets britanniques', 18 March 1942, F/1a/3729, AN.
3. Mack, 'Record of a Conversation with Pleven', 8 May 1941, FO 371/28321, PRO. There are a large number of entries on this subject in de Gaulle, *Lettres . . . juillet 1941–mai 1943.*
4. The most important scandal was that related to Dufour who had committed suicide after interrogation at Passy's offices. The documentation is in FO 371/36031, PRO.
5. Passy, 'Relations entre le BCRAM . . .' op cit.
6. W. P. Maddox, 'OSS Report on French Underground', August 1942, 851.00/2945, State Department Papers, NA.
7. 'La Résistance et SOE; la Résistance et OSS' in 'Histoire de la Résistance', (Official Anglo-Franco-American history) Ziegler Papers, Carton 1, Ministère de la Défense Nationale, Vincennes (henceforth cited as MDN).
8. Ibid.
9. For more on this see Passy? 'Memorandum pour Monsieur le Chef de l'Etat-Major Particulier', 8 May 1942, F/1a/3729, AN.
10. Maddox, 'OSS Report on French Underground', op cit.
11. 'Objective Consideration of the Report of March 27, 1943, entitled: "Survey of Underground Organisations in France" by OSS (Research and Analysis Branch)', 22 April 1943, F/1a/3729, AN.
12. Wiley (Murphy) to Secretary of State, 28 Aug 1943, 851.01/2799, State Department Papers, NA.
13. Henri Frenay, *The Night Will End* (English translation, New York, 1976) 124.
14. See de Gaulle to Moulin, 22 Oct 1942, de Gaulle, *War Memoirs, II, Documents*, 60.
15. Bernard, 'Note sur le problème syndical', 16 Oct 1942, F/1a/3730, AN.

16. Report by Rex, 7 May 1943, Emmanuel d'Astier de la Vigerie Papers, 72AJ/410, AN.
17. Kittredge, 'Report on Claudius of FTP', 15 Nov 1943, Box 10, Devers Papers, York County Historical Association, York, Pennsylvania.
18. 'Report on the Resistance', RG 218, Joint Chiefs of Staff, Geographic File 1942–5, 091.411 France (28 Aug 1943) Box 47, NA.
19. 'La Résistance et SOE . . .', op cit.
20. 'Resistance by the General Public in France', SHAEF/17253/1/OPS, 29 April 1944, WO 219/212, PRO.
21. Wilson to Secretary of State, 11 Jan 1944, *FRUS 1944, III, Europe,* 637.
22. Hull to Leahy, 20 March 1944, RG 218, US JCS, Geographic File 1942–5, 400 France (18 Jan 1944) Box 53, NA.
23. Joint Staff Planners, 'Report on the Resistance', 31 March 1944, Ibid.
24. Marshall to Hull, 17 April 1944, Ibid.
25. Hull to Marshall, 26 April 1944, Ibid., sec 2.
26. Eisenhower to Joint Chiefs of Staff, 1 May 1944, Ibid.
27. Murphy to Secretary of State, 12 May 1944, 851.001/50, State Department Papers, NA.
28. Joint Staff Planners, 'Allied Assistance to Resistance', 17 May 1944, RG 218, Georgraphic File, 1942–5, op cit.
29. Hull to Chapin, 30 May 1944, *FRUS, 1944, III: Europe,* 693.
30. Eisenhower to Marshall, 10 July 1944, Chandler, III, 1992.
31. Koenig to Smith, 24 May 1944, WO 219/14, PRO.
32. Koenig to Brigadier Mockler-Ferryman, 1 July 1944, Ibid.
33. Merlin to de Gaulle, confidential from Cléante, 2 Feb 1944, F/1a/3718, AN.
34. See, for example, OSS report, 7 June 1944, RG 218, Joint Chiefs of Staff, Chairman's file, Leahy 1942–8, Box 4, folder 19, NA.
35. Oronte to d'Astier, 2 July 1944, Emmanuel d'Astier de la Vigerie Papers, 72AJ/410/2, AN.
36. Marshall to Eisenhower and Devers, 9 July 1944, RG 218 Joint Chiefs of Staff, Geographic File 1942–5, 400 France (3 Nov 1942) sec 4.
37. SHAEF Psychological Warfare Division, Intelligence Section, 'Special Report (France) N° 10', N.D. (summer 1944?), WO 219/112, PRO.
38. Boris to d'Astier, 22 Aug 1944, F/1a/3716, AN.
39. SOE, 'Memorandum on FFI', 7 Oct 1944, FO 660/213, PRO.
40. 'Report to General de Gaulle by a high official touring the Midi', 6 Sept 1944, de Gaulle, *War Memoirs, III, Documents,* 13.

7 The Financial Link

1. Cabinet Conclusions, 13 July 1940, Cab 65/8, PRO.
2. Treasury Report, 'Memorandum on the Present Position of the Free French African Empire', n.d. (7 June 1941?), Z4643/4445/17, T160/1106/F17672, PRO.
3. De Gaulle to Governors of French Equatorial Africa, 24 March 1941, 382AP/63, Cassin Papers, AN.
4. 'Les réalisations coloniales de la France Combattante en AEF', 6 Jan 1943, 382AP/60/1, Cassin Papers, AN.

5. Kingsley Wood to Churchill, 12 June 1943, Prem 3 181/7, PRO.
6. 'Proceedings of the French National Committee', 19 Jan 1943, 72AJ/567, André Philip Papers, AN.
7. 'Pret-Bail', 20 Dec 1943, Monnet Dossier, F60/921, AN.
8. CFLN, Secrétariat du Comité, 30 Sept 1943, Ibid.
9. Joint Chiefs of Staff Memorandum, 'The Effect of Political Disturbances on Military Operations in North Africa', 23 Jan 1943, RG 218 JCS Papers, Central Decimal File 1942–5, CCS 385.7 (10 Oct 1942) sec 2, NA.
10. Cole to Hull from Murphy, 17 Nov 1942, *FRUS 1942, II: Europe*, 443.
11. Hull to Cole for Murphy, 18 Nov 1942, Ibid., 444.
12. Hull to Cole for Murphy, 21 Nov 1942, Ibid., 449–50.
13. Murphy to Smith, 2 Sept 1943, WO 204/239, PRO.
14. Deane to Hull, 12 Nov 1942, RG 218, USJCS, Central Decimal File, 1942–5, CCS 385.2 (24 June 1942) sec 4, NA.
15. Political Warfare Executive memorandum, 'Green Tea for French North Africa', n.d., FO 898/135, PRO.
16. Political Warfare Executive memorandum, 'Cotton Textiles for French North Africa', n.d., Ibid.
17. See 10 Nov 1943 entry, Macmillan, *War Diaries*, 287. Even such a sympathetic observer as Macmillan found that the French were 'better "takers" than "givers"' on this question.
18. Bernard Bernstein, 'Dollar–Franc Rate of Exchange in Africa', 16 Jan 1943, WO 204/239, PRO.
19. The standard work on this subject is Marcel Vigneras, *Rearming the French* (Washington, 1986). See also Chapter 5 in this book.
20. Eisenhower to Combined and British Chiefs of Staff, 4 Jan 1943, Chandler, II, 891.
21. 61st Meeting, Combined Chiefs of Staff, 19 Jan 1942, RG 218, USJCS, Geographic File 1942–45, 400 France, Box 54, sec 1, NA.
22. Marshall to McCloy, 4 Feb 1943, Ibid.
23. Adm. Leahy, at JCS, 64th Meeting, 3 Feb 1943, Ibid.
24. Vigneras, 36–7.
25. Forrest C. Pogue, *George C. Marshall: Organizer of Victory, 1943–1945* (New York, 1973) 233.
26. Sir John Dill at CCS, 74th Meeting, 3 May 1942, RG 218, USJCS, Geographic File, op cit.
27. General Macready at CCS, 75th Meeting, Supplementary Minutes, 12 March 1943, Ibid.
28. Eisenhower to Marshall, 18 Feb 1943, Chandler, II, 963.
29. Murphy to Secretary of State (signed Wiley), 18 Feb 1943, Map Room Papers, France and the Free French, 1942–45 (3) FDRL.
30. Roosevelt to Hull, draft of a letter to Murphy, 20 Feb 1943, Ibid.
31. 'Memorandum of a Conversation' between McCloy and Col. Swatland and State Department officials, 25 March 1943, 740.0011 EW/28900, State Department papers, NA.
32. Eisenhower to the Secretariat, Combined Chiefs of Staff, 1 Nov 1944, Chandler, IV, 2272.
33. BCRA, Memorandum, 26 June 1943, F/1a/3721, AN.
34. Etat-Major particulier de de Gaulle to Passy, 3 May 1943, Ibid.

35. D'Astier de la Vigerie to Boris, 18 Jan 1944, F/1a/3715, AN.
36. BCRA, 'Note: Financement de la Résistance: pourparlers avec la Trésorerie britannique', 21 Jan 1944, F/1a/3721, AN.
37. CFLN, Secrétariat Général du Comité, 30 Sept 1943, op cit.
38. Monnet to the Assistant Secreatry of State, Dean Acheson, 7 Jan 1944, *FRUS, 1944, III: Europe*, 748–9.
39. Department of State to French Supply Council, 15 March 1944, Ibid., 753–5.
40. Hull to President, 15 July 1944, President's Secretary's file, FDRL contains the draft memorandum which Roosevelt subsequently approved. The actual memorandum to the French Committee is dated 20 July 1944 and published in *FRUS, 1944, III, Europe*, 757–8.
41. Hull to President, 11 Sept 1944, Ibid., 761. It is interesting to note that Hull also writes in this memorandum: 'What seems to me necessary is to leave in your hands complete discretion to do what you may think necessary from time to time in the light of French behavior.' Hull clearly believes that financial assistance to France was, and should be, a useful lever to achieve some degree of control over the French.
42. Minutes of 15 Jan 1945 meeting of Economic Committee, F60/898, AN.
43. 'Note sur les Accords Prêt-Bail américain', 19? Feb 1945, Ibid.
44. Minutes of the 19 Feb 1945 meeting of the Economic Committee, 24 Nov 1945, Ibid.

8 The Provisional Government of France, 1944–45

1. Entry, 4 June 1944, Piers Dixon, *Double Diploma: The Life of Sir Pierson Dixon, Don and Diplomat* (London, 1968), 91.
2. Entry, 5 June 1944, Dilks, 634–5.
3. Coulet to Military Delegate, 18 June 1944, F60/892, AN.
4. Acting Secretary of State to Acting American Representative to FCNL (Chapin) 10 June 1944, *FRUS, 1944, III, Europe*, 705.
5. Acting Representative (Chapin) to Secretary of State, 12 June 1944, Ibid., 710.
6. 'Confidential Annex to Conclusions of the War Cabinet', 13 June 1944, Prem 3 177/2, PRO.
7. FCNL, Note to British and American Governments, 8 June 1944, de Gaulle, *War Memoirs, II, Documents*, 338.
8. Koenig to de Gaulle, 28 June 1944, F/1a/3716, AN.
9. 8 July 1944, 'Civil Affairs in Liberated France', XL1431, RG 226, OSS Papers, entry 17, NA.
10. Coulet to Koenig, 3 July 1944, & General Secretary of the Police in the Rouen area to the Assistant Director of the Sûreté, 9 July 1944, both in F60/892, AN.
11. Chevigné to Koenig, 'Rapport des activités, 14–25 June 1944', 8P8, MDN.
12. Transcript of interrogation of SS general, 22 Nov 1944, Martin Blumenson (ed.), *The Patton Papers* (Boston, 1974) 577–8.
13. OSS report, n.d., June 1944?, RG 218, US Joint Chiefs of Staff, Chairman's file, Leahy, Box 5, folder 20, NA. Other relevant documents are: Caffery to

Secretary of State, 3 Jan 1945, *FRUS, 1945 Europe, IV*, 661–5 and reports on interallied relations in F/1a/3304 and 3306, AN.

14. John Boyd, 'Political Tendencies in Marseille Region', 29 Dec 1944, 851.00/ 1–245, LM 108 microfilm roll 1, State Department Papers, NA.
15. Eisenhower to Bedell Smith, 22 Sept 1944, Chandler, IV, 2182.
16. Marshall, King and Arnold to President. S-53809, 13 June 1944, RG 218, Joint Chiefs of Staff, Chairman's file, Leahy, 1942–48, Box 4, folder 19, NA.
17. Memorandum for the President, President's Secretary's File, France, 1944– 45, FDRL.
18. Belladone to General Koenig and Comidac, N° 52–5, 17 Aug 1944, F/1a/ 3718, AN.
19. Belladone to Comidac, N° 60–1, 18 Aug 1944, Ibid.
20. Patton diary, 15 & 17 August 1944, Blumenson, 511 & 516.
21. SHAEF to War Department, 16 Aug 1944, N° S57762, Map Room Papers, 011, French Civil Affairs, FDRL.
22. Entry, 20 Aug 1944 Harvey, 352–3.
23. De Gaulle, *War Memoirs, II, Documents*, 403.
24. Eisenhower to Marshall, 21 Aug 1944, Chandler, IV, 2088.
25. Winant (Phillips) to Secretary of State (Dunn), 26 Aug 1944, *FRUS, 1944, III, Europe*, 731.
26. Eisenhower, *Crusade in Europe*, 297–8, de Gaulle in *The New York Times*, 7 Dec 1948. One thing seems certain: Eisenhower had no reason to invent such a story, while de Gaulle had every reason to deny it.
27. OSS report, 7 June 1944, and comment by OSS Berne, same date, RG 218, Joint Chiefs of Staff, Chairman's file, Leahy 1942–8, Box 4, folder 19, NA.
28. Memorandum of a conference between James Forrestal and Charles de Gaulle, 18 Aug 1944, Map Room, France and the Free French, 1942–45 (3) FDRL.
29. Harriman to the President and the Secretary of State, N° 4700, 8 Dec 1944, President's Secretary's File, France, 1944–45, FDRL.
30. Caffery to the Acting Secretary of State, 5 May 1945, *FRUS 1945, IV, Europe*, 686.
31. Report by Major J. R. Greenwood, n.d., RG 165 War Department, ABC Papers, 014 France, 17 Dec 43, Sec 1, NA.
32. Eisenhower to Joint Chiefs of Staff, N° S63111, 20 Oct 1944, Map Room, 011, Sec 2, French Civil Affairs, FDRL.
33. Memorandum by the Secretary of State to President Roosevelt, 17 Sept 1944, *FRUS, 1944, III, Europe*, 735–6.
34. Memorandum to President Roosevelt, 21 Sept 1944, Ibid., 737–8.
35. Churchill to Roosevelt, 14 Oct 1944, C-798, Kimball, III, 355–6.
36. Special information for the President, 13 April 1945, Records of Executive Secretariat (Dean Acheson), memorandums for the president, 1944–49, Lot 53D444, Box 1, Lot Files, State Department Papers, NA.
37. De Gaulle, *War Memoirs, III*, 169. For Eisenhower's account of this conversation see *Crusade in Europe*, 363.
38. Eisenhower to Marshall, 6 Jan 1945, Chandler, IV, 2399–2400.
39. Patton diary, 24 Jan 1944, Blumenson, 629.
40. Eisenhower to de Gaulle, 28 April 1945, Chandler, IV, 2657–8.
41. De Gaulle to Eisenhower, 1 May 1945, *War Memoirs, III, Documents*, 223.

42. De Gaulle to Truman, 4 May 1945, in Caffery to Secretary of State, 5 May 1945, *FRUS 1945, IV, Europe*, 685.
43. Alexander to the War Department, FX 74784, NAF 966, 13 May 1945, RG 218, Joint Chiefs of Staff, Chairman's File, Admiral Leahy, 1942–48, Box 4, Folder 18, NA.
44. Murphy to Matthews, 17 May 1945, *FRUS 1945, IV, Europe*, 728–9.
45. Truman to de Gaulle, *FRUS, 1945, IV, Europe*, 735.
46. Alexander to War Department, 9 June 1945, RG 218, Joint Chiefs of Staff, Chairman's File, Admiral Leahy, 1942–48, Box 4, Folder 18, NA.
47. Memorandum by President Roosevelt to the Secretary of State, 24 Jan 1944, *FRUS, 1944, III, Europe*, 773.
48. Much of the information in this paragraph comes from SOE reports on Indo-China, 'French Indo-China', 25 Nov 1945 & 'Notes on French Indo-China', 24 March 1945, both in HS1/94, PRO.
49. Edwin Wilson, Memorandum of a conversation with the President, 24 March 1944, 851.00/3185 1/2, State Department Papers, NA.
50. Wilson to Ismay, FMW 33, 27 March 1945, WO 106/3483, PRO.
51. Memorandum by the Under Secretary of State to President Roosevelt, 17 Feb 1944, *FRUS, 1944, III, Europe*, 774.
52. Hull to Roosevelt, 13 Oct 1944, Ibid., 776–7.
53. Report by Joint Staff Planners, 'Military Aspects of Resistance Groups in Indo-China', 16 March 1945, RG War Department, ABC Papers, 384 Indo-China (16 Dec 1944) Sec 1-B, NA.
54. This is what the Joint Chiefs of Staff explained to the French. See JCS to General Brossin de Saint-Didier, 4 Jan 1945, RG 218 US JCS, Geographic File 1942–5, 370 France Sec 1, NA.
55. State–War–Navy Coordinating Committee Directive, 13 March 1945, RG War Department, ABC, 384 Indo-China (16 Dec 1944) Sec 1-B, NA.
56. Joint Staff Planners Report, 'Use of Indo-China Resistance Forces', 15 Feb 1945, RG ABC Papers, 384 Indo-China (16 Dec 44) Sec 1-A, NA.
57. State–War–Navy Coordinating Committee Minutes, 16th Meeting, 13 April 1945, Ibid.
58. 'French Indo-China', 25 Nov 1945, op cit.
59. Mountbatten to British Chiefs of Staff, 14 Sept 1944, SEACOS 231, WO 106/4633, PRO.
60. 'French Indo-China', op cit.

9 'Our Mutual Headache': Churchill, Roosevelt and de Gaulle

1. De Gaulle termed him 'this artist, this seducer'. See *War Memoirs, II*, 270.
2. Entry, 22 May 1943, John Morton Blum (ed.) *The Price of Vision: The Diary of Henry Wallace* (Boston, 1967) 202. In other situations, Churchill was considerably cruder, stating that: 'I brought him up from a pup, but never got him properly trained to the house.' Dilks, 529.
3. For the most recent interpretation see Douglas Johnson, 'Churchill and France' in Robert Blake and William Roger Louis (eds) *Churchill* (Oxford, 1993).
4. Churchill to de Gaulle, 16 June 1944, de Gaulle, *War Memoirs, II, Documents*, 345.

5. Churchill, *Their Finest Hour* (London, 1949) 182.
6. Churchill to Ismay, 24 June 1940, SPRS1/134/2, CCAC.
7. De Gaulle, *Memoirs de guerre, L'appel* (Paris, 1954). The text of this speech is only available in the French edition.
8. Speech to House of Commons, 18 June 1940, in David Cannadine (ed.) *The Speeches of Winston Churchill* (Boston, 1989) 177.
9. Churchill, *Their Finest Hour*, 218.
10. De Gaulle to Catroux, 29 Aug 1940, *War Memoirs, I*,.
11. De Gaulle, *War Memoirs, I*, 58.
12. Entry, 26 May 1943, John Harvey (ed.) *War Diaries of Oliver Harvey 1941–45* (London, 1978) 262.
13. De Gaulle had an almost overwhelming psychological need to quarrel with older men who had assumed the role of mentor towards him – such as in the obvious cases of Pétain and Churchill. Of course, these two men were exceedingly different, but it would be quite interesting one day to compare de Gaulle's relationship with them.
14. Spears Diary, 23 Aug 1942, Spears Papers, Box 1, MECSAC.
15. Churchill to de Gaulle, 19 Jan 1943, and De Gaulle to Churchill, 20 Jan 1943, *War Memoirs, II, Documents*, 127–8.
16. De Gaulle to Giraud, 1 Jan 1943, Map Room, Torch I, Sec 5, FDRL.
17. De Gaulle, note on an interview with Winant, 21 May 1942, *War Memoirs, II, Documents*, 12.
18. Memorandum by Macmillan, 3 Jan 1944, Prem 3/182/6, PRO.
19. Entry, 7 June 1944, Lord Avon. *The Reckoning* (London, 1965) 455.
20. See Warren Kimball, *The Juggler* (Princeton, 1991). See also Mario Rossi, *Roosevelt and the French* (Westport, CT., 1993).
21. De Gaulle, *War Memoirs, II*, 271.
22. Roosevelt to Wilson, 5 Jan 1944, President's Secretary's File, France, 1944–5, FDRL.
23. In Roosevelt to Churchill, R-214, 17 Nov 1942, Kimball, II, 18–19.
24. Roosevelt to Churchill, R-250, 1 Jan 1943, Ibid., 104–5.
25. 'Mr. Robert Murphy', Elsey Papers, HSTL.
26. Roosevelt to Wilson, 5 Jan 1944, op cit.
27. Roosevelt to Churchill, R-210, 11 Nov 1942, Kimball, I, 669.
28. See Sumner Welles, Memorandum of a conversation between the president, Tixier, Philip and Welles, 20 Nov 1942, *FRUS, 1942, II Europe*, 547 and 851.01/798 1/2, State Department Papers, NA.
29. Eden wrote to Macmillan on 21 July 1943: 'The President has also not looked kindly upon the composition of the French Committee of National Liberation, particularly in view of the presence on it of Messieurs André Philip and Tixier.' FO 954/8, Avon Papers, PRO. See also Roosevelt to Churchill, R-275/2, 20 May 1943, Kimball, II, 215.
30. Roosevelt to Wilson, op cit.
31. Roosevelt to Churchill, R-275/1, 8 May 1943, Kimball, II, 210 (As Kimball notes, there is no record that this memorandum was actually given to Churchill.) and R-278, 4 June 1943, 229.
32. Roosevelt to Churchill, R-288, 17 June 1943, Kimball, II, 255.
33. Churchill to Roosevelt, 18 June 1943, C-318, Kimball, II, 262.
34. Churchill to Duff Cooper, ? October 1943, Duff Cooper Papers, 4/4, CCAC.

35. Entry for 21 Dec 1943, Macmillan, *War Diaries*, 332.
36. Churchill to Roosevelt, C-498, 10 Nov 1943, Kimball, II, 593 and C-504, 13 Nov 1943, 599.
37. Churchill to Eden, 30 July 1943, Prem 3/181/2, PRO.
38. Marshall, King and Arnold to the president, 13 June 1944, RG 218, JCS, Chairman's File, Leahy, 1942–8, Box 4, Folder 19, NA.

Bibliography and Manuscript Sources

MANUSCRIPT COLLECTIONS

I Archives Nationales, Paris (AN)

1. Public Papers
   F/1a   Ministère de l'Intérieur, objets généraux (Londres, Alger)
   F60   Secrétariat Général du Gouvernement (Londres, Alger)

2. Private Papers
   72/AJ   Comité d'histoire de la Deuxième guerre mondiale:
              Emmanuel d'Astier de la Vigerie
              Général de Larminat
              Général Catroux
              Jacques Soustelle
              André Philip
   334/AP   Cabinet Bluet (Haute Cour de Justice), procès de:
              Pierre Boisson
              Camille Chautemps
              Pierre-Etienne Flandin
              Général Noguès
              Marcel Peyrouton
              Amiral Robert
   382/AP   René Cassin Papers
   457/AP   Georges Bidault Papers

II Archives du Ministère des Affaires Etrangères, Paris (MAE)

1. Public Papers
   Guerre 1939–45, Londres/Alger

2. Oral Archives
   René Massigli
   Maurice Couve de Murville

188

III Archives du Ministère de la Défense Nationale, Vincennes (MDN)

1. Public Papers
   - 4P   Etat-Major, Général de Gaulle
   - 5P   Etat-Major Particulier, Général Giraud; Général Juin
   - 6P   Cabinet du Ministre (Alger, Paris)
   - 7P   Etat-Major Général, Guerre (Alger, Paris)
   - 8P   Mission de Liaison avec les Alliés
   - 10P   Armées et Corps d'Armées

2. Private Papers
   - 1K374   Général Ziegler

IV Library of Congress, Washington, D.C. (LC)

Cordell Hull Papers
Admiral Leahy Papers

V National Archives and Records Administration

1. National Archives, Washington, D.C. (NA)
   (a) Military Reference Section:
   - 165   The War Department, General and Special Staffs
   - 218   The US Joint Chiefs of Staff
   - 226   Office of Strategic Services
   (b) Civil Reference Section
   (i) State Department Papers:
   - 740.0011 EW
   - RG 59 General Diplomatic Files
   - Lot Files
   (ii) Treasury Department Papers

2. Dwight David Eisenhower Library, Abilene, Kansas (DDEL)
   Eisenhower Pre-Presidential Papers
   Walter Bedell Smith Papers

3. Franklin Delano Roosevelt Library, Hyde Park, New York (FDRL)
   Harry Hopkins Papers
   Map Room Papers
   Private Secretary's File, Roosevelt Papers

4. Harry S. Truman Library, Independence, Missouri (HSTL)
   George Elsey Papers
   James T. Quirk Papers

VI   Public Record Office Kew (PRO)

1. Foreign Office Papers
    FO 226   Beirut Legation
    FO 371   Political Departments: General Correspondence
    FO 660   British Minister in Algiers, then British Ambassador
    FO 892   The Spears Mission
    FO 898   Political Warfare Executive
    FO 921   Minister of State, Cairo
    FO 954   Avon Papers

2. Prime Minister's Papers
    PREM 3   Operational Papers
    PREM 4   Confidential Papers
    PREM 7   Desmond Morton

3. Cabinet Office Papers
    Cab. 65   War Cabinet Minutes
    Cab. 66   War Cabinet Memoranda

4. War Office Papers
    WO 106   Directorate of Military Operations and Intelligence
    WO 193   Directorate of Military Operations
    WO 204   Allied Forces in North Africa, Italy & France, 1942–5
    WO 219   SHAEF

5. Treasury Papers
    T 160   Foreign Economic Relations

6. SOE Papers
    HS1   Far East

VII   Private Archives

1. Churchill College Cambridge (CCAC)
    Lord Norwich (Duff Cooper) Papers
    Lord Halifax Papers
    Lord Swinton Papers
    Sir Edward Spears Papers

2. The Citadel, Military College of South Carolina, Charleston, S.C.
    Mark Clark Papers

3. Historical Society of York County, Pennsylvania
    Jacob Devers Papers

4. Middle East Centre, St Antony's College Oxford (MEC)
Sir Edward Spears Papers

NEWSPAPERS, PERIODICALS AND REPORTS

France
La France Libre
Free France
La lettre de la France Libre: News of the Free French Movement
La Marseillaise
Les cahiers français
Les documents: La France Combattante
The New York Times
The Times (London)

PUBLISHED PRIMARY SOURCES

I Official and Semi-official Documents

The Congressional Record.
Eade, Charles (ed.) *Winston Churchill's Secret Session Speeches* (New York, 1946).
Parliamentary Debates, House of Commons, 5th series.
US Department of State. *Foreign Relations of the United States, 1940–45* (Washington, 1959–69).
—*Foreign Relations of the United States, Conferences at Washington, 1941–2 & Casablanca, 1943* (Washington, 1968).
—*Foreign Relations of the United States, Conferences at Washington & Quebec, 1943* (Washington, 1970).
— *Foreign Relations of the United States, Conferences at Cairo & Tehran, 1943* (Washington, 1961).
— *Foreign Relations of the United States, the Conference at Quebec, 1944* (Washington, 1972).
— *Foreign Relations of the United States, Conferences at Malta and Yalta, 1945* (Washington, 1955).
USSR, Ministry of Foreign Affairs. *Stalin's Correspondence with Churchill & Attlee, 1941–45* (New York, 1965).
— *Stalin's Correspondence with Roosevelt & Truman, 1941–5* (New York, 1965).

II Letters and Private Papers

Bland, Larry, et al. (eds) *The Papers of George Catlett Marshall*, vol. 3 (Baltimore, 1986).
Bullitt, Orville (ed.) *For the President Personal and Secret: Correspondence between Franklin Roosevelt and William C. Bullitt* (Boston, 1972).

Chandler, Alfred D., et al. (eds) *The Papers of Dwight David Eisenhower: The War Years*, 5 vols (Baltimore, 1970).
Complete Presidential Press Conferences of Franklin D. Roosevelt, 25 vols in 12 (New York, 1972).
Coutau-Bégarie, Hervé & Claude Huan (eds) *Lettres et notes de l'Amiral Darlan* (Paris, 1992).
Gaulle, Amiral Philippe de, et al. (eds) *Lettres, notes et carnets de Charles de Gaulle* (Paris, Plon, 1980).
— *Discours et messages de Charles de Gaulle* (Paris, 1970).
Kimball, W. F. *Churchill & Roosevelt: The Complete Correspondence* (3 vols) (Princeton, 1984).
Nicholas, H. G. (ed.) *Washington Despatches 1941–5* (London, 1981).
Roosevelt, E. (ed.) *FDR: His Personal Letters 1928–45* (New York, 1950).
Rosenman, Samuel (ed.) *The Public Papers and Addresses of Franklin D. Roosevelt*, 13 vols (New York, 1938–50).

III Published Diaries

Blum, John Morton (ed.) *From the Morgenthau Diaries: Years of War; 1941–45* (Boston, 1967).
— (ed.) *The Price of Vision: The Diary of Henry Wallace* (Boston, 1973).
Blumenson, M. (ed.) *The Patton Papers* (Boston, 1974).
Butcher, Harry, *My Three Years with Eisenhower* (New York, 1946).
Campbell, Thomas & George C. Herring (eds) *The Diaries of Edward R. Stettinius, 1943–46* (New York, 1975).
Colville, John, *The Fringes of Power: Downing Street Diaries 1939–1955* (London, 1985).
Dilks, David (ed.) *The Cadogan Diaries, 1938–1945* (London, 1971).
Dixon, Piers, *Double Diploma: The Life of Sir Pierson Dixon, Don and Diplomat* (London, 1968).
Ferrell, Robert, *The Eisenhower Diaries* (New York, 1981).
Harvey, John (ed.) *War Diaries of Oliver Harvey (1941–45)* (London, 1978).
Macmillan, Harold, *War Diaries* (London, 1984).
Martin, Sir John, *Downing Street: The War Years* (London, 1991).
Moran, Lord, *Winston Churchill: The Struggle for Survival* (London, 1966).
Nicolson, Nigel (ed.) *Harold Nicolson, Diaries and Letters, 1939–1945* (London, 1967).

IV Memoirs

Aglion, Raoul, *Roosevelt and de Gaulle: Allies in Conflict* (New York, 1988).
Alexander, Harold, *The Alexander Memoirs, 1940–45* (London, 1962).
d'Astier de la Vigerie, Emmanuel, *De la chute à la libération de Paris* (Paris, 1965).
— *Les Dieux et les hommes* (Paris, 1952).
— *7 x 7 Days* (Eng. trans. London, 1958).
Cassin, René, *Des hommes partis de rien* (Paris, 1974).

Catroux, Général, *Dans la bataille de Mediterranée* (Paris, 1949).
Churchill, W. S., *The Second World War*, 6 vols (London, 1948–53).
Clark, Mark, *Calculated Risk* (New York, 1950).
Colville, John, *The Churchillians* (London, 1981).
Cooper, Alfred Duff (Viscount Norwich), *Old Men Forget* (London, 1953).
Cooper, Lady Diana, *Autobiography* (Salisbury, 1979).
Eden, Anthony (Lord Avon), *The Reckoning* (London, 1965).
Eisenhower, Dwight, *At Ease: Stories I Tell to Friends* (Garden City, New York, 1967).
— *Crusade in Europe* (Garden City, 1948).
Frenay, Henri, *The Night Will End* (Eng. trans. New York, 1976).
Gaulle, Charles de, *Mémoires de guerre*, 3 vols (Eng. trans. London, 1955–60).
Hull, Cordell, *The Memoirs of Cordell Hull* (New York, 1948).
Ismay, General Lord, *The Memoirs of General Lord Ismay* (New York, 1960).
Leahy, William, *I Was There* (New York, 1950).
Macmillan, Harold, *The Blast of War, 1939–45* (London, 1967).
Monnet, Jean, *Mémoires* (Paris, 1976).
Murphy, Robert, *Diplomat among Warriors* (Garden City, New York, 1964).
Pendar, Kenneth, *Adventures in Diplomacy: Our French Dilemma* (New York, 1945).
Spears, Edward Louis, *Assignment to Catastrophe* (London, 1954).
— *Fulfillment of a Mission* (London, 1977).
— *Two Men who Saved France: Pétain and de Gaulle* (London, 1966).

SECONDARY SOURCES

I Biographies

Ambrose, Stephen E., *Eisenhower: Soldier, General of the Army, President-elect* (New York, 1983).
— *The Supreme Commander* (London, 1971).
Blake, Robert and William Roger Louis (eds) *Churchill* (Oxford, 1993).
Blumenson, Martin, *Mark Clark* (New York, 1984).
Burns, James MacGregor, *Roosevelt: Soldier of Freedom, 1940–45* (London, 1970).
Callaghan, Raymond, *Churchill: Retreat from Empire* (Wilmington, Del., 1984).
Carlton, David, *Anthony Eden: A Biography* (London, 1981).
Charmley, John, *Churchill: The End of Glory* (London, 1993).
— *Duff Cooper: The Authorised Biography* (1986).
Cook, Don, *Charles de Gaulle: A Biography* (London, 1984).
Cordier, Daniel, *Jean Moulin*, 2 tomes (Paris, 1989).
Coutau-Bégarie & Claude Huan, *Darlan* (Paris,1989).
Cross, J. A., *Lord Swinton* (1982).
Crozier, Brian, *De Gaulle: The Warrier* (London, 1973).
Dunlop, Richard, *Donovan: America's Master Spy* (New York, 1982).
Ferro, Marc, *Pétain* (Paris, 1987).

Freidel, Frank, *Franklin Roosevelt: A Rendezvous with Destiny* (Boston, 1990).
Funk, A. L., *Charles de Gaulle: The Crucial Years* (Oklahoma, 1959).
Gilbert, Martin, *Winston S. Churchill: Finest Hour, 1939–1941* (London, 1984).
— *Winston S. Churchill, 1941–45: Road to Victory* (London, 1986).
Gough, Hugh & John Horne (eds) *De Gaulle and Twentieth Century France* (London, 1994).
Horne, Alistair, *Harold Macmillan, vol. 1 1894–1957* (London, 1988).
Jackson, Julian, *Charles de Gaulle* (London, 1990).
James, Robert Rhodes, *Anthony Eden* (London, 1986).
Kaspi, André, *Franklin Roosevelt* (Paris, 1988).
Kimball, Warren, *The Juggler: Franklin Roosevelt as Wartime Statesman* (Princeton, 1991).
Lacouture, Jean, *De Gaulle: Le rebelle* (Paris, 1984).
Ledwidge, Bernard, *De Gaulle* (London, 1982)
McJimsey, George, *Harry Hopkins* (Cambridge, Mass, 1987).
Michel, Henri, *François Darlan* (Paris,1993).
Parrish, Thomas, *Roosevelt and Marshall* (New York, 1989).
Pelling, Henry, *Winston Churchill* (London, 1974).
Pogue, Forrest C., *George C. Marshall*, 3 vols (New York, 1963–73).
Shennan, Andrew, *De Gaulle* (London, 1993).
Tournoux, J.-R. *Pétain et de Gaulle* (Paris, 1964).
Ziegler, Philip, *Diana Cooper* (London, 1981).
— *Mountbatten* (London, 1985).

II General Works

Anglin, Douglas *The St Pierre and Miquelon Affaire of 1941: A Study in Diplomacy in the North Atlantic Quadrangle* (Toronto, 1966).
Azéma, Jean-Pierre, *De Munich à la Libération* (Paris, 1979).
— & François Bédarida (eds) *Vichy et les Français* (Paris, 1992).
Baptiste, Fitzroy André *War, Cooperation & Conflict: The European Possessions in the Caribbean, 1939–45* (Westport, Conn, 1988).
Barker, Elisabeth, *Churchill and Eden at War* (London, 1978).
Blumenthal, Henry, *Illusion and Reality in Franco-American Diplomacy, 1914–1945* (Baton Rouge, 1986).
Bryant, Arthur, *The Turn of the Tide, 1939–1943* (London, 1957).
Calvi, Fabrizio, *OSS: La guerre secrète en France* (Paris, 1990).
Caroff, C. F., *Les débarquements alliés en Afrique du Nord* (Vincennes, 1960).
Cerny, P. G., *The Politics of Grandeur. Ideological Aspects of de Gaulle's Foreign Policy* (Cambridge, 1980).
Charlot, Jean, *Le phénomène gaulliste* (Paris, 1970).
Cointet, M & J.-P., *La France à Londres, 1940–1943* (Paris, 1990).
Cointet, J.-P., *La France Libre* (Paris, 1975).
Comité d'histoire de la Deuxième guerre mondiale. *La Guerre en Méditerranée* (Paris, 1971).
Dallek, R., *Franklin D. Roosevelt and American Foreign Policy 1932–1945* (New York, 1979).
— (ed.) *The Roosevelt, Diplomacy & World War Two* (New York, 1970).

Danan, Y.-M., *La vie politique à Alger de 1940 à 1944* (Paris, 1963).

Dansette, A., *Histoire de la libération de Paris* (Paris, 1966).

Debu-Bridel, J., *De Gaulle et le Conseil National de la Résistance* (Paris, 1978).

DePorte, A., *De Gaulle's Foreign Policy, 1944–46* (Harvard, 1968).

Duroselle, Jean-Baptiste, *L'Abîme, 1939–1945* (Paris, 1982).

Eubank, Keith, *Summit at Tehran* (New York, 1985).

Foot, M. R. D., *Resistance: An Analysis of European Resistance to Nazism* (London, 1976).

— *SOE in France* (London, 1973).

Funk, A., *Hidden Ally: The French Resistance, Special Operations and the Landings in Southern France, 1944* (Westport, CT., 1992).

— *The Politics of Torch* (Kansas University Press, 1968).

Hess, Gary, *The US's Emergence as a Southeast Asian Power, 1940–50* (New York, 1987).

Hoisington, William, *The Casablanca Connection* (Chapel Hill, 1986).

Howard, Michael, *The Mediterranean Strategy in World War II* (New York, 1968).

Howe, George, *Northwest Africa: Seizing the Initiative in the West* (Washington, 1957).

Hurtsfield, Julian, *America and the French Nation, 1939–1945* (Chapel Hill, 1986).

Kaspi, André, *La mission de Jean Monnet à Alger, mars-octobre 1943* (Paris, 1971).

Kedward, H. R., *Resistance in Vichy France* (London, 1988).

Keegan, John, *Six Armies in Normandy* (New York, 1982).

Kersaudy, François, *Churchill and De Gaulle* (London, 1981).

Kolko, Gabriel, *The Politics of War: Allied Diplomacy and the World Crisis of 1943–5* (London, 1969).

Langer, William, *Our Vichy Gamble* (New York, 1947).

Laqueur, W. (ed.) *The Second World War: Essays in Military and Political History* (London, 1982).

Larrabee, Eric, *Commander in Chief: FDR, His Lieutenants & Their War* (New York, 1987)

Marder, A. J., *Operation Menace* (Oxford, 1976).

Michel, Henri, *Histoire de la France Libre* (Paris, 1967).

— *Histoire de la Résistance française* (Paris, 1969).

— *Histoire de la Résistance en France* (Paris, 1972).

Noguères, H., *Histoire de la Résistance en France* (5 vols, 1967–81).

Paxton, Robert, *Vichy France* (New York, 1972).

Pogue, Forrest, *The Supreme Command* (Washington, 1977).

Rioux, Pierre, *La France de la 4e République, 1944–1952* (Paris, 1980).

Rossi, Mario, *Roosevelt and France* (Westport, CT., 1993).

Sainsbury, K., *The North African Landings 1942* (London, 1977).

— *The Turning Point* (Oxford, 1985).

Sherwood, R., *Roosevelt and Hopkins: An Intimate History* (New York, 1948).

Smith, Bradley F., *The Shadow Warriors: OSS and the Origins of the CIA* (NY, 1983).

Smith, Gaddis, *American Diplomacy During the Second World War, 1941–1945* (NY, 1965).

Sweets, John, *The Politics of Resistance in France, 1940–44* (N. Ill. Uni. Press, 1976).

Thomas, R. T., *Britain and Vichy* (London, 1978).

Touchard, J., *Le Gaullisme 1940–1969* (Paris, 1978).

Vernet, J., *Le réarmement & la réorganisation de l'Armée de Terre français (1943–46)* (Vincennes, 1980).

Vigneras, Marcel, *Rearming the French* (Washington, 1986).

Vincent, Jean-Noel, *Les forces françaises dans la lutte contre l'Axe en Afrique* (Vincennes, 1983).

Viorst, Milton, *Hostile Allies: FDR and De Gaulle* (New York, 1965).

Waites, N. (ed.) *Troubled Neighbours: Franco-British Relations in the Twentieth Century* (London, 1971).

Woodward, Sir Llewellyn, *History of the Second World War*, 5 vols (London: HMSO, 1971).

III Articles and Theses

Charmley, John, 'British Policy towards de Gaulle, 1942–4 (unpublished D.Phil thesis, Oxford, 1982).

— 'Harold Macmillan and the Making of the French National Committee of Liberation', *International History Review*, vol. iv (November 1982).

Funk, A. L., 'The Anfa Memorandum' in *Journal of Modern History* (1954).

— 'A Document Relating to the Second World War: The Clark – Darlan Agreement' in *Journal of Modern History* (March 1953).

— 'Negotiating the Deal with Darlan' in *Journal of Contemporary History* (1973).

— 'La "reconnaissance" du CFLN, Quebec, aout 1943' in *Revue d'Histoire de la deuxième guerre mondiale* (janvier 1959).

Hess, Gary, 'Franklin Roosevelt and Indochina' in *The Journal of American History* (September 1972).

LaFeber, Walter, 'Roosevelt, Churchill & Indochina, 1942–45' in *American Historical Review* (December 1985).

Maguire, Gloria, 'General Sir Edward Spears: 'Une certaine idée de la France' in *Frontières* (1994).

— 'La Nouvelle Grèce, la nouvelle Rome: Harold Macmillan et Dwight Eisenhower à Alger, 1943' in *Frontières* (1995).

Michelson, Martin, 'Operation Susan: The Origins of the Free French Movement' in *Military Affairs* (October 1988).

Munholland, Kim, 'The Trials of the Free French in New Caledonia, 1940–1942' in *French Historical Studies* (Fall 1986).

Thorne, Christopher, 'Indochina & Anglo-American Relations, 1942–45' in *Pacific Historical Review* (1976).

Index

Murphy, Robert (*continued*)
rearming the French 124–5
(*see also* North Africa;
Roosevelt, Franklin; State
Department; Hull, Cordell)
Murphy–Weygand Accords 57, 59
Musée de l'Homme group 97
Muselier, Admiral Emile 7, 13–15,
27–8, 171
Muslim Community in Lebanon 47,
48, 52
Mutual Aid *see* Reciprocal Aid

Naccache, Alfred 43
National Front 101, 114, 141
National Resistance Council
*see Conseil National de la
Résistance*
National Revolution 58
Navy Department (US) 161
Nehru, Jawaharlal 44, 174
NEF (earlier name for MUR) 103
Netherlands 1, 93, 96, 132
Neutrality Act 21
New Caledonia 8, 29–31, 94, 164
New Deal 24, 78
New Hebrides rallies to de Gaulle
8
New York Times 27
New Zealand 8
Noguès, General Charles 64
Normandy Landings *see* D-Day;
'Overlord'
North Africa 18, 34, 36, 101, 108,
110, 127, 158, 162, 164; and
General Weygand 11; strategic
importance of 20; debate over
whether American aid should be
given 25; plans for Allied
invasion 33, 46, 77, 175; Allied
invasion of 56–74, 79, 158,
160; and Allied rivalry 80, 121;
and economic life after Allied
invasion 119–22, 127–8;
liberalisation of 83, 84–6;
exchange rate in 121–2; Pétain
authorises transfer of part of
government there 170 (*see also*
Weygand, Maxime; Murphy,

Robert; Eisenhower, Dwight;
Arabs)
North African Economic Board 81,
121
Norway 93, 132

Office of Strategic Services (OSS)
44, 57, 98, 99–100, 102, 109,
111, 137, 141–2, 150
Operational Groups (OGs) 106
Oran (attack on French fleet) 5, 7,
16, 58, 96, 170; de Gaulle on
2, 3, 75, 156; Allied landings
there 62
Organisation civile et militaire
(OCM) 101
Orthodox Community in Lebanon
52
Ottoman Empire 35
Oubangui-Chari 8, 116
'Overlord', Operation 91, 110
Oxford University 81, 156

Pacific Fleet 28, 152
Pacific War 30, 35, 149, 151
Palestine 35, 36, 49, 52, 53
Palewski, Gaston 7, 50
Paris, liberation of 112, 138–41
Paris, Henri d'Orléans, Count of 58,
72, 73, 74
Parr, Robert 12
Passy *see* Dewavrin, André
Patch, General Alexander 29–31
Patton, General George 64, 136,
139, 144–5
Pearl Harbor 20, 28, 30, 100
Pétain, Marshal Philippe 12, 17, 61,
142; comes to power 1; and de
Gaulle 2, 170, 186; de Gaulle's
response to his actions 2–4;
meeting with Hitler at Montoire
3; and France's role in a Nazi
Europe 5; and Egypt 9–10;
British hopes of assistance from
11; and Americans 18–20; and
North Africa 59, 65, 176;
viewed as a saviour in France
96; authorises Massilia 170
(*see also* Vichy)

Vichy *(continued)*
  German invasion of unoccupied
  zone 68; arrest of former
  officials of 90; and STO
  104–5; accuse French of being
  British organisation 5, 115;
  and British blockade 116; and
  West Africa 117; 'shield
  theory' of 171 *(see also*
  Pétain, Philippe)
Viet-Minh 149

Wadsworth, George 45, 53
Wallace, Henry 24, 76, 154
War Department (US) 27, 139, 161;
  attitude to Free French 24, 26,
  32–3; and North African
  invasion 60, 62, 63, 74, 79;
  and role in making foreign
  policy 78, 79, 82, 88; and
  recognition of FCNL 89, 92–3;
  and resistance 93; and civil
  affairs directive 93; and
  exchange rate in North Africa
  121; and Indochina 151–2

(see also Marshall, George;
  Eisenhower, Dwight; McCloy,
  John)
War Office (GB) 22, 37
Wedemeyer, General 149
Wehrmacht *see* German Army
Weller, George 26
Welles, Sumner 25, 34, 78, 88, 144,
  164, 172
West Africa 58, 59, 65, 69, 77,
  80–1, 84, 117, 121, 158, 163
Weygand, General Maxime 11, 25,
  56, 57, 58–9
Wilkie, Wendell 46
Wilson, Edwin 91, 94, 161, 162, 165
Wilson, General Sir Maitland 37,
  39, 110, 138
Winant, John 24, 159
World War I 26, 35, 118, 129

Yalta Conference 142, 144, 145,
  146, 168
Yugoslavia 148

Zionism 53